THE ELIZABETHAN COUNTRY HOUSE ENTERTAINMENT

Print, Performance, and Gender

This is the first full-length critical study of country house entertainment, a genre central to late Elizabethan politics. It shows how the short plays staged for the Queen at country estates like Kenilworth Castle and Elvetham shaped literary trends and intervened in political debates, including whether women made good politicians and what roles the church and local culture should play in definitions of England. In performance and print, country house entertainments facilitated political negotiations, rethought gender roles, and crafted regional and national identities. In its investigation of how the hosts used performances to negotiate local and national politics, this book also sheds light on how and why such entertainments enabled female performance and authorship at a time when English women did not write or perform commercial plays. Written in a lively and accessible style, this is fascinating reading for scholars and students of early modern literature, theater, and women's history.

ELIZABETH ZEMAN KOLKOVICH is an Assistant Professor of English at The Ohio State University. She has published essays on pageantry and Renaissance drama in *Shakespeare Quarterly*, *English Literary Renaissance*, and elsewhere. A conference paper relating to this book won the Agnes B. Strickland Award for best paper from the Queen Elizabeth I Society in 2011. Her research has been funded by short-term residential fellowships at the Huntington Library.

THE ELIZABETHAN COUNTRY HOUSE ENTERTAINMENT

Print, Performance, and Gender

ELIZABETH ZEMAN KOLKOVICH

Ohio State University

CAMBRIDGE
UNIVERSITY PRESS

CAMBRIDGE
UNIVERSITY PRESS

University Printing House, Cambridge CB2 8BS, United Kingdom

Cambridge University Press is part of the University of Cambridge.

It furthers the University's mission by disseminating knowledge in the pursuit of
education, learning and research at the highest international levels of excellence.

www.cambridge.org
Information on this title: www.cambridge.org/9781107134256

First published 2016

Printed in the United States of America by Sheridan Books, Inc.

A catalogue record for this publication is available from the British Library

ISBN 978-1-107-13425-6 Hardback

For Elliot and Teddy

Contents

Acknowledgments

I began this project at the University of Illinois at Urbana-Champaign under the expert guidance of Carol Neely. Without her early belief in its merits, tireless readings of drafts, and judicious advice, this book never would have been written. Zachary Lesser was also a wonderful mentor whose advice improved this book in countless ways, and I benefited immensely from conversations with and feedback from Catharine Gray and Lori Newcomb. At Illinois I was extremely fortunate to be surrounded by a group of brilliant new scholars. Sara Luttfring, Tara Lyons, and Alli Meyer inspired and strengthened my work, and along with Anne Brubaker and Kim O'Neill, they provided respite and support at crucial moments. The University of Illinois Graduate College funded travel to archives in early stages of my research.

I completed this book with the support of another vibrant scholarly community at Ohio State. One of the best parts of teaching at the small Mansfield campus is engaging with faculty across disciplines, and that environment enriched this book and my methods. Rachel Bowen, Terri Fisher, and Heather Tanner listened and advised when needed, and my amazing English colleagues at Mansfield – Cynthia Callahan, Susan Delagrange, Norman Jones, Barbara McGovern, and Carolyn Skinner – read drafts and shared wisdom and laughter that made my days brighter. A Mansfield Campus Seed Grant funded additional travel and writing time. For energizing exchanges and excellent fellowship, I thank Columbus colleagues Richard Dutton, Alan Farmer, Hannibal Hamlin, Jennifer Higginbotham, Chris Highley, and Luke Wilson – all of whom improved early drafts with generous, rigorous comments. I thank my research assistants Katie Pfahler, who checked many original-spelling quotations, and Chelsea Chafin, whose meticulous editing saved me from many errors. Any that remain are, of course, my own.

Parts of every chapter originated as conference papers, and I am grateful to those who responded, especially members of the Queen Elizabeth I

Society and Shakespeare Association of America. Jaime Goodrich, Gabriel Heaton, Leah Knight, Carole Levin, Erin McCarthy, Kirk Melnikoff, Tim Moylan, Niamh O'Leary, and Linda Shenk deserve special mention for their comments or willingness to share materials and expertise. Peter Greenfield, Alexandra Johnston, Sally-Beth MacLean, and other editors of the Records of Early English Drama project generously shared unpublished findings and recommended archives. I received aid from many librarians at the University of Illinois, Ohio State, the British Library, Lambeth Palace Library, Royal Collections at Windsor, several county record offices, Folger Shakespeare Library, and Huntington Library. The Huntington provided a fellowship that made Chapter 3 possible. Harmony Bench, David Cook-Martin, and Victor Quintanilla encouraged me in countless ways. I thank Sarah Stanton, Rosemary Crawley, and Sarah Starkey at Cambridge University Press for their guidance, as well as the two anonymous readers whose suggestions made this book stronger.

My scholarly network has enriched and inspired me, but my family has sustained me. The unfailing support (and child care) of my mom, Candy Zeman, made my life and work immensely better. My husband, Elliot, made sacrifices in support of my career and this project, and his optimism and confidence in my abilities have made me a better person. For me, this book is strongly tied to the birth and early years of my son, Teddy. His arrival made me newly appreciate the parents featured in this book who went to great lengths to secure their children's futures. He and his dad have made my home a very happy one, and I dedicate this book to them with gratitude and love.

An early draft of a section of Chapter 2 was published as "Lady Russell, Elizabeth I, and Female Political Alliances through Performance" in *English Literary Renaissance* 39.2 (2009): 290–314. A few paragraphs in "Pageantry, Queens, and Housewives in the Two Texts of *The Merry Wives of Windsor*" in *Shakespeare Quarterly* 63.3 (2012): 328–54 are substantially revised and expanded in Chapters 3 and 4. Chapter 5 contains material published in "Elite Pageantry as Popular News: Elvetham House, John Wolfe and Country-House Entertainment in Print" in *The Intellectual Culture of the British Country House, 1500–1700*, edited by Matthew Dimmock, Andrew Hadfield, and Margaret Healy (Manchester University Press, 2015), 146–59. I thank the publishers for their permission to use revisions of these essays.

Abbreviations

BL	London, British Library
HEH	San Marino, Henry E. Huntington Library
LPL	London, Lambeth Palace Library
OED	*Oxford English Dictionary*
SP	London, National Archives, State Papers
STC	*A Short-Title Catalogue of Books Printed in England, Scotland, & Ireland and of English Books Printed Abroad, 1475–1640*, ed. A. W. Pollard, et al., 2nd edn (London: Bibliographical Society, 1976–91)

Note on Transcription and Citation

I quote early modern texts in their original spelling, including i/j and u/v. I silently expand abbreviations (including ampersands) and change long s to short, and I normalize titles of printed books according to modern standards of capitalization. I have included *STC* numbers in citations of early modern books to help those wishing to locate a particular edition.

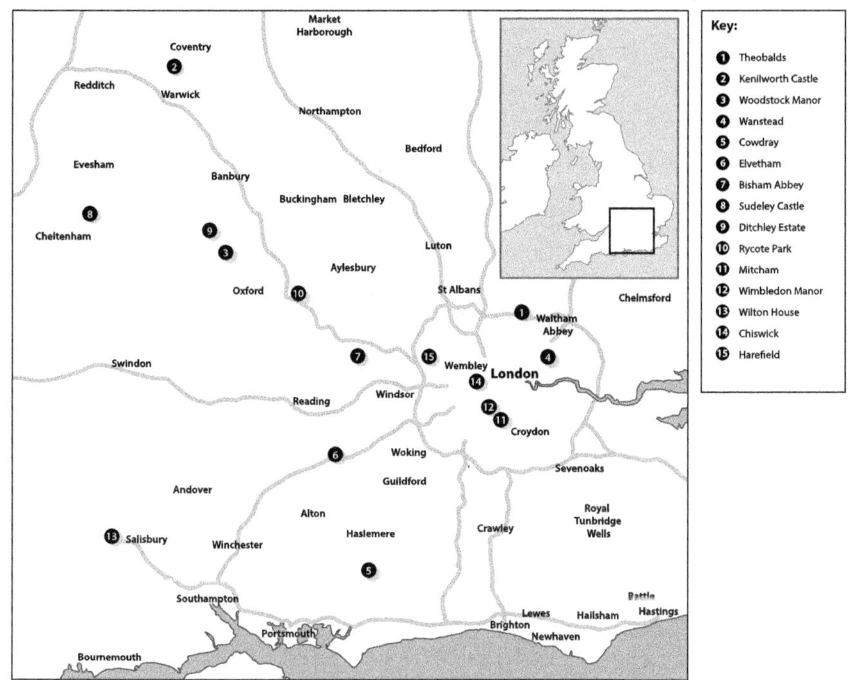

Map showing the location of Elizabethan country house entertainments.

Introduction

In September 1575, Queen Elizabeth visited the royal residence at Woodstock in Oxfordshire as part of a lengthy journey through several English counties. As she entered the grounds, two men jousted before her, and a hermit welcomed her to the residence, currently kept by her lieutenant, Sir Henry Lee. With her entourage trailing behind her, Elizabeth dismounted her horse and walked with the hermit from the park entrance to the manor, as he delivered a chivalric tale about knights in love with women above their station or beyond their reach. When Elizabeth and the others approached the house, they admired the ivy, flowers, and "glimering" gold plate that covered the path and door, and they could see a crescent-shaped table just inside the house set with many "diuers" and "dainty" dishes.[1] At the manor entrance stood an oak tree covered with paintings featuring "men of great credite," many of whom "were in loue."[2] Seventeen years later, when Lee hosted Elizabeth at Woodstock and at his nearby Ditchley estate, he had these paintings appear once again. On this second occasion, a page claimed that the "charmed picturs" held "some secreats" that only the Queen could unlock.[3] No account of either performance describes the paintings in further detail, and the pamphlet of the earlier entertainment adds by way of explanation: "the Allegories are hard to be vnderstood, without some knowledge of the inuentors."[4]

Lee's indecipherable paintings serve as an apt metaphor for Elizabeth's entertainments at country houses. Little information has survived about many of them, and the meanings of an ephemeral performance designed for an "in crowd" at a specific political moment can easily elude us.

---

[1] *The Queenes Maiesties Entertainment at Woodstocke* (London, 1585; *STC* 7596), sig. B4r.

[2] Ibid., sig. B4v.

[3] I quote from Gabriel Heaton's newly edited text, "Sir Henry Lee's Entertainments for the Queen at Ditchley and Woodstock, 20–21 September 1592" in Elizabeth Goldring, et al., eds., *John Nichols's The Progresses and Public Processions of Queen Elizabeth I: A New Edition of the Early Modern Sources* (Oxford University Press, 2014), 3:687.

[4] *Woodstocke*, sig. B4v.

Additionally, as Lee's entertainments reveal, narrators of printed and manuscript accounts described only certain details. Curtis Breight has argued that these pageants "must be approached particularly, not monolithically; historically, not generically."[5] I propose that we need both at once – a methodology that analyzes the genre to understand better each individual instance of it. To unlock the secrets of a country house entertainment, we need to study its "inventors" and their political agendas, its language, its conventional features, and relevant archival materials to assess what that specific performance and its subsequent texts meant at those particular times. But to appreciate fully these entertainments' political interventions, we also need to analyze them as a group. This approach best enables us to examine their "social force and function" as their original audiences would have understood them.[6]

Although long unrecognized as a literary genre, the country house entertainment – the episodic pageantry performed at country estates during royal "progresses" – was practiced as one in Elizabethan England. Composed of historically specific conventions that grew out of "social contracts" and advanced social relations among multiple collaborators and audiences, this genre carried unique cultural and political functions.[7] Recent scholarship has shown increasing interest in individual Elizabethan country house performances as important events, but no one has yet analyzed the genre's features and development more fully.[8] By doing so, we gain new insights

[5] Curtis Breight, "Realpolitik and Elizabethan Ceremony: The Earl of Hertford's Entertainment of Elizabeth at Elvetham, 1591" in *Renaissance Quarterly* 45 (1992): 20.

[6] I take the phrase "social force and function" from Rosalie Colie, *The Resources of Kind: Genre-Theory in the Renaissance*, ed. Barbara K. Lewalski (Berkeley: University of California Press, 1973), 114.

[7] My definition of genre builds on Alastair Fowler's identification of literary kinds as historical and dynamic in *Kinds of Literature: An Introduction to the Theory of Genres and Modes* (Cambridge, Mass.: Harvard University Press, 1982) and Frederic Jameson's description of genres as "social contracts" between writers and their audience in *The Political Unconscious: Narrative as a Socially Symbolic Act* (Ithaca: Cornell University Press, 1982), 106.

[8] Examples of this recent interest include the newly edited texts of country house entertainments in *John Nichols's The Progresses*; Gabriel Heaton, *Writing and Reading Royal Entertainments From George Gascoigne to Ben Jonson* (Oxford University Press, 2010); Janette Dillon, *The Language of Space in Court Performance, 1400–1625* (Cambridge University Press, 2010); Jayne Elisabeth Archer, Elizabeth Goldring, and Sarah Knight, eds., *The Progresses, Pageants, and Entertainments of Queen Elizabeth I* (Oxford University Press, 2007); Rachel Kapelle, "Predicting Elizabeth: Prophecy on Progress" in *Medieval and Renaissance Drama in England* 24 (2011): 83–105. In earlier studies, David Bergeron, Bruce R. Smith, and Michael Leslie each briefly approached country house entertainment as a distinct kind of drama, but they did not examine the genre's development, involvement of women, agendas in print, or specific insights into Elizabethan literature and culture. Bergeron, *English Civic Pageantry, 1558–1642* (Columbia: University of South Carolina Press, 1971); Smith, "Landscape with Figures: The Three Realms of Queen Elizabeth's Country-house Revels" in *Renaissance Drama* n.s. 8 (1977): 57–115; Leslie, "Something Nasty in the Wilderness: Entertaining Queen Elizabeth on her Progresses" in *Medieval and Renaissance Drama in England* 10 (1998): 47–72.

into Elizabethan England's political trends, its theatrical genres, the functions of printed pageantry, and the collaborative nature of Renaissance authorship. This book places country house entertainment in two different and equally crucial contexts: as part of a performance genre and as printed texts that helped to form publishers' lists. The first half examines surviving records of a performance along with hosts' biographies, family papers, and other contextual materials to reconstruct what might have happened during that event. The second half examines how Elizabethan stationers made country house entertainments widely appealing in print. Although scholars have often misunderstood these entertainments as simple propaganda with limited cultural significance, they debated local and national politics in the guise of light-hearted praise. As Elizabeth's hosts used performances to lobby for personal gains, and publishers later used entertainment texts to develop their specialties, the genre intervened in political debates, including whether women made good politicians and what roles the church and local culture should play in definitions of England. This introduction defines the genre's features and functions, identifies the conditions in which it emerged, and considers how its engagement with related genres encourages us to look anew at Elizabethan politics.

Setting the Stage: Defining Country House Entertainment in Performance

Elizabethans described country house performances as "speeches," "pleasures," "dialogues," "spectacles," "devices," and "shows," but they most often used the word "entertainment" to encompass the range of revelry and hospitality that hosts extended to the Queen. This revelry included banquets, music, hunting, dancing, fireworks, and various spectacles and sports. All encoded political meanings, but the dramatic pageants announced the event's political stakes most directly. Each performance, designed and executed for a single event, was staged in the gardens, parks, and courtyards of a country estate. This aspect of the genre – its occasion-specific, site-specific location at country estates where people lived and worked – was its most crucial defining element.[9] A large country estate

---

[9] I use the term "site-specific" to highlight connections between my approach and contemporary performance studies, in which the term describes performances staged in spaces other than a standard theater. Some scholars of early modern theater have begun thinking about site-specificity in the English Renaissance, and my study shows that Elizabethan country house entertainment is an especially apt example. See especially Anna Birch and Joanne Tompkins, eds., *Performing*

signified a family's social status and power in local, regional, and national communities, and it became, on the arrival of the court, simultaneously provincial and courtly.[10] Audiences arrived with set ideas about the place and its inhabitants, and the performance exploited or rewrote that existing history as its hosts and audiences moved between the fictional world of the entertainment and the real world of the country estate.

A country house performance also required significant physical movement from its actors and audience as they performed and experienced a sequence of pageants consisting of songs, speeches, and dialogues in verse and prose. Elizabeth arrived on horse and was greeted at the gate by a poetic invocation that introduced her hosts and the performance's tone and agendas. As the pageantry progressed to new episodes, actors guided Elizabeth and the rest of the audience toward the manor, and Elizabeth typically stepped off her horse to walk with them. The country location inspired the use of elements from English popular pastimes and seasonal festivals such as feasts of misrule, morris dancing, and May Day festivities, while the presence of the monarch enabled the genre to employ and rework courtly praising conventions, especially pastoral and Petrarchan ones. Elizabeth met shepherds, porters, gardeners, and other characters whose presence highlighted the pastoral, domestic location. She also met figures from classical mythology and English lore who helped construct a narrative of Elizabethan England's cultural eminence. Once inside the house, she was treated to a grand feast. Other pageants might follow if she stayed for multiple nights and, at her departure, a final pageant bid farewell and mourned the loss of her presence.

Each performance was the collaborative enterprise of a collection of "devisers," an Elizabethan term for those who invented pageantry, all of whom contributed personal and political agendas.[11] These devisers typically included several members of the host family, writers, actors, composers, and musicians. Because Elizabeth often traveled with a large retinue, her hosts — sometimes a single male householder or female widow, but most often a

---

Site-Specific Theatre: Politics, Place, Practice (Basingstoke: Palgrave, 2012); Susan Bennett and Mary Polito, eds., *Performing Environments: Site-Specificity in Medieval and Early Modern English Drama* (Basingstoke: Palgrave, 2014); Julie Sanders, *The Cultural Geography of Early Modern Drama, 1620–1650* (Cambridge University Press, 2011).

[10] Matthew Johnson, *Behind the Castle Gate: From Medieval to Renaissance* (London and New York: Routledge, 2002), 1–18.

[11] Court entertainments were often called "devices" in early modern England, and the Woodstock entertainment refers to its "deuisors" (sig. c3r). Modern performance studies also use the term to describe someone who invents and plans a performance, especially one generated collaboratively. See, e.g., Emma Govan, Helen Nicholson, and Katie Normington, *Making a Performance: Devising Histories and Contemporary Practices* (Abingdon and New York: Routledge, 2007), 4–7.

husband–wife team – relied on many household servants and laborers to produce an entertainment, and some records highlight the contributions of food and supplies by neighboring gentry. Elizabeth's hosts served as lead devisers; they financed and supervised the event, including plans for meals, sleeping quarters, and entertainment. The Crown paid some expenses and a royal advance team traveled ahead to help secure supplies, but the hosting family generally bore the brunt of the cost and stress.[12] The entertainments at Kenilworth Castle in Warwickshire and at Harefield in Middlesex cost their hosts more than their households normally spent in a year.[13] In part, country house owners hosted the court because they had no choice. Elizabeth did not need to be invited; she and her advisors arranged the itinerary, called a "gest," and announced where they would travel. But householders who staged dramatic productions chose to do so because they hoped their investment would produce intangible rewards such as increased honor and favor. Hosts had the most to gain or lose from an entertainment's relative success, so their preferences and ambitions typically determined its content.

They collaborated with writers and players to produce this content. Surviving Elizabethan expense records include entries for food and other provisions, but none for writers, actors, costumes, or dramatic properties beyond gifts for the Queen, so we cannot be certain whether writers and players received monetary compensation.[14] Perhaps they were "paid" in meals, lodging, and the prospect of future patronage. A few hosts wrote pageants themselves; others commissioned writers or collaborated with courtly poets, who contributed verses in the hopes of royal preferment. All entertainment writers had the opportunity to lobby for royal favor and advertise their skill at penning courtly verse, as the few entertainment texts that mention writers demonstrate. But most hired writers primarily carried out their patrons' wishes. A letter from John Davies to his patron about a pageant draft exemplifies the typical writer–patron relationship in this genre: "I humbly beseech your honour to lett your eie passe a little over it; and to lett me know what your Judgment mislikes, and I shall quickly

---

¹² For more about preparations for royal visits, see Mary Hill Cole, *The Portable Queen: Elizabeth I and the Politics of Ceremony* (Amherst: University of Massachusetts Press, 1999), 41–6.

¹³ See Chapters 1 and 3.

¹⁴ Some records associated with Jacobean country house entertainments show payments to writers and other devisers. For example, Robert Cecil paid Ben Jonson and Inigo Jones sizable sums to devise entertainments at Theobalds in 1606 and 1607. But later practices do not necessarily indicate what happened in Elizabeth's reign. For more on the Cecilian expense records, see Scott McMillin, "Jonson's Early Entertainments: New Information from Hatfield House" in *Renaissance Drama* n.s. 1 (1968): 153–66.

correct it ... I am not ambitios to be reputed the autor of a speech, but am zealous to have things donne according to your honours pleasure."[15] Most Elizabethan country house entertainments did not mention their writers but instead presented themselves as gifts poured directly from their hosts' hearts to the Queen. Each performance also showed off the host family's patronage of professional and amateur actors. Hosts sometimes employed traveling companies – the pageantry at Kenilworth and at Elvetham in Hampshire probably featured the hosts' own companies of players – and other times patched together casts of individual performers.[16] Elite members of the household regularly acted in entertainments. They sought political reward rather than payment, while professional actors and lower-ranking amateur performers from neighboring towns could receive monetary compensation from Elizabeth.[17] Some questions remain impossible to answer with certainty, including who assigned roles, selected costumes, and directed rehearsals.[18]

Country house performances were as interactive as they were collaboratively prepared. Because Elizabeth walked with performers and spectators more often than she sat apart from or above the action, she mingled with subjects on their level and at their homes. She and other audience members were not passive spectators; they interacted, responded, and moved in ways that shaped the performance. A single entertainment produced numerous meanings for multiple audiences. Because the lowest ranking guests were excluded from indoor areas, banquets, and certain gated outdoor spaces, they experienced the performance differently from those with

---

[15] Davies to Robert Cecil, Hatfield House Archives, Cecil Papers, 90/69. Qtd. in Heaton, *Writing and Reading*, 101.

[16] We lack direct evidence that Leicester's Men performed at Kenilworth or that Hertford's Men performed at Elvetham, but there is also no evidence that either company was elsewhere during these performances. See E. K. Chambers, *The Elizabethan Stage* (Oxford: Clarendon, 1923), 1:88–9, 1:117; Sally-Beth MacLean, "Tracking Leicester's Men: The Patronage of a Performance Troupe" in Paul Whitfield White and Suzanne R. Westfall, eds., *Shakespeare and Theatrical Patronage in Early Modern England* (Cambridge University Press, 2002), 263–4; MacLean, "Adult Playing Companies, 1583–1593" in Richard Dutton, ed., *The Oxford Handbook of Early Modern Theatre* (Oxford University Press, 2011), 49.

[17] Printed accounts of the Kenilworth and Elvetham entertainments reveal that Elizabeth gave actors money for their performances. *A Letter Whearin Part of the Entertainment vntoo the Queenz Maiesty at Killingwoorth Castl in Warwik Sheer in this Soomerz Progress 1575 is Signified* (London, n.d.; *STC* 15190.5), sig. E4v; *The Honorable Entertainement Gieuen to the Queenes Maiestie in Progresse, at Eluetham in Hampshire by the Right Honorable the Earle of Hertford. 1591* (London, 1591; *STC* 7583), sig. D2r.

[18] Only one record mentions rehearsal; it describes an unperformed pageant as "being prepared and redy (euery Actor in his garment) two or three dayes together." "A Briefe Rehearsall, or Rather a True Copie of as Much as Was Presented before Her Maiesties at Kenelworth" in *The VVhole Woorkes of George Gascoigne Esquyre* (London, 1587; *STC* 11638), sig. c2v.

greater access and proximity to the Queen. Likewise, audience members might interpret the same pageant differently, depending on their education, gender, social rank, and the "horizon of cultural and ideological expectations" they brought to the performance.[19]

To please their most demanding and powerful guest, devisers carefully choreographed nearly all aspects of an entertainment. When Elizabeth hunted, deer appeared in her sightline.[20] When she stayed overnight, she often slept in newly built or renovated apartments. When she ate, she enjoyed exquisite banquets. When she walked or rode into new spaces, she encountered pageants and music. But devisers' carefully laid plans often needed to be altered at the last minute in response to two sources of unpredictability: the weather and the Queen. Parts of several entertainments were canceled or postponed owing to wet conditions, and the Harefield entertainment included an entire pageant about the nuisance of persistent rain. The comments and corrections of the vocal guest of honor also affected the content of pageantry, and even more uncertain was whether and when she would arrive. Her gests often show multiple possible paths because court business, infections, food shortages, fears about her security, and her own changing preferences could all alter the plan, and several letters complain about the frustrating lack of "certayntie" about her progresses.[21] Hosts, writers, and performers prepared as well as they could, improvised when needed, and hoped in all cases to present themselves as accommodating and clever.

The genre's defining elements – its provincial landscape setting, episodic and mobile structure, characters and tropes from courtly and popular literature, collaborative authorship, and interactive and somewhat improvised performance – combined to enable public negotiations among senior courtiers and Elizabeth. With the exception of Woodstock, a royal residence, the genre's performance sites were estates managed by aristocrats but officially owned by the monarch. This space, together with the interaction central to the genre, offered heightened opportunities for shared and contested authority. During a country house entertainment, Elizabeth was more accessible than usual, and her hosts took advantage of these

---

[19] Susan Bennett, *Theatre Audiences: A Theory of Production and Reception* (Abingdon and New York: Routledge, 1990), 107.

[20] In *Shakespeare and the Hunt: A Cultural and Social Study* (Cambridge University Press, 2001), Edward Berry notes that Elizabeth's progress hosts often used either bow-and-stable hunting, where they brought deer before Elizabeth, or coursing, a spectator sport (1–37). Both were carefully arranged in advance to ensure success in hunting.

[21] I quote from Gilbert Talbot's letter to Shrewsbury on July 6, 1576, LPL, Manuscript 3197, f. 157. For an example of a gest with multiple paths, see BL, Lansdowne Manuscript 19.

circumstances to advance their own ambitions and to negotiate the roles of monarch and advisor, of region and nation, and of men and women. These political negotiations were rooted in personal relationships and goals. Elizabeth sought pleasure, productive alliances with her elite subjects, and the opportunity to monitor and solicit her subjects' obedience. Likewise, her hosts sought enhanced status, court positions or successful marriages for their children, and heightened influence over policy-making. As entertainments questioned policies and proposed new ones, they offered advice about how Elizabeth might best manage the poor, Catholic recusants, her advisors, foreign policy, and especially her gender.

Setting the Type: Defining Country House Entertainment in Print

Devisers and audience members recorded aspects of these ephemeral performances in printed and manuscript texts. These texts allow us to access the genre in performance, but they also carried new agendas. Of the seventeen entertainments I have identified, nine survive as printed books, five as manuscripts, and three in both forms (see Appendix 1). Elizabethans shared manuscript texts of country house pageantry either as separates, which letter-writers enclosed in correspondence for those who could not attend, or as small pamphlets that served as keepsakes for the hosting family or Elizabeth. In both formats, manuscript copies include pageantry dialogue but few to no narrative descriptions of the actors' movements or audiences' responses. Gabriel Heaton has analyzed the manuscript circulation of various kinds of Elizabethan pageantry at length.[22] *The Elizabethan Country House Entertainment* focuses on the less studied printed texts, which brought country house entertainments to wider audiences and which reveal how contemporary publishers and later readers encountered and exploited the genre.

These printed accounts appeared as pamphlets, in poetry anthologies, and as part of authorial collections. All formats mixed narrative description with pageantry dialogue. Some examples include only a short header declaring the performance occasion and focus on literary devices, while others offer detailed narration of the event's sights and sounds. In print the genre retained several of its defining features, including central tropes, collaborative authorship, and a fragmented structure. The miscellanies that print fragments of entertainments reveal that the genre was an excellent example of *genera mixta* because it derived from several other literary

---

[22] Heaton, *Writing and Reading*, 1–116. He discusses some printed pamphlets but does so briefly (93–100).

kinds – pastoral lyric, encomia, dramatic comedy, songs, and eclogues – but carried its own unique combination of elements and utilities.[23] Scholarship on Elizabethan pageantry still tends to treat these texts mostly as windows onto the performances they describe, but readers experienced printed country house entertainment differently from those who saw the performances.[24] The contributions of eyewitnesses, scribes, editors, and publishers altered an entertainment's meaning, and printed accounts removed the pageantry from its original location and hosts' individual concerns to place it in new contexts. Sometimes a narrator's prose even instructs readers how to interpret aspects of the pageantry. Because the printed records involved new devisers and reached even more diverse audiences, they carried new functions.

Contrary to popular assumption, the Crown did not commission these texts as official propaganda. There is no evidence that the Queen, her advisors, or her royal printer had a hand in any of the publications I examine.[25] Instead, publishers – the lead "devisers" of printed entertainments – invested money in their production because they identified existing markets for them. Entertainment hosts might have occasionally helped finance these publications in order to advertise widely their own wealth and status, but even the books that might have been subsidized by hosts show evidence of their publishers' involvement and aims. In this way, printed country house entertainment differs from several other kinds of Elizabethan pageantry. Printed Lord Mayors' shows, for example, were financed by companies and printed hastily on demand, but publishers identified country house entertainment as attractive to wider audiences.[26]

---

[23] Colie identifies *genera mixta* as typical of many Renaissance works in *Resources of Kind*, esp. 76–102.

[24] The few scholars who have considered certain Elizabethan entertainment texts (especially those about Kenilworth) as unique rhetorical projects include Heaton, *Writing and Reading*, 1–116; Wendy Wall, *The Imprint of Gender: Authorship and Publication in the English Renaissance* (Ithaca: Cornell University Press, 1993), 111–67; Elizabeth Goldring, "'A mercer ye wot az we be': The Authorship of the Kenilworth *Letter* Reconsidered" in *English Literary Renaissance* 38.2 (2008): 245–69; and Sandra Logan, *Text/Events in Early Modern England: Poetics of History* (Aldershot: Ashgate, 2007), 93–183.

[25] Helen Watanabe-O'Kelly identifies Continental festival books as official, usually commissioned accounts of pageantry in "The Early Modern Festival Book: Function and Form" in J. R. Mulryne, Helen Watanabe-O'Kelly, and Margaret Shewring, eds., *Europa Triumphans: Court and Civic Festivals in Early Modern Europe* (Aldershot: Ashgate, 2004), 1:3–18. Several scholars have assumed the same is true in England. See, e.g., Axel Stähler, "Imagining the Illusive/Elusive? Printed Accounts of Elizabethan Festivals" in Christa Jansohn, ed., *Queen Elizabeth I: Past and Present* (Munster: Lit Verlag, 2004), 65–7; Jean Wilson, *Entertainments for Elizabeth I* (Woodbridge: D. S. Brewer, 1980), 10. Heaton determines in *Writing and Reading*, as I have, that this was not the case in England (96–100).

[26] Tracey Hill is probably right to speculate that printed Lord Mayors' shows served as programs or souvenirs because their lack of narrative detail implies a knowing audience familiar with their performances. Hill, *Pageantry and Power: A Cultural History of the Early Modern Lord Mayor's Show, 1585–1639* (Manchester University Press, 2011), 220, 232–3.

Furthermore, unlike some Continental festival books that were published in advance to be distributed at performances, Elizabethan country house entertainments were printed after the performances they describe.[27] The only example included in the Stationers' Register was the Elvetham pamphlet, which John Wolfe entered on October 1, 1591, shortly after the late September performance.[28] Elizabethan entertainment pamphlets typically offer titles that indicate past action, such as *Speeches Delivered to Her Maiestie This Last Progresse* (1592), refer to weather conditions and other occurrences that could not have been predicted, and describe audience reactions.

Drawing on evidence of early readers and owners, I demonstrate that printed country house entertainments served many functions for multiple audiences: they were collected as part of an emerging national literature, helped define regional culture, offered court gossip to the elite insider, functioned as news for the common reader, and were sometimes treated as literary works that helped define authorial identity. Printed entertainments tended to highlight the genre's negotiations of regional and national identities – a feature present in performance but accentuated in the printed texts. Entertainments used the words "nation," "country," "empire," and "English" – all unstable concepts in the Elizabethan period. As these terms merged discourses of localism, royal loyalty, and emerging nationalism, the genre debated to what extent England should be defined by and centered on its monarch.[29]

The Emergence and Development of Country House Entertainment

Like other genres, country house entertainment developed gradually and evolved over time, and although it shared certain features with earlier, adjacent, and later genres, there was nothing else exactly like it. It grew

---

[27] Watanabe-O'Kelly, "Early Modern Festival Book," 1:9.

[28] *Stationers' Register: A Transcript of the Registers of the Company of Stationers of London, 1554–1640, A.D.*, ed. Edward Arber (1875; reprint, New York: Smith, 1950), 2:596. Because no entries survive from 1571 to July 1576, we do not know whether anyone entered texts about the 1570s entertainments at Theobalds, Kenilworth, or Woodstock.

[29] Country house entertainment underscores that Elizabethans did not consistently differentiate between the state (royal authority) and the nation (the people and the land) and supports Andrew Hadfield's claim that various conceptions of the nation coexisted in this period. Building on studies by Hadfield, Richard Helgerson, Claire McEachern, and other literary scholars who identify the beginnings of a national rhetoric in Tudor England, this book treats Elizabethan royal patriotism as a kind of early nationalism. Andrew Hadfield, *Literature, Politics and National Identity: Reformation to Renaissance* (Cambridge University Press, 1994), esp. 1–3; Richard Helgerson, *Forms of Nationhood: The Elizabethan Writing of England* (University of Chicago Press, 1992); Claire McEachern, *The Poetics of English Nationhood, 1590–1612* (Cambridge University Press, 1996).

out of multiple dramatic precedents, especially Continental and English civic entries and entertainments at Continental royal palaces – all of which anticipated the country house entertainment's outdoor, episodic celebration of a visiting monarch but none of which staged as interactive a political negotiation.[30] Civic entries enacted exchanges between city officials and the monarch, but their structure often kept the royal guest apart from the performers and audience. Actors delivered speeches on carts and stages to a monarch observing the action from within a litter, whereas country house entertainments solicited more intimate interaction when actors and spectators walked together. Progress entertainments sponsored by Queen Mary of Hungary in 1549 and Catherine de Medici in 1564 anticipated this intimate structure, but, because members of the royal family directed these pageants at royal residences and had the literary components composed by official court poets, they served more as royal propaganda and less as dialogues with subjects than did Elizabethan country house pageants.[31] Although other Tudor monarchs went on progress and Henry VIII visited country houses with some frequency, no country house entertainments appear to survive from his or any other earlier English monarch's visits to provincial estates. From the beginning of her reign in 1558, Elizabeth traveled often, enjoyed banquets and short revels at country estates, and reveled in interactive pageantry and public performance. Yet the earliest known country house pageants did not appear until the 1570s, when William Cecil, Lord Burghley, welcomed Elizabeth to his house at Theobalds in 1571 and Robert Dudley, Earl of Leicester, entertained her at Kenilworth in 1575.[32]

The genre materialized in response to specific historical circumstances and helped shape monarch–subject relations and the English theater at a crucial time. The 1570s marked a turning point from Elizabeth's status

---

[30] For more on early Tudor revels, see especially Sydney Anglo, *Spectacle, Pageantry, and Early Tudor Policy*, 2nd edn. (Oxford: Clarendon, 1997), 21–34; Roy Strong, *Art and Power: Renaissance Festivals, 1450–1650* (Berkeley and Los Angeles: University of California Press, 1984); W. R. Streitberger, *Court Revels, 1485–1559* (University of Toronto Press, 1994), 3–22.

[31] Mary of Hungary's entertainment at Binche celebrated the visit of her brother Charles V of Spain and his son Philip II; Catherine de Medici sponsored several "magnificences" to promote the regime of her son, Charles IX, during their grand tour of France from 1564 to 1566. For more on these entertainments, see Victor E. Graham and W. McAllister Johnson, eds., *The Royal Tour of France by Charles IX and Catherine de Medici: Festivals and Entries, 1564–6* (University of Toronto Press, 1979), 23–9; Strong, *Art and Power*, 91–3.

[32] Elizabeth's hosts entertained her with banquets during her first progress at Nonsuch Palace in April 1559 and Baynard's Castle in August, she was entertained in some fashion at Hunsdon House (1571) and Warwick Castle (1572), and she enjoyed "Princely Sports" at Kenilworth Castle in 1572. No pageantry survives from any of these events, but brief descriptions can be found in *The Diary of Henry Machyn: Citizen and Merchant-taylor of London, from A.D. 1550 to A.D. 1563*, ed. John Gough Nichols (London, 1848), 196–206.

as a marriageable young woman to her new role – not yet established at this point – as Virgin Queen.[33] Country house entertainment enabled her high-ranking subjects to manage the unprecedented circumstance of an unmarried female ruler and to help define the terms of her new role. Entertainments in the 1570s often debated her marital prospects, used language of chivalry to represent political ambition, and urged her to listen to male advisors and put her country's needs above her own. Additionally, the earliest examples of the genre reveal that it emerged as a harbinger of the establishment of permanent commercial playhouses in England.[34] In 1576, James Burbage built the Theatre, the first permanent outdoor playhouse, and the Chapel Children leased the first Blackfriars, the first indoor commercial playhouse.[35] Some of the factors that created the conditions for viable commercial theater in London also contributed to the development of country house entertainment. Reforms in the Revels Office included a reduction in money for court masques, which helped inspire new dramatic forms, and both the Kenilworth entertainment and the construction of the Theatre might be linked to the royal patent Elizabeth granted Leicester's players, managed by Burbage, in May 1574.[36] This legislation, the first royal patent for a company of adult players, gave Leicester's company royal privilege to perform throughout England, including at Kenilworth and at commercial theaters, and it may have helped precipitate willingness to invest in a permanent playhouse.[37]

[33] See especially John N. King, "Queen Elizabeth I: Representations of the Virgin Queen" in *Renaissance Quarterly* 43.1 (1990): 30–74; Susan Doran, *Monarchy and Matrimony: The Courtships of Elizabeth I* (Abingdon and New York: Routledge, 1996), 10–11. Both dispute the notion that Elizabeth constructed the image of Virgin Queen herself by vowing celibacy at the beginning of her reign. King locates the shift to Virgin Queen in the 1579–83 marriage negotiations with Francois, the Duke of Anjou, and Doran finds an early representation of Elizabeth as Virgin Queen in the Norwich civic entry of 1578. I propose that country house entertainments played a major role in establishing this image.

[34] Public playing was not new and the construction of the semi-permanent Red Lion playhouse in 1567 suggests that other temporary playing spaces may have existed earlier, but the mid-1570s was a crucial period of growth for multiple kinds of dramatic entertainment. See especially W. R. Streitberger, "Adult Playing Companies to 1583" in Dutton, ed., *The Oxford Handbook of Early Modern Theatre*, 19–38; Jean E. Howard, *Theater of a City: The Places of London Comedy, 1598–1642* (Philadelphia: University of Pennsylvania Press, 2009), 14–16.

[35] Andrew Gurr, *The Shakespearean Stage, 1574–1642* (Cambridge University Press, 1992), 113–56.

[36] Streitberger, "Adult Playing," 19–38.

[37] Gurr, *Shakespearean Stage*, 29–31. Scott McMillin and Sally-Beth MacLean argue against this theory in *The Queen's Men and their Plays* (Cambridge University Press, 2006) and emphasize that the Crown issued the patent to limit, not to encourage the growth of commercial theater (1–36). But Streitberger, "Adult Playing" notes that although the council regulated the theater to benefit the court, it still created the conditions that encouraged development in the theater industry (24–6).

No record of country house entertainment survives from the 1580s, at least partially because Elizabeth traveled less for fear of political unrest, and when the genre reappeared in the altered climate of the 1590s, new motifs emerged as devisers sought nuanced strategies to praise an aging queen and to dramatize increased conflict at and beyond the court. Marriage gave way to chastity as a central theme, and it became fashionable to represent Elizabeth as a beloved, ever-youthful monarch ruling in England's golden age. We can attribute the genre's growth partially to changing times and partially to the involvement of female devisers, who sought alternatives to the gendered language of Petrarchan courtiership. Although some feminist critics have argued that Elizabeth's queenship made no difference in the status of English women, this book demonstrates otherwise.[38] The lengthy rule of a single female monarch seems to have inspired other elite women to engage in political diplomacies through country house performance.

Women's contributions to country house entertainments became especially visible in Elizabeth's last decade, but the genre always included female devisers. Other kinds of contemporary drama mostly performed masculinity – only men wrote and acted in university and commercial plays, jousted, devised royal entries, and performed in masques during Elizabeth's reign – but Elizabethan country house entertainment offered women opportunities to plan, write, and perform drama.[39] Elite household women stood behind nearly every progress visit; they planned meals, prepared the house for visitors, and perhaps supervised the production of pageantry. Because the genre was staged at country houses for the court, these housewives performed political roles while carrying out domestic duties. At least two

[38] See, e.g., Allison Heisch, "Queen Elizabeth I and the Persistence of Patriarchy" in *Feminist Review* 4 (1980): 45–56; Joan Kelly-Gadol, "Did Women Have a Renaissance?" in Renate Bridenthal and Claudia Koonz, eds., *Becoming Visible: Women in European History* (Boston: Houghton, 1977), 148–52.

[39] Women sometimes contributed to other kinds of Tudor pageantry, but they played less central roles than they did in country house entertainment. Aristocratic women danced in early Tudor mummings and masquerades, and female domestic laborers were silent performers in the 1578 civic pageantry at Norwich when they sat knitting and spinning on stage as part of a tableau. As is well known, women would later help devise and perform in court masques during the Stuart period, although Elizabethan court masques appear to feature only male devisers. Skiles Howard, *The Politics of Courtly Dancing in Early Modern England* (Amherst: University of Massachusetts Press, 1998), 26–45; Natasha Korda, "Staging Alien Women's Work in Civic Pageants" in Michelle M. Dowd and Natasha Korda, eds., *Working Subjects in Early Modern English Drama* (Aldershot: Ashgate, 2011), 53–68; Leeds Barroll, *Anna of Denmark, Queen of England: A Cultural Biography* (Philadelphia: University of Pennsylvania, 2001); Clare McManus, *Women on the Renaissance Stage: Anna of Denmark and Female Masquing in the Stuart Court (1590–1619)* (Manchester University Press, 2002); Sophie Tomlinson, *Women on Stage in Stuart Drama* (Cambridge University Press, 2005).

women – Lady Elizabeth Russell and Mary Sidney, Countess of Pembroke – wrote country house pageants. Female hosts and writers used entertainments to lobby for favor and power just as men did, but they also reshaped praising conventions to make space for female authority and negotiations between women. Some elite women performed speaking parts that gave voice to their goals and political concerns. Lower-ranking women contributed folk dances and plays that allowed them opportunities to represent the interests of their localities. As alternating cross-dressed male actors with female players drew attention to gender as culturally produced, the dialogue within several entertainments challenged gender roles or displayed female alliances as key to England's successful governing. Through country house entertainment, female hosts, writers, and performers participated in debates about war and policy-making that we might wrongly assume were off limits for Elizabethan women.

Meanwhile, the printed books recording these performances were at the forefront of an important period of growth for printed pageantry and other drama in the 1570s. The desire to record and print royal festivities was not entirely new, as printed narratives of Anne Boleyn's and Elizabeth's coronation pageants were published in the 1530s and 1550s, but printed country house entertainments were among the first examples of English pageantry to appear as literary playbooks with dialogue, speech prefixes, and stage directions. The earliest Theobalds entertainment appeared as a broadside in 1571, a few years before George Gascoigne included his masque for the wedding of Viscount Montague's daughter in *A Hundreth Sundrie Flowres* (1573) and Thomas Churchyard included the civic entertainment at Bristow in *The Firste Parte of Churchyardes Chippes* (1575).[40] Fuller texts of the Kenilworth and Woodstock entertainments then appeared as single playbooks in the mid-1570s to 1580s, and together with Gascoigne's inclusion of an account of the Kenilworth performance in his authorial collection in 1587, they argued for the literary value of printed pageantry. They also served as early news books, as did the country house entertainment pamphlets published in the 1590s. The popularity of printed country house entertainment as pamphlets and as part of three poetic miscellanies paved the way for the later publication of Stuart court masques in similar formats.[41] They showed future publishers and authors

---

[40] George Gascoigne, *A Hundredth Sundrie Flowres Bounde Vp in One Small Poesie* (London, 1573; *STC* 11635), sig. Aa3v–Cc1v; Thomas Churchyard, *The Firste Parte of Churchyardes Chippes* (London, 1575; *STC* 5232), sig. N4v–O6v.

[41] A dialogue from the Woodstock/Ditchley entertainment appears in *The Phoenix Nest* (London, 1593; *STC* 21516); excerpts from the Elvetham, Bisham, and Sudeley entertainments are included

that pageantry was widely appealing and could serve purposes beyond royal propaganda.

With the exception of a brief, forward-looking epilogue, this book ends with Elizabeth's final progress in 1602, which concludes the genre's period of greatest influence. The country house entertainment became less influential after Elizabeth's death, but it did not die with her. It continued to change in response to shifting historical circumstances, especially monarchical preference, for another three decades. Members of the royal family visited private estates on progress in Stuart England, but they became less interested in impromptu performance and interactive negotiation. James I preferred to connect with his elite subjects by knighting them rather than by performing public dialogues.[42] Charles I was even less interested in interacting with his subjects on progress; he preferred to travel with speed and privacy.[43] Yet at least twelve performance texts survive that we might identify as Stuart country house entertainments. As this book's epilogue explains, these texts reveal hosts' desires for both continuity and change in governing styles and the performance of gender roles since the Elizabethan period.

The court masque succeeded the country house entertainment as the most influential kind of English pageantry and remains the most canonical one today. Both court masques and country house entertainments served as sites for policy debate and social change as they celebrated monarchs, yet their locations and conventions produced different relations to the monarch, roles for women, and forms of Englishness. Compared to masques and other kinds of royal performance, the country house entertainment offered less a presentation *to* the Queen and more an interaction *with* her. When Elizabeth watched masques, tilts, and university performances, she usually sat in one central location as the action unfolded before her, and she appeared visually as the court's powerful center. *The Masque*

in *Englands Helicon* (London, 1600; *STC* 3191); the unperformed Wilton entertainment was published in *A Poetical Rapsody* (London, 1602; *STC* 6373); and the second edition of *A Poetical Rapsodie* (London, 1608; *STC* 6374) includes an excerpt from the Harefield entertainment. For more on the publication of Stuart masques and their function as news, see Lauren Shohet, *Reading Masques: The English Masque and Public Culture in the Seventeenth Century* (Oxford University Press, 2010).

[42] See the descriptions of James' progresses compiled by John Nichols in *The Progresses, Processions, and Magnificent Festivities of King James the First, His Royal Consort, Family, and Court* (London, 1828), 4 vols.

[43] R. Malcolm Smuts, *Court Culture and the Origins of a Royalist Tradition in Early Stuart England* (Philadelphia: University of Pennsylvania Press, 1987), 286; James Knowles, "'In the Purest Times of Peerless Queen Elizabeth': Nostalgia, Politics, and Jonson's Use of the 1575 Kenilworth Entertainments" in Archer, Goldring, and Knight, eds., *The Progresses, Pageants, and Entertainments*, 247–67.

of Proteus (1594) even compared her to an adamantine rock, an image of impenetrable stability.[44] Hierarchical seating at masques displayed a fixed social order.[45]

Under the Stuart kings, the court masque gained popularity because it better suited their governing styles. A masque allowed the monarch to separate his role as head of state from his physical body; the monarch could occupy a fixed position of authority without making himself vulnerable in the way that a fluid, spontaneous country house entertainment did.[46] Work by Clare McManus, Leeds Barroll, Sophie Tomlinson, and Karen Britland on the Stuart masque has laid important groundwork for this study by showing how Stuart women could intervene in politics through court performance. This book underscores that the Stuart court masque did not initiate female performance in Renaissance England, but adapted a tradition from earlier country house entertainment.[47]

The genre's development also paralleled or contributed to the emergence of two non-dramatic genres: sonnets and country house poems. Sonnet sequences emerged, peaked, and waned in the late Elizabethan period, roughly the same time as did this genre.[48] Some of the earliest country house entertainments helped create the Elizabethan convention of using love poetry to express ambition at court, and sonnets and later entertainments alternately employed and rethought that language. Although both genres shared a common language of Petrarchan love that engaged with the court politics of late Elizabethan England, country house entertainments offered devisers a more direct conversation with the Queen and a heightened opportunity to influence policy and court culture. The declining popularity of country house entertainment – and the grand hospitality it enacted and

---

44 This masque was performed as part of the Inner Temple Revels and was published nearly a century after its performance in *Gesta Grayorum* (London, 1688).

45 Martin Butler, *The Stuart Court Masque and Political Culture* (Cambridge University Press, 2009), 48–51; John R. Elliott, Jr., "Plays, Players, and Playwrights in Renaissance Oxford" in John A. Alford, ed., *From Page to Performance: Essays in Early English Drama* (East Lansing: Michigan State University Press, 1995), 184–5; Siobhan Keenan, "Spectator and Spectacle: Royal Entertainment at the Universities in the 1560s" in Archer, Goldring, and Knight, eds., *The Progresses, Pageants, and Entertainments*, 89–97.

46 Kenneth Robert Olwig, *Landscape, Nature, and the Body Politic: From Britain's Renaissance to America's New World* (Madison: University of Wisconsin Press, 2002), 89–92.

47 Clare McManus, *Women on the Renaissance Stage*; Barroll, *Anna of Denmark*; Tomlinson, *Women on Stage in Stuart Drama*; Karen Britland, *Drama at the Courts of Queen Henrietta Maria* (Cambridge University Press, 2006).

48 On the social functions of sonnet sequences, see especially Arthur F. Marotti, "'Love is Not Love': Elizabethan Sonnet Sequences and the Social Order" in *ELH* 49.2 (1982): 396–428; Christopher Warley, *Sonnet Sequences and Social Distinction in Renaissance England* (Cambridge University Press, 2005).

represented – helped create the circumstances that launched the country house poem in the early seventeenth century. The later genre's nostalgic rewriting of a lost country house era responded to claims the earlier genre made about the importance of elite hospitality and country house owners' local governance. But it did so in a somewhat less vexed way because it did not need to engage with a physically present monarch and thus balance multiple authorities.[49] A more thorough understanding of country house entertainment will help illuminate the political conditions in which the English sonnet, country house poem, and court masque gained and lost popularity.

Throughout its brief history, the genre of country house entertainment intervened in a wide range of political issues and literary trends. In the first half of this book, each chapter analyzes one of the genre's praising strategies and the political negotiations it facilitated in performance. Chapter 1, "Negotiating in a 'strange Country': Theobalds, Kenilworth, and the Local Politics of Country House Performance," examines how the genre used pastoral devices in country spaces to define local authorities and to debate Elizabeth's control over the provinces. While the entertainment at Theobalds (1571) insisted on Elizabeth's centrality, the one at Kenilworth (1575) exposed the court's vulnerability in an unfamiliar setting. Chapter 2, " 'Your Maiesty on my knees will I followe': Performing Gender and the Courtier–Monarch Relationship," analyzes how performances fostered and critiqued political Petrarchism to reframe images of Elizabeth's relations to her elite subjects. Some entertainments urged the Queen to employ male courtiers who used love poetry as a metaphor for political desires, while a group of 1592 entertainments proposed alternative definitions of political service that made space for female courtiers. Chapter 3, "An 'abundance of dainties': Hospitality and Housewifery at Elvetham, Mitcham, and Harefield," explores how devisers used language of generosity to build reciprocal relationships with the Queen. The three entertainments analyzed in this chapter sought either to preserve or to reimagine the declining tradition of hospitality, and they together defined it as an elite but not necessarily masculine virtue.

The second half of the book moves from performance to print. Chapter 4, "'Pleasures by a profitable publication': Publishers and Readers

---

[49] On country house poetry as a genre, see G. R. Hibbard, "The Country House Poem of the Seventeenth Century" in *Journal of the Warburg and Courtauld Institutes* 19.1/2 (1956): 159–74; Alastair Fowler, "Country House Poems: The Politics of a Genre" in *The Seventeenth Century* 1.1 (1986): 1–14; Hugh Jenkins, *Feigned Commonwealths: The Country-House Poem and the Fashioning of the Ideal Community* (Pittsburgh: Duquesne University Press, 1998).

of Printed Entertainment," examines the careers of the first publishers who financed printed country house pageants to consider why they reached print and how contemporary readers responded to them. This chapter reveals that several publishers identified value in entertainments' literary devices and sometimes marketed them in ways that ran counter to their politics in performance but appealed to new audiences. Chapter 5, "'Set this downe in English': Cowdray, Elvetham, and Printed Pageantry as National News," analyzes two popular books that functioned as news and cultivated a national readership. Their multiple editions offer different interpretations of these performances as well as disparate definitions of England that reveal an ongoing debate about what it meant to be English in the late Elizabethan period. Chapter 6, "'This paper, which carieth so base names': The Sidneys, Authorship, and Printed Pageantry as Literature," explores how the Sidney family used printed entertainments to bolster authorial identity, despite the genre's collaborative nature. When Mary Sidney included her brother's entertainment at Wanstead (1578) in the 1598 Folio of *Arcadia* and her entertainment at Wilton (1599) in a section of anti-court pastoral poems in the anthology *A Poetical Rapsody* (1602), she highlighted their critiques of Elizabeth's refusal to offer preferment. Both publications expose the genre's function as politically engaged literature.

The book ends with an epilogue that considers what happens to the genre after Elizabeth's death and proposes directions for future research, including how Elizabethan country house entertainment can help us understand John Milton's household entertainments in new ways. Together with the chapters that precede it, the epilogue underscores that country house entertainment flourished briefly in late Elizabethan England but carried more lasting influences. Likewise, the genre offers today's scholars a fresh perspective on Elizabethan drama, politics, gender, and cultural identity.

PART I

Performance

CHAPTER I

Negotiating in a "strange country"
Theobalds, Kenilworth, and the Local Politics of Country House Performance

Everyone who participated in a country house entertainment had needs and vulnerabilities, and each performance negotiated power with gains and losses on each side. The genre's location, its most important defining characteristic, enabled these collaborative exchanges, and the word "country" and its nexus of meanings are essential to understanding the politics of country house performance. At the end of the sixteenth century, "country" designated a rural area distant from courts and cities. The same word could mark a region or district, similar to our current use of "county," and it began to describe the territory or land of a nation. In all cases, "country" identified an area of land with specific boundaries. It should come as no surprise, then, that country house entertainments were obsessed with defining and testing boundaries. They emphasized how houses, gardens, and ordered landscapes reflected their owners' values and ambitions, and as they tried to balance royal and local claims to authority within these spaces, they negotiated the terms of Elizabeth's public relationships with her country gentry and aristocracy.

This chapter analyzes how early examples of the genre used their performance space to explore ownership as a metaphor for political security. It focuses on entertainments hosted by two of Elizabeth's top courtiers: William Cecil, Lord Burghley, who welcomed her to his Hertfordshire estate at Theobalds in 1571, and Robert Dudley, Earl of Leicester, who entertained her at Kenilworth Castle in Warwickshire in 1575. As these highly personal entertainments crafted certain images for their hosts, they revealed divergent strategies that reflected their hosts' personalities and ambitions. By the 1570s, both Burghley and Leicester had long and deeply dependent relationships with the Queen that carried mutual investments and responsibilities. Burghley had served as one of her top advisors since the beginning of the reign, and in his first major post as secretary he was positioned at the center of all political business. Leicester held the somewhat

less secure but influential position of Elizabeth's "favorite," and although
he possessed several titles and responsibilities, he sought increased power.
Elizabeth relied on these men for advice and companionship as much as
they needed her favor. Although both entertainments negotiated the terms
of these men's status and relationships with the Queen, they displayed different interpretations of what it meant to negotiate and balance authority in
the "country." Their entertainments and others in the genre – performances
that were at once provincial and courtly – reveal how discourses of royal
allegiance and national identity were intertwined with "local consciousness"
in Renaissance England.[1] The genre underscores the importance of local
identity to the Elizabethan experience and illustrates how devisers evoked
regional pride to engage in various ways with developing definitions of the
nation.

Location, Location, Location: The Use of Landscape in Country House Entertainment

Unlike progress pageants in cities or at universities, royal entertainments
at country estates exploited and developed the pastoral mode. Country
house entertainment was at the forefront of this literary movement in
Elizabethan England. "The Lady of May," an early country house entertainment at Leicester's Wanstead estate in Essex that was written by Philip
Sidney and performed one year before the publication of Spenser's seminal *Shepheardes Calender* (1579), featured what may have been the first
pastoral singing match in English.[2] Elizabethan writers described pastoral
literature as a vehicle for hidden political commentary. In the *New Arcadia*,
Sidney introduces pastoral eclogues as a kind of therapeutic exercise when
he explains that shepherds used them to "under hidden forms utter such
matters as otherwise they durst not deal with."[3] William Webbe notices
something similar in *Shepheardes Calender*: "much matter vttered somewhat couertly, especially the abuses of some whom he would not be too
playne withall."[4] In *The Arte of English Poesie* (1589), George Puttenham

---

[1] I take the phrase "local consciousness" from John Adrian, *Local Negotiations of English Nationhood, 1570–1680* (Basingstoke: Palgrave, 2011), 3.

[2] W. A. Ringler, ed., *The Poems of Sir Philip Sidney* (Oxford: Clarendon, 1962), 362.

[3] Philip Sidney, *The Countess of Pembroke's Arcadia (The New Arcadia)*, ed. Victor Skretkowicz (Oxford: Clarendon, 1987), 33–4. In the *Old Arcadia* the line reads: "under hidden forms utter such matters as otherwise were not fit for their delivery." Sidney, *The Countess of Pembroke's Arcadia (The Old Arcadia)*, ed. Katherine Duncan-Jones (Oxford University Press, 1990), 50.

[4] William Webbe, *A Discourse of English Poetrie* (London, 1586; *STC* 25172), sig. E4v.

describes the eclogue's function as "vnder the vaile of homely persons, and in rude speeches to insinuate and glaunce at greater matters, and such as perchance had not bene safe to haue beene disclosed in any other sort."[5] Like other kinds of pastoral literature, country house entertainments reveal complex layers of cultural criticism – which William Empson has called "the pastoral process of putting the complex into the simple" – beneath their deceptively simple verses and apparent celebration of an idyllic setting.[6] Country house pageantry did not offer Elizabeth a retreat from politics, but used the pastoral style to impart political instruction and critique.[7] The performances themselves enacted a conventional pastoral narrative – evident in *Arcadia*, Shakespeare's *As You Like It*, and other fictional texts – of courtly figures journeying to the country to gain new perspectives on the court. Their seeming triviality made the perfect cover for their directives and criticism, and because pastoral literature traditionally highlighted opposing voices and unresolved debates, it could be a safe space in which to voice concerns or unpopular opinions without being tied to them.[8]

Elizabethan pastoral was not about real shepherds or the rights of laborers, as Raymond Williams and Louis Montrose have noted, and country house entertainments broadcast "a particular version of country life," mostly from the perspective of the country gentry.[9] Entertainments talked extensively about houses and man-made additions to landscapes but rarely mentioned the land itself. When the Elvetham pageantry (1591) drew attention to surrounding plants and animals, it did so to claim that Elizabeth had influence over nature. Country house entertainments routinely played out this fiction by offering Elizabeth a carefully orchestrated hunting experience. At Cowdray in 1591, Elizabeth was taken to a bower and given a crossbow to shoot at the thirty deer paraded before her. One of our records

---

[5] George Puttenham, *The Arte of English Poesie* (London, 1589; *STC* 20519.5), sig. F4r.

[6] William Empson, *Some Versions of Pastoral* (Norfolk: New Directions, 1960), 23.

[7] Previous scholars have identified political and cultural critique as a defining characteristic of pastoral literature. Empson suggests that it includes a main figure who is "always ready to be the critic" (in *Some Versions*, 118). See also Michael Everton, "Critical Thumbprints in Arcadia: Renaissance Pastoral and the Process of Critique" in *Style* 35.1 (2001): 1–16; Louis Adrian Montrose, "'Eliza, Queene of Shepheardes' and the Pastoral of Power" in *English Literary Renaissance* 10.2 (1980): 153–82.

[8] Louis Montrose calls Elizabethan pastoral "an authorized mode of discontent" because it was an aspect of court culture rather than true opposition to the court. Montrose, "Of Gentlemen and Shepherds: The Politics of Elizabethan Pastoral Form" in *ELH* 50.3 (1983): 427.

[9] Raymond Williams, *The Country and the City* (London: Chatto & Windus, 1973), 27; Montrose, "Of Gentlemen," 415–59.

of the entertainment notes that the host's son, Henry Browne, "ordered" the hunting, an apt term that emphasizes its construction as deliberate and methodical.[10] Although several pageants highlighted the hosts' supervisory work as a way to showcase their loyalty to the Queen, only the Harefield pageantry (1602) alluded briefly to the actual labor behind such hospitality when the opening episode mentioned the workmen who renovated the house and joked about putting visitors to work.[11] Yet because these entertainments were performed in a genuinely rural environment and sometimes by actual country folk, they potentially exposed more than idealized views of the country.[12] In various deliberate and accidental ways, country house entertainments revealed that the natural landscape resisted order. The frequent presence of wild men and repeated complaints about the weather's interference underscored that nature could not be fully controlled, despite hosts' attempts to manage a certain space. Likewise, when the court was displaced to a new setting, its stability became vulnerable.

As a location for royal performance, the country landscape enabled manifold negotiations among Elizabeth and her elite subjects about authority, status, favor, policy, and various personal and political petitions. Entertainments often amplified the differences between the court and the country by depicting the Queen and country folk as foreigners to one another. Strange characters jumped out from behind trees or appeared suddenly in the Queen's path. Lowly shepherds and domestic servants recognized her beauty and importance, but not her identity. Country house performances repeatedly underscored that Elizabeth was a stranger in a new landscape, and they highlighted her dependence upon her subjects as characters guided her through unfamiliar places. As entertainments praised her, they hoped to influence her. In the Woodstock/Ditchley entertainment (1592), a knight led the Queen into a strange grove while explaining, "this I dare promise you (wich is somewhat worth in a straunge countrye) that so longe as I lead you you shall not lose your waye."[13] As it insisted on Elizabeth's need for male guidance, it hinted at the particular challenges of

---

[10]   *The Honorable Entertainment Giuen to the Queenes Maiestie in Progresse, at Cowdrey in Sussex, by the Right Honorable the Lord Montecute. 1591* (London, 1591; *STC* 3907.5), sig. A3v.

[11]   "The Queen's Entertainment at Harefield, 31 July–2 August, 1602," ed. Gabriel Heaton in Elizabeth Goldring, et al., eds., *John Nichols's The Progresses and Public Processions of Queen Elizabeth I: A New Edition of the Early Modern Sources* (Oxford University Press, 2014), 4:174–95.

[12]   See also Ken Hiltner, *What Else is Pastoral? Renaissance Literature and the Environment* (Ithaca: Cornell University Press, 2011). Hiltner argues that pastoral literature was often about literal landscapes and ecological problems even as it used shepherds and country settings to mask its discussion of other concerns.

[13]   "Sir Henry Lee's Entertainments for the Queen at Ditchley and Woodstock, 20–21 September, 1592," ed. Gabriel Heaton in Goldring, et al., eds., *John Nichols's The Progresses*, 3:686.

a female monarch, and when the knight described the surrounding area as "a straunge countrye," he revealed the form's potential for questioning the stability of Elizabeth's control over the provinces.

The invocations that welcomed Elizabeth to country estates especially evoked themes of ownership. A speaker typically stopped her at the gate to deliver an opening address, and the ubiquitous focus on possession was based in part on a genuine and potentially contentious legal issue. All land belonged to the monarch in principle. Although individuals could purchase land, English law did not recognize absolute ownership; instead, land was held, or "seized," in tenure from the Crown.[14] The Tudors evoked this theory, based in feudal law dating from the Norman Conquest, to institute what historians now call "fiscal feudalism," the Crown's use of feudal law to collect taxes from landowners.[15] This fundraising strategy carried larger implications, as it reminded English landowners that they were not outright owners, but tenants of the monarch. Elizabeth endorsed this theory, and she interpreted other claims to ownership as a challenge to her power. When a character in the Kenilworth entertainment introduced herself as "the Lady of this pleasant Lake" and told Elizabeth that "the Lake, the Lodge, the Lord, are yours for to commande," Elizabeth apparently responded: "we had thought indeed the Lake had been oours, and doo you call it yourz noow?"[16] Her tongue-in-cheek reaction exemplifies her view of aristocratic estates as always already owned by her, as does a 1570 letter she wrote from the Russell family's estate, in which she dated herself from "our manor of Cheneys."[17]

Yet the emphasis on ownership in country house entertainment also stood for political clout. In her study of Tudor architecture and gardens, Paula Henderson notes that the gate or gatehouse, which introduced the house and regulated incoming and outgoing traffic, signified status. It was

---

[14] Christopher W. Brooks, *Law, Politics, and Society in Early Modern England* (Cambridge University Press, 2008), 322–41; A. R. Buck, "The Politics of Land Law in Tudor England, 1529–1540" in *Journal of Legal History* 11.2 (1990): 200–17.

[15] For a succinct explanation of how this concept operated in Tudor England, see J. H. Baker, *An Introduction to English Legal History*, 4th edn. (Oxford University Press, 2007), 253–7.

[16] George Gascoigne, "A Briefe Rehearsall, or Rather a True Copie of as Much as Was Presented before Her Maiesties at Kenelworth" in *The VVhole Woorkes of George Gascoigne Esquyre* (London, 1587; *STC* 11638), sig. A2v–A3r; Robert Langham, *A Letter: Whearin, Part of the Entertainment vntoo the Queenz Maiesty, at Killingwoorth Castl, in Warwik Sheer, in this Soomerz Progress. 1575. iz Signified* (London, n.d.; *STC* 15190.5), sig. B4v–B5r. Although some modern sources refer to the letter's author as Robert Laneham, I follow Elizabeth Goldring's persuasive argument for Langham in "'A mercer ye wot az we be': The Authorship of the Kenilworth Letter Reconsidered" in *English Literary Renaissance* 38.2 (2008): 245–69. Gascoigne's "A Briefe Rehearsall" was also printed with a different title page as *The Pleasauntest Workes of George Gascoigne Esquyre* (London, 1587; *STC* 11639).

[17] Qtd. in E. K. Chambers, *The Elizabethan Stage* (Oxford: Clarendon, 1923), 1:118.

the first opportunity for an owner to display pride, loyalty to the Crown, or various themes that would be repeated in the house.[18] The same argument applies to the unfolding of a country house entertainment. Nearly every example referred to the host as the estate's "owner" and had the potential to evoke a disgruntled response from Elizabeth. In these statements of ownership we can most clearly see the hosts' own insecurities and desires, and the entertainments at Theobalds (1571) and Kenilworth (1575) are particularly instructive examples. While the former ceded authority to Elizabeth and revealed Burghley's confidence in his political position, the latter's bold statements of ownership and ongoing revisions demonstrated a less secure relationship between Leicester and Elizabeth.

Burghley and the "rising roofs" of Theobalds

When Elizabeth arrived at Theobalds on September 22, 1571, she got her first glimpse of the new house. She had visited only once, just before construction began in 1564. At her arrival, Burghley and his family welcomed her with a short Latin address spoken by the personified house. The thirty-two-line entertainment survives as a printed broadside. Its title, which translates to "Congratulatory Poem of the House of Cecil on the Arrival of the Fairest Queen 22 September 1571," identifies its occasion but neither its method of transmittal nor its author.[19] This text has received very little critical attention and, to my knowledge, no one writing about progress entertainment has identified it as a performance. One record explains that Elizabeth was "presented" this poem on arrival.[20] Although the word "present" could designate either the distribution of a written manuscript or the performance of a speech, its language and occasion make it likely that someone read it aloud. In his study of Elizabethan courtier poets, Steven May briefly mentions this text and proposes that Burghley may have

---

[18] Paula Henderson, *The Tudor House and Garden: Architecture and Landscape in the Sixteenth and Early Seventeenth Centuries* (New Haven: Yale University Press, 2005), 66.

[19] *Carmen Gratulatorium Aedium Cecilianarum in Aduentum Serenissimae Reginae. 22. Sept. 1571* (London, 1571; *STC* 4896). I quote from a new translation of this text, prepared for me by Jaime Goodrich. I include the full text as Appendix 2.

[20] John Nichols, *The Progresses and Public Processions of Queen Elizabeth* (London, 1823), 1:291. Drawing evidence from Burghley's diary, Nichols says that certain verses were presented to Elizabeth during her 1571 visit along with a portrait of the house, but he does not include a text of these verses. See also James Sutton, *Materializing Space at an Early Modern Prodigy House: The Cecils at Theobalds, 1564–1607* (Aldershot: Ashgate, 2004), 88–9. Sutton mentions Elizabeth's visit to Theobalds in 1571. He suggests that the event recognized Cecil's new status as Baron Burghley and celebrated Anne's wedding to the Earl of Oxford, but he assumes the entertainment text does not survive.

written it.[21] Even if Burghley hired someone else to pen the verses, the poem and performance spoke for him, and he undoubtedly had control over its content.

This very personal entertainment focused not on policy, but on Burghley's family and his gratitude for his own rise. Elizabeth had elevated him to Baron Burghley in February, and both of them were deeply invested in his acceptance by the court and aristocracy as a newly titled noble. He was intimately involved in decision-making at court, and his mutual confidence with Elizabeth meant that he felt able to challenge her without much fear of losing his place in her inner circle.[22] He might have felt especially triumphant about the reform bills he pushed through Parliament in April and May, which strengthened penalties for practicing Catholics. There was plenty more Burghley aimed to accomplish in terms of legislation: he believed firmly that Elizabeth should marry, and he was invested in ecclesiastical, political, and economic reform.[23] But because he had the Queen's ear nearly all the time, he did not need to take advantage of the intimate circumstances of a progress visit to push these kinds of agendas, nor did he need to cloak his political aims in Petrarchan or pastoral tropes. Hence his entertainment did not lobby for specific policies or offer potential challenges to Elizabeth's ownership over the estate. Instead, it demonstrated a man secure in his political position who desired to elevate his family. Burghley's promotion meant security for him, but it did not necessarily mean the same for his line. His entertainment reveals his attempts to transition the Cecils from country gentry to wealthy nobility with lasting social and political influence.

As it celebrated his new position as a member of the peerage, the entertainment also introduced his new house to Elizabeth and the court. The short performance must have been delivered just in front of Theobalds House, which represented visually Burghley's rise, ambitions, and hope that his family would retain a high social standing after his death. Its location signified Burghley's demanding responsibilities at court. His inherited estate, Burghley House in Lincolnshire, was too remote given his constant need to be with the Queen, and Cecil House in Westminster was a city residence. Theobalds was both a country retreat and a nearby place only

---

[21] Steven May, *The Elizabethan Courtier Poets: The Poems and Their Contexts* (Columbia: University of Missouri Press, 1991), 50.

[22] For more on Burghley's life and relationship with Elizabeth, see Stephen Alford, *Burghley: William Cecil at the Court of Elizabeth I* (New Haven: Yale University Press, 2008); Conyers Read, *Lord Burghley and Queen Elizabeth* (New York: Knopf, 1960).

[23] Read, *Lord Burghley*, 51–65; Alford, *Burghley: William Cecil*, 151–66.

about a half-day's ride from London. The house itself was already an impressive display but very much a work in progress. Its relatively modest structure as a Renaissance family home rather than a grand palace revealed Burghley's persona at this moment: a grateful courtier with substantial ambition but willingness to submit. The entertainment praised the house in humble terms, calling it "not badly built by a private man," but emphasized that the house was incomplete. Burghley spent increasingly large amounts of money on construction each year from 1564 to 1572, and in the late summer of 1571, he was planning an elaborate new court and gatehouse.[24] The improvement and decoration of Theobalds took more than twenty years, and although Burghley might not have anticipated such extensive renovation, the entertainment presented Theobalds' unfinished state as a symbol for Burghley's own aspirations. The opening line introduced the house to Elizabeth as "the rising Roofs of your CECIL," and the character "Theobalds" grieved because "we do not meet the master's desire, / Alas, he says, the house is not great enough now."

Most of the speech apologized for the house's inadequacies, as became conventional in later entertainments, but in this case, the personified house promised to improve and asked for Elizabeth's patience during an early stage of construction. The house explained that "here we have poured forth all [our] might for the time being" and that fate "forbids us to convey more." One of its final lines repeated this sentiment: "Neither do you seek more, nor are we able to give more, / O may Master please, if the roofs [please] you less." Besides signifying Burghley's continued ambition, the emphasis on the house's shortcomings might have reflected genuine anxiety about Elizabeth's displeasure or others' mockery at the state of his house. When Elizabeth visited Thomas Gresham at Osterley five years later, she reportedly suggested that the house would look more handsome if divided by a wall, and Gresham hired workers to partition the space overnight so the Queen would awake to find her recommendation fulfilled.[25] Gossip about this notoriously difficult guest's high expectations might help explain why some country house owners tried to avoid a royal visit by starting rumors about poor accommodations or by petitioning top advisors to take Elizabeth elsewhere.[26] As one of those advisors, Burghley would have been less anxious than many hosts were, but the stakes were still high because his new house embodied his future hopes. By announcing further renovation

[24] Sir John Summerson, "The Building of Theobalds, 1564–1585" in *Archaeologia* 97 (1959): 107–26.
[25] Ian Dunlop, *Palaces and Progresses of Elizabeth I* (London: Cape, 1962), 119–20.
[26] For more on reluctant hosts, see Mary Hill Cole, *The Portable Queen: Elizabeth I and the Politics of Ceremony* (Amherst: University of Massachusetts Press, 1999), 85–94.

plans, Burghley might have hoped to undercut the impression that he could not afford to build something grander.

Where the entertainment captured Burghley's ambition, it underscored that he desired to improve his house so he could serve Elizabeth better. The house called itself "not great enough / Either for you, ELIZABETH, or for your merits" and "lesser than your splendor." It stated simply, "The master has given these commands. You deserve more." The poem made clear that the house, although inadequate for Elizabeth's greatness, became hers when she arrived: "Roofs, doors, gates, all things revealed lie open. / To meet you, VIRGIN, we run up with peaceful arms, / The brow is happy, the appearance fair, the face rejoicing." A few lines later it continued: "And to you we give the master with the house, the children with the dear wife, / Steadfast bodies, faithful hearts. / Here all things obey your power." This welcome address did not contest Elizabeth's authority; instead, it smoothly handed over dominion of the full estate. It suggested slight skepticism about absolute hospitality when it worried that "because we lie open" the house might not be great enough for the Queen, but it never hesitated to grant her unconditional access. Burghley also presented Elizabeth a portrait of the house, a small token to represent Theobalds as his grand gift to her.[27] The welcome address introduced Theobalds less as a noble family's estate than as a budding provincial palace, kept for Elizabeth by Burghley. Likewise, it represented Burghley as her possession by naming him "your CECIL."

The "children with the dear wife" would have been present at the occasion. Burghley took the opportunity to announce with great pride the betrothal of his daughter Anne to Oxford:

> Here an EARL, here OXFORDIAN Atlas is present:
> To whom our ANNA has now been betrothed with matrimonial promise,
> A cherished girl has brought great honor to us.
> That young man serves you with youthful strength,
> BURGHLEY serves you with an aged mind.

The entertainment hoped this marital alliance would "promise" more secure standing for the Cecil family. It continued to claim that all of the family's movements were motivated by the desire to serve Elizabeth; Burghley arranged a marriage for his "cherished" daughter with a man poised to offer Elizabeth military and political service. When the poem was printed as a broadside, Burghley's name here and "Cecil" in the first line were

---

[27] As far as I know, the portrait is not extant. For a reference to it, see the Theobalds documents edited by Jayne Elisabeth Archer in Goldring, et al., eds., *John Nichols's The Progresses*, 1:706.

printed in small caps, a calculated show of modesty that extended the performance's emphasis on humility.[28] The Queen's name and title, along with those of Anna and Oxford, were printed in large caps. Still, even with a humble tone and perhaps a joke about his age, Burghley emphasized that his wisdom and experienced political mind would continue to serve Elizabeth well.

His decision to present this poem in Latin, the language of law and court politics, reveals that the performance was designed for political insiders rather than for the masses. The Latin presentation highlighted Burghley's humanist learning, as well as the excellent classical education of his wife Mildred, the eldest daughter of Sir Anthony Cooke. Both Burghley and Mildred were fluent in Latin and Greek and owned a substantial collection of classical books.[29] The entertainment, delivered to an exceedingly well-educated Queen, presented an image of a learned couple who positioned themselves as Elizabeth's best, most educated servants and parents to equally capable children. The entertainment did not mention Robert, the politically successful son who would take over Theobalds after Burghley's death, because he was only eight years old. It also excluded Thomas, Burghley's son by his late wife, who may or may not have attended. By 1571, Burghley had already determined with great disappointment that Thomas, then in his early twenties, was unfit for a political career, and Burghley's Latin entertainment indicates that he rested his hopes instead in his daughter and the new kinship alliances resulting from her marriage.[30] By dedicating Theobalds and all future construction to Elizabeth as its rightful owner, the entertainment promised steadfast loyalty and good political service from all family members in exchange for Elizabeth's continued favor and facilitation of the Cecils' rise.

When we examine this speech as part of the genre of country house entertainment, it stands out as decidedly not about the country landscape. It did not highlight local customs or use conventional pastoral devices. It

---

[28] Jaime Goodrich brought this to my attention in private correspondence.

[29] For more on Mildred as a writer, reader, and patron, see Gemma Allen, *The Cooke Sisters: Education, Piety, and Politics in Early Modern England* (Manchester University Press, 2013); Louise Schleiner, *Tudor and Stuart Women Writers* (Bloomington: Indiana University Press, 1994), 34–51; Jane Stevenson, "Mildred Cecil, Lady Burleigh: Poetry, Politics, and Protestantism" in Victoria E. Burke and Jonathan Gibson, eds., *Early Modern Women's Manuscript Writing: Selected Papers from the Trinity/Trent Colloquium* (Aldershot: Ashgate, 2004), 51–73; Caroline Bowden, "The Library of Mildred Cooke Cecil, Lady Burghley" in *The Library* 6.1 (2005): 3–29; Pauline Croft, "Mildred, Lady Burghley: The Matriarch" in *Patronage, Culture and Power: The Early Cecils 1558–1612* (New Haven: Yale University Press, 2002), 283–300.

[30] David Loades, *The Cecils: Privilege and Power Behind the Throne* (Kew: National Archives, 2007), 173–9; G. Ravenscroft Dennis, *The Cecil Family* (Boston and New York: Houghton Mifflin, 1914), 79–89.

represented Theobalds as an extension of Elizabeth's court rather than a country estate distant from London, and it emphasized the house's and Burghley's constant accessibility and ability to serve her needs. Country house owners were essential to the Crown's maintenance of outlining regions, as Chapter 3 explores in greater detail, but Elizabeth repeatedly made clear that she preferred Burghley by her side at court. His 1571 entertainment implied that his travels to Theobalds would not operate as removals from the Queen and her court, but instead as short journeys to a place rather like the court where he continued to serve her. It represented the renovation of Theobalds, although a symbol of Burghley's personal ambition, as evidence of his dedication to Elizabeth. Its insistence that this country was familiar rather than strange facilitated its representation of Elizabeth's authority as centralized and unwavering. It did not engage explicitly in a conversation about national identity. The community it defined was neither England nor Hertfordshire, but simply one elite house occupied by one elite family that revered Elizabeth as she should be honored. It implicitly held up this house as a microcosm for an ideal England in which royal allegiance mattered above all else. Although the disastrous marriage between Anne and Oxford was not at all what Burghley hoped, the entertainment succeeded in two main ways.[31] Elizabeth apparently accepted its representation of Theobalds because she would travel there a record thirteen times on progress, and it laid important groundwork for Robert's eventual political rise.

Leicester, Elizabeth, and Kenilworth Castle

The performance at Kenilworth Castle four years later was more elaborate and public than the one at Theobalds. Because it negotiated a more delicate relationship and placed greater emphasis on the landscape and surrounding region, the Kenilworth entertainment seemed to equivocate about Elizabeth's authority in the provinces. It included a dizzying array of festivities spanning her nineteen-day stay, including a dozen pageants written and performed by court poets, hopeful courtiers, and local men and women of the lower ranks. These diversions cost Leicester an estimated and wildly extravagant £1000 per day, not counting gifts and improvements to the estate.[32] The Kenilworth entertainment also became a popular

---

[31] For more on Anne's marriage to Oxford, see Alford, *Burghley: William Cecil*, 206–22.

[32] Mary E. Hazard, "A Magnificent Lord: Leicester, Kenilworth, and Transformations in the Idea of Magnificence" in *Cahiers Elisabethains* 31 (1987): 11–35, esp. 22. As a point of comparison, Leicester's annual revenue from land and rent in the 1580s was £5000, according to William Dugdale, *The Antiquities of Warwickshire Illustrated* (London, 1656).

cultural event. Its audience was probably wider and more diverse than that at Theobalds, and its multiple printed accounts reached numerous readers. Discussions of many country house performances must rely on single accounts, but the two surviving Kenilworth texts enable us to experience the entertainment from multiple perspectives.[33] I will return to the individual texts' interpretations and goals in the second half of this book.

Because it was such a significant cultural event and because it left behind two full records, the Kenilworth entertainment has attracted substantial critical attention. Most scholars focus on the power dynamics in Leicester's relationship with Elizabeth. Susan Frye calls it a "competition" or "struggle" for authority.[34] However, Leicester's and Elizabeth's interests were not diametrically opposed, and Frye reads certain moments as more combative than either account presents them. Sandra Logan and Janette Dillon each interpret this relationship as more cooperative and mutually beneficial. When Logan proposes that Leicester presents himself as Elizabeth's ally, she downplays aspects of the performance that voiced his frustrations about Elizabeth's hesitancy to heed her courtiers' advice.[35] Dillon's emphasis on the entertainment's fraught negotiation of a "balance of lordship" between Elizabeth and Leicester most accurately captures the pageants' tone, yet when Dillon emphasizes the Queen's stable position of power, she underestimates how the performance unsettled that power in various subtle and bold ways.[36] As these three theorists demonstrate, the entertainment defined Leicester's relationship with Elizabeth with enough ambiguity to enable divergent interpretations. I propose that its approach can seem uneven, at times bold and at times submissive, because the performance was constantly under revision by Leicester, Elizabeth, and others as they collaborated and resisted, queried and responded to one another.

The entertainment aimed to establish a new public image for Leicester, one that provided him a sense of ownership and individual identity apart from his odd, unprecedented position as the male favorite of a single, female

[33] Langham, *A Letter*; Gascoigne, "A Briefe Rehearsall." See Chapter 4 for more on these texts.

[34] Susan Frye, *Elizabeth I: The Competition for Representation* (New York: Oxford University Press, 1993), 92. For other interpretations of the Kenilworth entertainment as a gendered battle of wills, see Catherine Bates, *The Rhetoric of Courtship in Elizabethan Language and Literature* (Cambridge University Press, 1992), 47–60; Diana E. Henderson, *Passion Made Public: Elizabethan Lyric, Gender, and Performance* (Urbana: University of Illinois Press, 1995), 68–79; Ilana Nash, "'A Subject Without Subjection': Robert Dudley, Earl of Leicester, and *The Princely Pleasures at Kenelworth Castle*" in *Comitatus* 25.1 (1994): 81–102.

[35] Sandra Logan, *Text/Events in Early Modern England: Poetics of History* (Aldershot: Ashgate, 2007), 93–105.

[36] Janette Dillon, *The Language of Space in Court Performance 1400–1625* (Cambridge University Press, 2010), 49–75, esp. 59.

monarch. The struggles Frye identifies show evidence not of competition with the Queen, but of Leicester's attempts to define himself before the court and a wider public in a way that appeared a little less dependent upon his royal mistress. He already enjoyed in 1575 a long list of political duties, titles, and land that the Queen had awarded him, yet he sought more responsibility and respect from Elizabeth and from his fellow courtiers.[37] His entertainment revealed his insecurity and desire to be heard. The stakes were high for Elizabeth as well. Rumors had circulated about a romantic affair between the two – including lovers' trysts, the birth of illegitimate children on progress, and suspicious circumstances surrounding the death of Leicester's late wife – and they both needed to negotiate the terms of their relationship in a public setting.[38] Leicester risked upstaging the Queen by presenting an especially extravagant production that emphasized his resources and proudly asserted his status, and unlike the Theobalds entertainment, Leicester's pageantry highlighted and exploited the Queen's vulnerability on progress.

The specific image Leicester crafted was that of a military leader. He aimed to transition from Elizabeth's pet to a respected authority figure in the masculine, moral enterprise of religious war. This goal was not necessarily at odds with what Elizabeth wanted. Logan has identified that Elizabeth needed Leicester as a Protestant military leader, a kind of front man for her foreign policy.[39] However, the entertainment declared Leicester's own authority too boldly at times and pushed for military intervention more aggressively than she preferred. Leicester had been a Protestant activist from the beginning of the reign, and by the middle of the 1570s he was passionately committed to international Protestantism.[40] The Kenilworth performance might implicitly advocate a more militant Protestant foreign policy, but it made no explicit argument for England's need to engage in any specific war. Frye and Jim Ellis are able to identify different possible contexts (including Dutch–Spanish and Anglo–Irish relations) because the

---

[37] Elizabeth named him Master of the Horse on the first day of her reign, appointed him to the Privy Council in October 1562, granted him the lordships of Denbigh and Chirk in 1563, and gave him the earldom of Leicester in 1564. He was also the greatest landholder in North Wales. For a fuller list of Leicester's lands and offices, see Simon Adams, *Leicester and the Court: Essays on Elizabethan Politics* (Manchester University Press, 2002), 200–1.

[38] Susan Doran, *Monarchy and Matrimony: The Courtships of Elizabeth I* (London and New York: Routledge, 1996), 41–72; Carole Levin, *The Heart and Stomach of a King: Elizabeth I and the Politics of Sex and Power* (Philadelphia: University of Pennsylvania Press, 1994), 81.

[39] Logan, *Text/Events*, 100–2.

[40] Paul E. J. Hammer, *Elizabeth's Wars: War, Government and Society in Tudor England, 1544–1604* (Basingstoke: Palgrave, 2003), 85–7; Alan Haynes, *The White Bear: Robert Dudley, The Elizabethan Earl of Leicester* (London: Owen, 1987), 54–5.

entertainment's treatment of war remained vague rather than tied to a particular location.[41] The performance simply represented war as heroic and Leicester as ready to take command of an army. From his perspective, this new position was ideal because it would allow him to strike out on his own while still serving Elizabeth.

The estate at Kenilworth encoded Leicester's desire to redefine his public image as a strong military leader who owned an important regional center. While Theobalds was a modest Renaissance family home in 1571, Kenilworth was an elaborate castle with a long military and royal history. It was built as a Norman keep in the twelfth century, received improvements under the ownership of King John and John of Gaunt, and was a favorite residence of the Lancastrian kings.[42] Kenilworth remained a royal residence until Henry VIII gave it to Leicester's father in 1553. Queen Mary took it back when she executed John Dudley, and Elizabeth gave it to Leicester in 1563. Elizabeth had already visited three times since then, but in 1575 Leicester could finally show off the full scale of his improvements. He was clearly proud to display the estate, which included a recently renovated castle, expanded chase, and extravagant gardens featuring sand-filled walkways bordered by grass, fruit trees, flowers, sculptures, and a fountain – the effect of which led Robert Langham in his account of the event to describe the Kenilworth grounds as "Paradis" (see Figure 1.1).[43] The entertainment exploited the many historical associations with its performance space. Kenilworth Castle was simultaneously an ancient military fortress, a royal castle, his father's home now rightfully restored under a Protestant queen, a mark of his family's status, and a symbol of Elizabeth's trust and favoritism.[44] Leicester was eager to put his own mark on it and show his large audience how to interpret his and Kenilworth's status.

When Elizabeth arrived at Kenilworth in the evening of Saturday, July 9, she encountered a series of opening pageants that repeatedly called Leicester the estate's "owner" and used Kenilworth's military history to present him as a potential wartime hero. Elizabeth heard speeches by a sibyl and Hercules outside the estate entrance, and as she and her entourage progressed through a series of gates and bridges to the castle, she was welcomed by the Lady of the Lake floating on an island in the castle pool and received baskets of

---

[41] Frye, *Elizabeth I*, 56–96; Jim Ellis, "Kenilworth, King Arthur, and the Memory of Empire" in *English Literary Renaissance* 43.1 (2013): 3–29.

[42] Richard K. Morris, *Kenilworth Castle* (London: English Heritage, 2006).

[43] Langham, *A Letter*, sig. J2v–K1v.

[44] Matthew Johnson makes a similar point when he argues that the estate and entertainment created a complex image of Leicester, part ancient and part modern, in *Behind the Castle Gate: From Medieval to Renaissance* (London and New York: Routledge, 2002), 136–60.

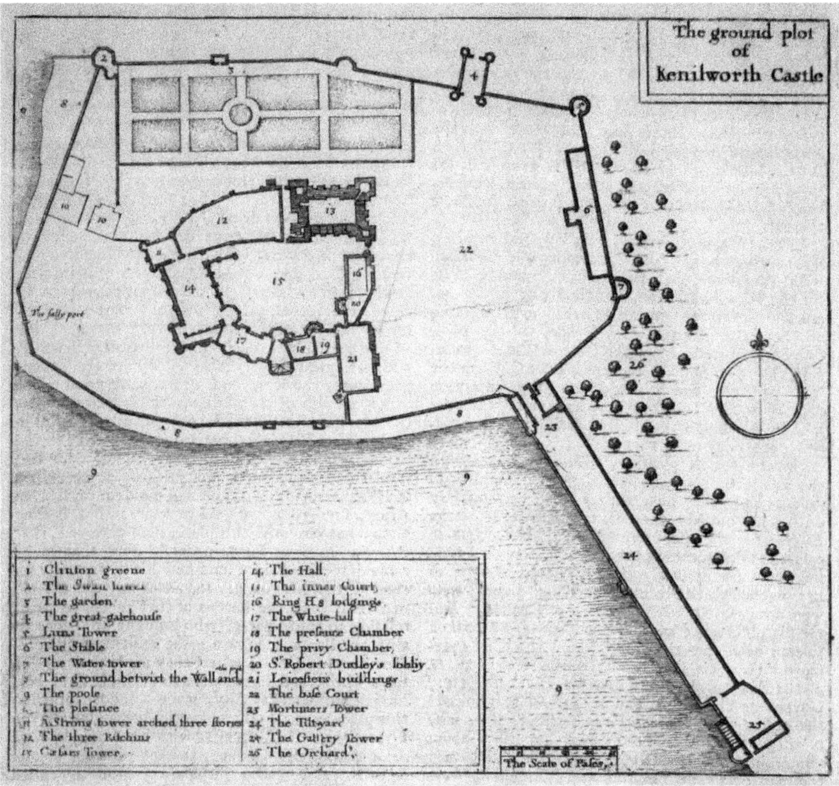

1.1 Plan of Kenilworth Castle, drawn by Wenceslas Hollar in the middle of the seventeenth century. The Thomas Fisher Rare Book Library, University of Toronto.

gifts and a poem attached to the castle gate. These pageants celebrated her arrival with effusive flattery but hinted that the transition of authority from householder to royal guest would not be as smooth as that at Theobalds. The linked tropes of ownership and military prowess appeared throughout the sibyl's prophecy. She foresaw that Elizabeth would never be stirred by "rage of warre" but instead be known as "the Prince of peace" whose "eyes shal neuer see / the broyles of bloody field."[45] The emphasis on Elizabeth's reign as peaceful, which became a conventional trope in country house entertainment, complimented her ability to rule effectively and to protect her people. Because Elizabeth's contemporaries debated whether a woman could govern an army and a country, the sibyl's promise that she would

[45] Gascoigne, "A Briefe Rehearsall," sig. A1r.

never experience battle firsthand could have alluded to those debates and suggested that she was not equipped to lead an army. At least it implied that Leicester stood at the ready to protect England's and Elizabeth's peace. The speech ended with these lines:

> If perfect peace then glad your minde
> he ioyes aboue the rest:
> Which doth receiue into his house,
> so good and sweete a guest.[46]

By introducing Leicester directly after its discussion of war and peace, the pageant positioned him as an advisor ready to ensure "perfect peace," or to tackle whatever military or political issues Elizabeth would or could not. The final two lines, although framed by praise of Elizabeth's virtues and celebration of her arrival, identified Kenilworth as Leicester's possession and introduced ownership as a central theme. They presented Leicester as a gracious, hospitable householder who identified Elizabeth as "good" and "sweete," though not necessarily powerful or above his station.

Other moments during the first day of performance represented Kenilworth as a military fortress and Leicester as its proud protector. As held true in many later entertainments as well, Elizabeth met with a guarded entrance to the estate that visually declared ownership for the host, and Hercules stood as porter. He had an imposing presence; the actor who played him was "tall of parson, big of lim and stearn of coountinaus."[47] While the sibyl emphasized the importance of war by celebrating its absence, Hercules indicated his readiness for violence by holding a club in addition to keys to the gate. His oration matched his appearance: "a roough speech full of passions" that began when he "burst out in a great pang of impaciens too see such vncooth trudging too and fro."[48] Like many other wild characters who greeted Elizabeth on progress, Hercules appeared untamed so that he could yield to her on Leicester's behalf. Once he noticed her appearance as a "soueraigne Goddes," Hercules surrendered "both club and keyes / my selfe, my warde I yeelde, / Euen gates and all, yea Lord him selfe, / submitte and seeke your sheelde."[49] These lines nearly echoed the language of Burghley's entertainment; they presented Kenilworth as open to her and Leicester as her obedient subject. Yet they did so within a different context. The Kenilworth entertainment emphasized ubiquitous violence and Elizabeth's need for protection by strong figures like Hercules and Leicester. The welcoming pageants opened Kenilworth to her, but

---

[46] Ibid., sig. A1r.   [47] Langham, *A Letter*, sig. B3v.
[48] Ibid., sig. B3v.   [49] Gascoigne, "A Briefe Rehearsall," sig. A2r.

required her first to pass through multiple closed gates and receive permission to enter.[50] Later that evening when she passed over the bridge from the outer court to the castle gate, she saw bowls and trays filled with gifts on the bridge posts. These gifts included food, drink, musical instruments, and "beautifully glittering of armoour thervpon depending, Bowz, Arroz, Spearz, Sheeld, Head pees, Gorget, Corselets, Swoords, Targets, and such like for *Mars* gifts the God of war."[51] Langham notes that this gift of martial tools was especially fitting because the posts seemed "naturally meet for the bearing of armoour," indicating that Kenilworth Castle looked like a military fortress, and that they might be used to protect Elizabeth, who "so benignly pleazed her to take herboour."[52] At least in his interpretation, these instruments were not for Elizabeth's own use, but for Leicester to defend her.

Several pageants together established Kenilworth Castle as the continuation of King Arthur's legacy, and the entertainment's praise of dual owners Leicester and Elizabeth at first made unclear which one was the rightful heir to the fictional and ideal king. The Arthurian figure the Lady of the Lake first appeared floating on an island in a pond in the outer courtyard. She said that she resided at Kenilworth "since the time of great king Arthures reigne / That here with royal Court aboade did make."[53] When she explained that previous Kenilworth owner Roger Mortimer was Arthur's heir, she connected Leicester to that lineage. The Lady's final stanza is worth quoting at length:

> Wherefore I wil attend while you lodge here,
> (most peereles Queene) to Court to make resort,
> And as my love to Arthure dyd appeere,
> so shalt to you in earnest and in sport,
> Passe on Madame, you neede no longer stand,
> the Lake, the Lodge, the Lord, are yours for to commande.[54]

Although these lines might appear simply as a gracious welcome, Elizabeth's response ("doo you call it yourz now?") indicates that she identified within them a potential slight against her authority. She is likely to have delivered her line as a joke, but it reveals a more serious issue as it highlights the risks involved in negotiating dual authorities of host and monarch. Indeed, the Lady made two errors. First, although she claimed that Elizabeth was "peereles," she compared her to Arthur as an equal. By connecting Leicester

---

[50] See also Johnson's discussion of the Kenilworth gates and access in *Behind the Castle Gate*, 136–60.
[51] Langham, *A Letter*, sig. B5v–B6r.   [52] Ibid., sig. B6r.
[53] Gascoigne, "A Briefe Rehearsall," sig. A2v.   [54] Ibid., sig. A3r.

to Arthur as well, the first several pageants potentially implied that Leicester also stood as her peer. Second, the Lady ordered the Queen forward boldly and offered her rule over entities Elizabeth believed she already owned.

Leicester overreached in these early pageants by welcoming the Queen as a near equal, and after he met with some resistance, later episodes revealed a shift in tone and approach. As the entertainment gradually ceded ownership to Elizabeth on Leicester's behalf, later speeches stopped referring to Kenilworth as his possession and represented him more clearly as a submissive subject. The differences between early and late pageants were partially a result of generic structure, as country house performances enacted the transfer of ownership. We also might attribute the development in tone to different composers; aspiring courtiers like George Gascoigne might have been more cautious than were more established courtly poets when defining the relationship between Leicester and Elizabeth. However, several moments revealed evidence of revision, probably initiated and at least supervised by Leicester. He may have tried to correct slight missteps early in the entertainment by commissioning his writers to compose new pieces that clarified his submissive position. At least two pageants were planned but not performed, and Leicester ordered at least one additional episode after Elizabeth arrived. One of our records specifies that he directed Gascoigne to write a new farewell episode after a lengthy pageant about Zabeta's marriage was canceled owing to poor weather.[55] This text explains, "The Queenes Maiestie hasting her departure from thence, the Earle commanded master *Gascoigne* to deuise some Farewel worth the presenting."[56] When Elizabeth did not stop to listen to Gascoigne's new farewell address, he improvised by chasing her horse while shouting a summary of the canceled show's plot. Country house performance was always an interactive, collaborative work in progress.

Later pageants indeed reveal evidence of revision based on Elizabeth's reactions. When she joked that a character who praised her beauty must be blind, a later episode represented him as such. After the first day's entertainment, several characters explained that the Lady of the Lake desired only to serve the Queen in a humble fashion and that Leicester did not genuinely claim ownership over Kenilworth Castle. Triton insisted that the

---

[55] Ibid., sig. C2v. I explain in Chapter 4 that although many others speculate that Elizabeth censored this pageant because it lobbied too boldly for royal marriage, there is no direct evidence that she did so. Instead, we might simply take the statement as genuine, especially because both extant texts attribute its cancelation to the weather.

[56] Gascoigne, "A Brief Rehearsall," sig. C2v.

Lady's statements meant no challenge: "Who when your highnesse hither came, / dyd humbly yeeld her Lake: / And to attende vpon your Court, / did loyall promise make."[57] He explained that she needed the Queen's help because only "a worthier maide then she" could turn away her pursuer, "Sir Bruce sans pittie."[58] The Savage Man explained that the Lady desired only to serve the Queen and that Leicester was not the castle's owner, but the person who "did lay" there – a pun on his name – and who "gave him selfe and all."[59] The final pageant noted that Leicester "keepes" the castle for Elizabeth to command.[60] In these later pageants, Leicester gradually resituated himself as Elizabeth's submissive favorite. The entertainment's final image of him was not the bold military leader of the first day, but a frustrated lover named Deep Desire, whose cruel mistress had imprisoned him by withholding favor.

Yet even at its end the entertainment revealed some unsettling of Elizabeth's authority through emphasis on the pastoral landscape. When Gascoigne jumped out at her and chased her to deliver his speech, one of our records explains, "Here her maiestie stayed her horse to fauour *Sylvanus*, fearing least he should be driuen out of breath by following her horse so fast."[61] As he intruded on her ride, Sylvanus made clear that the woods at Kenilworth were unfamiliar territory to Elizabeth. His sudden appearance and speech intimated that she was not wholly in control of her surroundings in this strange space, which she needed guidance to navigate. Sylvanus further claimed that she needed protection; he offered to serve as her footman so he could "conduct your Maiestie in safetie from the perillous passages which are in these Woods and Forrests."[62] Soon after Sylvanus declared himself keeper of the forest: "whiles I walke in these woods and wildernes (wherof I haue the charge) I haue often mused with my selfe that your Maiesty being so highly esteemed, so entirely beloved, and so largely endued by the Celestial powers: you can yet continually give eare to the councel of these terrestrial companions, and so consequently passe your time wheresoeuer they deuise or determine that it is meete for your royal person to be resident."[63] These lines positioned Elizabeth as powerful and gracious by praising her decision to follow counsel and the schedule of her host.

When it referred to the local "Countrey" and Elizabeth's relationship to it, Sylvanus' speech brought into focus the genre's emphasis on regional identities. Sylvanus added that if Elizabeth understood her people's joy

---

57 Ibid., sig. A8r.   58 Ibid., sig. A8r.   59 Ibid., sig. A6r.   60 Ibid., sig. C7v.
61 Ibid., sig. C4r.   62 Ibid., sig. C3r.   63 Ibid., sig. C2v.

at her presence and sorrow at her absence, then she should feel "resolute determination for euer to abide in this Countrey, and neuer to wander any further by the direction and aduice of these Peeres and Councellers. Since thereby the heauens might greatly be pleased, and most men throughly recomforted."[64] He claimed that the inhabitants of this region would so miss their honored guest that she should resolve to stay forever. His comment exemplifies the genre's emphasis on Elizabeth's transformative presence, which several Kenilworth pageants stressed; her appearance alone imbued nature with new life and rescued the Lady of the Lake from men who threatened her chastity. The desire for Elizabeth to stay certainly flattered her and argued for her importance, but it also encapsulated the entertainment's main theme: the desire of Leicester and other advisors to captivate and influence her. Because Kenilworth Castle was the center of a staunchly Puritan area, the local advice tended to serve militant Protestant interests. Sylvanus alluded to this underlying Protestant agenda when he entreated Elizabeth to be ruled by her male advisors, which he claimed would please both God and her subjects.

Whereas the 1571 Theobalds entertainment represented Burghley as the head of a family dedicated to serving the Crown's interests, the Kenilworth performance portrayed Leicester as the head of a region filled with petitioners eager to preserve their unique traditions. The entertainment included a rustic bride-ale with a morris dance and tilt, along with a Hock Tuesday play.[65] Both are likely to have been performed by men and women from the area, who used their participation to express their commitment to Elizabeth and assert local tensions in the hopes of resolving them.[66] These country pageants shared themes with the rest of the entertainment, but neither offered Elizabeth explicit advice. The mock battle might have supported intervention in the Netherlands because it represented English soldiers as triumphant over another nation. Yet it also maintained that women could be brave warriors – the battle ended when the Danes were

---

[64] Ibid., sig. C2v–C3r.

[65] A bride-ale consisted of secular festivities after a country wedding. The traditional English dance known as morris dancing (which involved leaping, jerky movements, and the wearing of bells) probably began as a courtly dance but by 1575 was identified as a rural sport. The Coventry Hock Tuesday play, a folk play traditionally presented on the second Tuesday after Easter, dramatized the town's victory over the Danes at the beginning of the eleventh century.

[66] Logan (in *Text/Events*, 150) proposes that the bride-ale was a self-conscious parody performed by professional actors; I disagree. Langham's descriptions, which heckle the actors, instead reveal an elitist eyewitness recording (and exaggerating the faults of) a performance by those of the lower ranks. For an extended discussion of the two rustic plays and their likely performance by commoners, see Alex Davis, *Chivalry and Romance in the English Renaissance* (Cambridge: Brewer, 2003), 73–98.

"beaten doown, ouercom and many led captiue for triumph by our English weemen" – and implied that Elizabeth could handle the role of military commander.[67] Primarily the Hock Tuesday play advanced a more local concern by offering its citizens the opportunity to lobby for the resumption of a yearly hock tide performance at a time when the city of Coventry was in economic crisis.[68] Event eyewitness Robert Langham interpreted the entire event as a successful display of Leicester's hospitality and eminence, his "honorabl, frank, freendly & nobl hart toward all estatez" and ability to unify a regional population harmoniously.[69] The Kenilworth entertainment positioned Leicester as a powerful local magnate and suggested that Elizabeth needed country house owners like him to understand and govern England well. As it did so, it revealed the complexity of the project of defining Elizabeth's England and implicitly asked to what extent Elizabeth could control her regional authority figures. By emphasizing differences between London and the provinces, the Kenilworth performance risked making the Queen appear out of touch and revealed a strained relationship between Crown-centered patriotism and regional pride.

The Cecils and Theobalds Entertainments in the 1590s

The early entertainments at Theobalds and Kenilworth both proved successful. Elizabeth eventually gave Leicester the military leadership position he desired, although his 1585–6 expedition to the Netherlands was far from successful, and references to his entertainment in Shakespeare's *Midsummer Night's Dream* and a seventeenth-century jest book, among others, reveal that people continued to talk about this popular cultural event.[70] Meanwhile, Burghley continued to hold an influential position at Elizabeth's court, advocate his family's interests, and expand Theobalds. In 1585, Burghley defended himself from "backbyters" who accused him of overreaching his relatively low-born status and building an excessively showy

---

[67] Langham, *A Letter*, sig. E4r. Langham reports that Elizabeth was delighted by this demonstration of "how valiantly oour english weemen for looue of theyr cuntree behaued themselues" (sig. E2r).

[68] Davis, *Chivalry and Romance*, 85–9; Logan, *Text/Events*, 141–2.

[69] Langham, *A Letter*, sig. K3r. Langham also reveals that he feels indebted to Leicester, who served as his patron. Although their relationship likely influenced his interpretation of the event, his perspective helps illustrate how country house entertainments bolstered their hosts' local power.

[70] Adams, *Leicester*, 176–95; *A Midsummer Night's Dream*, 2.1.148–54; BL, Harley MS 6395, item 221. The jest book is attributed to Nicholas L'Estrange. His anecdote and Oberon's reminiscing in *Midsummer* seem to recall the same episode: an actor singing on a dolphin's back during the Kenilworth water pageant.

house.[71] He wrote of Theobalds as "begun by me with a meane mesure, but Increased by occasions of hir Maiesties often coming, whom to please I neuer would omitt to strayne myself to more charges than buylding it and yet not without some speciall direction of hir Maiesty."[72] Burghley claimed that he felt content with a modestly sized house but was "forced to enlarg a room" to please the Queen, who complained about the small size of her chamber.[73] He maintained that Theobalds developed into a royal palace by chance, and its renovations were simply Elizabeth's orders. The later pageants of 1591 and 1594 maintained the idea that Elizabeth controlled Theobalds and Burghley, but they petitioned her with mounting urgency as the aging Burghley pleaded for retirement and as his son Robert took an increasingly leading role. Both entertainments promoted Burghley's plea and Robert's political ambition, and the Queen responded to their requests with playfulness and a little resistance.

When Elizabeth arrived on May 10, 1591, the house must have changed substantially since her Latin welcome twenty years earlier. Now her path to the house took her along a tree-lined driveway and through multiple gates and courtyards. Just as at Kenilworth, the gates could have appeared as obstacles as they offered several opportunities for welcome. An actor playing a Hermit stopped Elizabeth and her entourage in the Middle Court, a place of great ceremony with classical architecture meant to impress. It was also a space where the estate's dual purposes came into sharp focus. On one side of the courtyard stood a gallery with many pillars and arches, and with the Cecil family crest positioned atop the central arches. On the opposite side was a second gallery with the royal arms under its central arch.[74] Behind this gallery stood the clock tower, which had three gilded dials that probably tracked the hours, months, and zodiac signs.[75] Beyond both was the house entrance. As the Hermit spoke, the audience saw a visual representation of the blended or dueling authorities of Burghley and Elizabeth. At best, as the visitors passed from the Cecil crest to the royal arms, they performed the event's transition of power from Burghley to Elizabeth. At worst, the two galleries showed competing heads of the household.

Extending the approach Burghley used in his 1571 entertainment, the Hermit's speech emphasized eager transition of power much more than it

---

[71] SP Domestic, Elizabeth I, 12/181, f. 159r. Burghley wrote this letter to William Herle and dated it August 14, 1585.

[72] Ibid., f. 159r.   [73] Ibid., f. 159r.

[74] Sutton, *Materializing Space*, 42–4; Summerson, "Building of Theobalds," 118. Their sources postdate 1607, so it is possible the royal arms were not yet present, but Sutton argues persuasively that they were an important feature of the 1591 entertainment (44, n. 42).

[75] Summerson, "Building of Theobalds," 118; Sutton, *Materializing Space*, 45.

revealed a competitive stance. The 1591 pageantry called Burghley "owner" of Theobalds only once in a later episode; it mostly represented the house as kept and improved for Elizabeth. The Hermit addressed her without delay: "My souerayn lady and most gratious Queene / be nott displeased that won so meanly clad / presumes to stand this bowldly In the way / that leades into this howse accowntted yours" (3:530).[76] Unlike many other characters who welcomed the Queen or obstructed her path on progress, the Hermit showed no uncertainty about the guest's identity or the implications of his actions. He explained that Burghley had retreated from public view following the deaths of his wife, mother, and daughter and had entreated the Hermit to "gouern this his howse and family" in his absence – a task the Hermit felt unsuited to fulfill (3:531). Here Burghley was not an owner or a governing head, but simply "the gardiian of this howse Increast for your delyghtt" (3:533). The Hermit in turn asked Elizabeth to let Burghley retire from active duty at court.

The end of the Hermit's speech introduced several of Burghley's family members, who probably gathered to greet the Queen as they did in 1571, and although its language emphasized Elizabeth's great power, the performance suggested intimacy with the family. She had dismounted her horse by this point and stood on equal footing with the rest.[77] In response to the Hermit's petition, she drew up a mock charter, signed and perhaps read aloud by Lord Chancellor Christopher Hatton, requesting Burghley to return to public life.[78] This interactive exchange performed between the two galleries established with special clarity the possibilities for cooperation and critique present in all country house entertainment. James Sutton argues that although Theobalds may have been designed for the Queen, her dominion there was "always secondary to the Cecils' proprietary claims."[79] He emphasizes how the house displayed Burghley's power and influence, and by carefully allocating sleeping arrangements and provisions for the

[76] I cite the 1591 Theobalds entertainment from Marie-Louise Coolahan's edited text in Goldring, et al., eds., *John Nichols's The Progresses*, 3:529–41. The Hermit's speech survives in one manuscript: BL, Egerton MS 2623, f. 15–16. For critical discussions of the entertainment, see Sutton, *Materializing Space*, 100–26; Curtis Breight, "Entertainments of Elizabeth at Theobalds in the Early 1590s" in *REED Newsletter* 12.2 (1987): 1–6; Marion Colthorpe, "The Theobalds Entertainment for Queen Elizabeth I in 1591, with a Transcript of the Gardener's Speech" in *REED Newsletter* 12.1 (1987): 2–9; Gabriel Heaton, *Writing and Reading Royal Entertainments From George Gascoigne to Ben Jonson* (Oxford University Press, 2010), 168–9.

[77] Sutton, *Materializing Space*, 98–9.

[78] The mock charter is now in the collection of the Elizabethan Club at Yale University. See also Coolahan, ed., "Mock-Charter," in Goldring, et al., eds., *John Nichols's The Progresses*, 3:538–41; *Sotheby's Catalogue of Valuable Autograph Letters, Literary Manuscripts, and Historical Documents* (London, 15–16 December 1980), 141–2.

[79] Sutton, *Materializing Space*, 55.

royal entourage, Burghley used the space at Theobalds to manage Elizabeth and others' access to her.[80] Sutton's claims speak to the management of space in country house performance more broadly. As host, Burghley held great control over the event and used it to promote his son in a space he had carefully designed. But as the 1591 pageantry insisted that the house only served Elizabeth, it offered fewer ambiguities about ownership than did many others in its genre.

A later pageant performed in the Great Garden made explicit the entertainment's primary goal: to present Robert Cecil as poised to take over Theobalds and his father's place in Elizabeth's favor. In speeches by a Gardener and a Molecatcher, Elizabeth heard how Robert transformed a wild plot of land "ouergrowne with thistles and turned vp with moles" at his nearby estate at Pymmes into an ordered garden filled with native English flowers: roses, pansies, and eglantine, the tenacious English rose frequently associated with Elizabeth (3:535).[81] Especially because the praise of Robert's successful management of this small garden was delivered in the meticulously organized seven-acre Great Garden, the pageant suggested that Robert was ready to transition to greater responsibility.[82] His older brother Thomas would inherit Burghley House, and this pageant claimed Theobalds for Robert. The praise of Robert's gardening served as a thinly veiled metaphor for his skill as a political advisor: just as he was preparing to move from Pymmes to Theobalds, he was eager to increase his responsibilities at court. By this time Robert had started taking over duties associated with the secretarial post left vacant after Sir Francis Walsingham's death, but Elizabeth had not yet officially appointed him. The Molecatcher alluded to late Elizabethan dissension when he noted that "moles in fildes [fields] were like ill subiectes in commonwelthes, which are alwyes turninge vp the place in which they are bredde" (3:538). The entertainment argued that Robert would help Elizabeth rule England as efficiently and successfully as he transformed an infested garden into a fertile one. Curtis Breight has noted

---

[80] Ibid., 84–5.

[81] Both speeches survive in BL, Egerton MS 2623, f. 17–18, and a variant of the Gardener's speech appears in Hatfield House Archives, Cecil Papers, 140/94. Elizabeth and her courtiers often employed the eglantine rose in her imagery, and some portraits have her flanked by branches of eglantine and Tudor roses. See Roy Strong, *The Cult of Elizabeth: Elizabethan Portraiture and Pageantry* (London: Thames and Hudson, 1977), 68–76; Maria Hayward, "The 'Empresse of Flowers': The Significance of Floral Imagery in Two Portraits of Elizabeth I at Jesus College, Oxford" in *Costume* 44 (2010): 20–7.

[82] Sutton, *Materializing Space*, 48; Henderson, *Tudor House and Garden*, 85, 206–7. The Theobalds garden was twice the size of Henry VIII's garden at Hampton Court. Its seven acres were divided into nine knots, each of which was seventy square feet, and the knots were separated by walks twenty-two feet wide.

that Robert's methods might be brutal; when the entertainment promised that Robert would manage domestic traitors, it alluded to intelligence-gathering about Catholic recusants and vowed he would aggressively root out anyone found to be "turninge vp the place."[83]

The entertainment's goal of urging Burghley's retirement and Robert's official promotion was tied to its larger political message. The opening speech primed the audience for allusions to Anglo–Spanish relations when the Hermit praised the Lord Admiral, who was in attendance, for "your famous victorye ore that spannishe Nauye / which by them sellues was termed Inuyncyble" (3:533). The Gardener then reported that Robert said eglantine was a flower "I moste honor, and yt hathe bene towlde mee that the deeper yt is rooted in the grounde the sweeter it smelleth in the flower, makinge it ever so greene, that the Son of spaine att the hotteste cannot parche itt" (3:536). With a pun on "Son" and "sun," this line boasted that the failure of King Philip's navy was brought about by the strength of Elizabeth and her England. As the entertainment celebrated England's improved international status following its encounter with the Spanish Armada, it defined England as a firmly Protestant nation headed by a powerful monarch, and it promoted Robert as an anti-Catholic advisor ready to seek and destroy traitorous recusants. This perspective posed a striking contrast to the Cowdray entertainment, performed three months later at the Sussex estate of known Catholics Anthony and Magdalen Browne, Viscount and Lady Montague. As Chapter 5 explains in greater detail, their entertainment argued for leniency in Elizabeth's treatment of Sussex Catholics, whom it represented as loyal supporters of the Crown. The Cecils' pageantry advocated the opposite and reminded the audience of the continued possibility of Spanish invasion. In the Privy Council's three sessions during Elizabeth's stay at Theobalds, members discussed concerns about Spain and the possibility of gathering troops in southern England.[84] The Theobalds pageantry might not have said explicitly that the Queen should stay forever and be advised by her protectors there, but its pageantry implied the same. The Hermit, Gardener, and Molecatcher speeches together asserted that the Cecils would provide security for Elizabeth and England if she heeded their advice.[85]

The garden pageantry also offered fascinating commentary on the issue of legal ownership. The Gardener and Molecatcher speeches claimed that when the laborers constructed the garden at Robert's orders, they uncovered

---

[83] Breight, "Entertainments of Elizabeth," 1–6.   [84] Sutton, *Materializing Space*, 104, n. 63.
[85] Breight makes a similar argument in "Entertainments of Elizabeth," 4–5.

a box of treasure, and the Molecatcher spoke of the property and land laws
that the genre alternately evaded and confronted:

> I cam not to clayme anie right for my selfe, but to geue you yours, for that,
> had the bickeringe bene betweene vs, there shoulde haue needed noe other
> Iustice of peace then *this*, to haue made him a mittimus, to the first gardner
> that euer was Adam. I went to Lawyers to aske coansell, who made lawe
> Lyke a playce, a blacke syde and a whitte, for saide one yt belongeth to the
> Lorde of the soile by the custome of the manor: nay saide the other, yt is
> Treasure trove, whats that quoth I? mary all monye or Iewlls hidden in the
> earthe is the Queenes, *noli me tangere* I let go my houlde, and desire your
> maiestie that you will houlde youres. (3:537)

As the Molecatcher relayed a debate with the Gardener about possession
of the treasure, his speech identified two competing theories of property
ownership: Burghley could claim any materials discovered on land he held,
or the Queen held rights to all property in England. The entertainment
underscored that his conclusion, that Elizabeth laid claim to all English
goods, was based on legal precedent rather than mere desire to please her.
Many entertainments claimed to teach others how to praise Elizabeth; this
one offered lessons in law and politics to demonstrate Robert as a shrewd
advisor whose alliance with her was deeply rooted in family tradition.
The Molecatcher returned focus to the relationship between Burghley and
Elizabeth when he said, "next your majestie I honor the owner of that
howse wishinge that his vertues maye duble his yeares, and yours treble"
(3:537). Like the rest of the entertainment, this line praised Elizabeth while
acknowledging Burghley's central role in her life and government. Although
it called Burghley "owner" of Theobalds, it made clear that Elizabeth held
possession of the place and the Cecils.

In terms of the tenuous issues of power and entitlement, the 1591
Theobalds entertainment was among the most prudent in its genre. Yet
it was only partially successful in accomplishing what its hosts hoped it
would. Elizabeth's mock charter made clear that she would not allow Burghley complete retirement, and she never did. She knighted Robert before
leaving Theobalds and admitted him into the Privy Council three months
later, and at least one contemporary letter suggests that others assumed
his promotion was imminent: "I suppose you have heard of her Majesty's
great entertainment at *Tibbuls*; of her knighting Sir Robert Cecil, and of
the expectation of his advancement to the Secretaryship."[86] But Elizabeth
did not formally appoint Robert to the secretaryship until 1596.

---

[86] Qtd. in Nichols, *Progresses*, 3:74.

When the Cecils hosted Elizabeth again in 1594, another Hermit speech continued to represent her as Theobalds' true owner as it even more urgently promoted Burghley's retirement and Robert's skills as a political advisor. Robert was especially involved in the devising of this pageant; one manuscript copy identifies it as "penned by Sir Robert Cecill," and although his father still technically served as host, the entertainment revealed that Robert was beginning to step into the role of estate master.[87] After the Hermit welcomed back Elizabeth and praised her youthfulness and political success, he asked "to trouble your Maiestie, with another peticion, not much differing from the former" (3:736).[88] The speech then emphasized Burghley's age and Robert's readiness to take over Theobalds and solidify his rise into a position as one of Elizabeth's top advisors. The Hermit drew parallels between himself, a retired "old aged man," and Burghley, whom he described as near death and struggling to fulfill his political duties: "when his body being laden with yeares, oppressed with sicknes, having spent his strength for publick service desireth to be ridd of wordly cares, by ending his dayes, Your Maiestie, with a band of princlie, kindnes even when he is most greviosly sicke, and lowest brought, holdes him back and ransometh him" (3:736). These lines represented Burghley as resistant to continued political service but did not make him seem ungrateful or disloyal. The Hermit implicitly asked on Burghley's behalf for retirement by describing himself as follows: "howsoeuer I live obscure, I may be quiet and secure, not to be driven to seeke my grave which though it may be euery where, yet I desire it to be here. This may be done, if yow will enioyne him for your pleasure, whose will is to him a Law" (3:737). Especially because the Hermit already discussed his and Burghley's meditative age in similar terms, this self-description as a man pleading to retire in peace at Theobalds clearly stood for Burghley's own request.

Robert was the "him" who treated Elizabeth's will as "Law," and the Hermit's speech positioned Robert as his father's familial and political successor. The Hermit spoke of the future, when Robert would govern Theobalds, with great optimism. When he predicted that Robert would use Theobalds rather "for a place of recreation then of meditacion," he implied that Robert's youthful energy would make him a more effective head of Theobalds, an estate designed for royal entertainment, than did

---

[87] LPL, Tracts & Treatises MS 2858, f. 188v.

[88] I quote this speech from Marie-Louise Coolahan's edited version in Goldring, et al., eds., *John Nichols's The Progresses*, 3:734–8. Besides the Lambeth Palace Library manuscript cited above, manuscript copies of the 1594 Hermit's speech include Oxford, Bodleian Library, Rawlinson MS D 692, f. 106–9; Dublin, Trinity College, MS 802, f. 60–2; BL, Additional MS 73087, f. 170–4.

Burghley's years (3:737). As Burghley lobbied for personal space, he and Robert continued to advance his agenda from twenty years earlier: the securing of their family's status. The Hermit told Elizabeth that Burghley, "to Leave all free for yow, and your Trayne," had sent his grandchildren to the Hermit's residence (3:737). As the previous Theobalds pageants also illustrated, Burghley wanted Elizabeth to imagine the manor as always open to her. The Hermit described Burghley's grandchildren as "all his vnfledged birds being the Comfort of his age, and his pretious Iewells" and added: "a man must pluck their quilles, orels they will daylie fly out to see your Maiestie, such is the working of the grandfathers affection in them, and your vertue and beautie" (3:737). The pageant promoted Burghley's issue as naturally drawn to Elizabeth's virtue and educated on how to serve her by their patriarch. The Hermit said of Robert, "although his experience and Iudgment, be noe waie comparable, yett as the report goeth, he hath something in him like the Child of such a Parent" (3:737). Burghley asked in turn that Elizabeth allow him to retire from public service and that she continue to show his family favor. The 1590s Theobalds pageants expanded the 1571 representation of Burghley as a "private man" by transitioning him to a hermit. Whereas the personified house asked Elizabeth not to seek more than it could offer in 1571, the later entertainments presented a similar plea from an advisor who insisted he had already given everything he could.

When Burghley died in August 1598, Robert had already been made secretary and was settling in to a secure position at court that would last well into James' reign. The eldest son, Thomas, then inherited Burghley's title and family estate, but he apparently desired to establish his own identity somewhat apart from his father and brother. His many letters to Robert reveal that he relied on his brother's position and access to Elizabeth, but his own country house and royal entertainment imply that he hoped to earn some degree of favor and clout himself. Elizabeth must have known his father's disappointment in him, and Thomas must have felt he had a fair amount to prove. When his Wimbledon estate appeared on the 1599 progress gest, he gathered provisions and prepared entertainment. Elizabeth deferred her arrival four times, and Thomas grew tired both of hearing of changes "by chaunce" and of large quantities of food spoiling in the heat.[89] He wrote to his brother Robert that the Queen's "so often commyng and not commyng so distemprith all thyngs with me as vppon euery chang

---

[89] Hatfield House Archives, Cecil Papers, vol. 179, f. 37, 41, Microfilm Reel 48, BL.

of commyng I doo nothyng but giue directions into the country for new prouysyons."[90]

When Elizabeth finally arrived at Wimbledon manor in Surrey in late July 1599, a Porter greeted her at the entrance. Only a short welcome address survives from the visit; it might have been a brief standalone pageant modeled after his father's 1571 entertainment, or it might have served as an introduction to other, now-lost pageants. The estate entrance sat on top of a hill and was surrounded by impressive gardens and landscaping in an Italianate style, and a dramatic stairway led to the house.[91] Against this showy backdrop, the Porter welcomed the Queen with humility and excitement on behalf of Thomas, now Lord Burghley, and his wife Dorothy. He said:

> The bunch of keyes that comands euery gate
> dewty, love, loyalty, constancye to the state
> If any will ask whoe wrought these keyes
> the vertues of your minde the faire power of your eyes
> It is the fittest and the finest smith
> to bolt and lock in mens harts therewith
> But that your highnes may not stay to knock
> take this double key and open euery lock
> Even the lock of his hart to whose house you ar come
> where of fayth you shall finde a sound built Rome.[92]

Like his father's and brother's earlier entertainments, this invocation ceded ownership to the Queen and invited her to command all inside – not because Thomas and Dorothy were simply being hospitable, but because they acknowledged that Elizabeth already owned Wimbledon. Although the speech briefly referred to the house as Thomas' possession ("whose house you ar come"), an extended metaphor about Elizabeth's creation and possession of all keys overshadowed this small claim. It stated directly that Thomas' heart, like the house, remained open to Elizabeth and her authority. It is likely that Dorothy and their eleven children stood poised to greet Elizabeth at her arrival, but the welcoming speech did not mention them. Instead, it highlighted Thomas' devotion because advancing his political career was the family's top priority. Thomas had been corresponding with

---

[90] Hatfield House Archives, Cecil Papers, vol. 199, f. 60, Microfilm Reel 53, BL.

[91] Henderson, *Tudor House and Garden*, 89–90.

[92] Oxford, Bodleian Library, Tanner MS 306, f. 266. See also Marion Colthorpe, "An Entertainment for Queen Elizabeth I at Wimbledon in 1599" in *REED Newsletter* 10.1 (1985): 1–2. Her transcription first brought this text to my attention.

his brother about the possibility of his becoming President of the Council of the North, a post he dearly sought.[93] Through his entertainment, Thomas hoped to prove himself valuable, and shortly after Elizabeth's visit, she granted him the presidency.

Although the Cecils did not always rise as quickly as they wished, their country house performances revealed their successful navigations of the genre's particular challenges and rewards. Together with Leicester's entertainment at Kenilworth, the Theobalds and Wimbledon entertainments revealed how all country house pageantry merged the personal and the political. They demonstrated how the genre's structure and location could lead to tensions about competing authorities, and entertainments that emphasized the local and pastoral space tended to exhibit more ambiguity about Elizabeth's role. This collection of entertainments focused on the role of Elizabeth's elite advisers in governing and defining England. They together created an image of a heterogeneous nation in which the monarch and her subjects engaged in ongoing public conversations, localities proudly embraced their differences, and aristocrats governed locally in Elizabeth's absence but also carried their own agendas that made them more than simple mouthpieces for the Crown. As Chapters 4 and 5 will reveal, the printing of country house performance further engaged with the linked but sometimes conflicting identities and authorities of region and nation. The performances analyzed in this chapter featured hosts with well-established relationships with Elizabeth who had other outlets for influencing policy. Even Thomas Cecil, who had more to prove than did his father or Leicester, had a nearly direct line to the Queen through his brother and would not have needed to prove his strong family line. As the next two chapters turn to the genre's definitions of courtiership and hospitality, they offer several examples of hosts far less secure than were the Cecils or Leicester in their social and political positions.

---

[93] Hatfield House Archives, Cecil Papers, vol. 199, f. 60, Microfilm Reel 53, BL; Hatfield House Archives, Cecil Papers, vol. 73, f. 73, Microfilm Reel 14, BL.

CHAPTER 2

"Your Maiesty on my knees will I followe"
Performing Gender and the Courtier–Monarch Relationship

Devisers of country house entertainment used their performances to audition for royal appointments and to promote certain policies. As they did so, they debated the best way to serve and advise a single female monarch. Especially early in the genre, many country house entertainments employed what Leonard Forster has called "political Petrarchism," or the use of unrequited romantic love as a metaphor for the relationship between an unmarried queen and her male courtiers.[1] This praising strategy was incredibly popular at the Elizabethan court. In sonnets, tilts, and other kinds of texts and performances, male courtiers represented themselves as love-struck suitors enamored with a desirable, unattainable, and sometimes cruel mistress, and they described Elizabeth as an incarnation of Petrarch's idealized Laura.[2] In many country house pageants, male courtiers used rhetoric of sexualized desire to describe and act upon their political ambition. This chapter begins by exploring how two of Elizabeth's repeat hosts – Robert Dudley, Earl of Leicester, and Sir Henry Lee – relied on Petrarchan rhetoric to define the role of courtier during the late 1570s and early 1590s. Although their pageants exploited similarly sexualized language, Leicester and Lee offered competing models of political service: outspoken, self-promoting advisor or submissive servant focused on Elizabeth's agendas.

I then turn to three 1592 performances at Bisham Abbey in Berkshire, Sudeley Castle in Gloucestershire, and Rycote Park in Oxfordshire, all of which highlighted the contributions of female devisers and aimed to

---

[1] Leonard Forster, "The Political Petrarchism of the Virgin Queen" in *The Icy Fire: Five Studies in European Petrarchism* (Cambridge University Press, 1969), 122–47. Forster argues that Elizabeth, who read the "suggestive" combination of Machiavelli and Petrarch, implemented this strategy as a mode of political control when she adopted the role of Petrarch's Laura. However, country house entertainments underscore that her courtiers often directed the conversation. See also Susan Frye, *Elizabeth I: The Competition for Representation* (Oxford University Press, 1996), esp. 3–21.

[2] See especially Arthur F. Marotti, "'Love is Not Love': Elizabethan Sonnet Sequences and the Social Order" in *ELH* 49.2 (1982): 396–428; Richard C. McCoy, *The Rites of Knighthood: The Literature and Politics of Elizabethan Chivalry* (Berkeley: University of California Press, 1989).

build political alliances among household women and Elizabeth. These entertainments continued to debate the two models of courtiership presented by Leicester and Lee but reimagined the courtier–monarch relationship beyond Petrarchism. Each advertised young members of the household for new or sustained employment, and in bolstering the social and political futures of this new generation, each promoted a gendered alternative to political Petrarchism.[3] The Bisham and Sudeley performances asserted that chaste, educated, and politically savvy young women – those fashioned in the Queen's image – made the best courtiers. Young women performed speaking roles in both. The Sudeley entertainment represented its female performer as an apt servant, while the Bisham pageantry presented its teenaged women as capable political advisors. The Rycote entertainment argued that ideal service to the Queen was male military duty – not the kind of aggressive commander that Leicester imagined at Kenilworth, but a role that illustrated absolute submission to Elizabeth. This model validated her authority as a wartime monarch but left little room for female courtiership. All three entertainments creatively rewrote the position of Elizabethan courtier to suit the host families' personal goals. As they urged Elizabeth to reevaluate how she chose her servants and advisors, they enabled her iconographic shift from marriageable young queen to ageless Virgin Queen and offered her a range of possibilities for redefining her role as a single woman in power.

Petrarchan Courtiership: Leicester, Lee, and Their Mistress

Several scholars have identified Elizabeth's relations with her male courtiers as tense and competitive. Catherine Bates and Richard McCoy have both suggested that court rituals enabled male courtiers to release aggression about their subordinate roles as they sought influence and compromise, and some country house entertainments did just that.[4] Male hosts often configured themselves as suitors desperately in love with Elizabeth. Rhetoric of desire and despair abounded, and many entertainments coupled declarations of painful unrequited love with fantasies of fulfilled desire or pleas for something to change. Such complaints often emerged in songs played

---

[3] I use the word "alternative" in a similar way to how Heather Dubrow uses "counterdiscourse." As she explains, the term "anti-Petrarchan" can be problematic because of the diverse ways critics use it. Dubrow, *Echoes of Desire: English Petrarchism and Its Counterdiscourses* (Ithaca: Cornell University Press, 1995), 6–8.

[4] Catherine Bates, *The Rhetoric of Courtship in Elizabethan Language and Literature* (Cambridge University Press, 1992), 45–88; McCoy, *Rites of Knighthood*, 9–27.

outside Elizabeth's window or while she hunted or took garden walks. For example, the 1591 Cowdray entertainment featured a Petrarchan song while Elizabeth shot at deer. It called her "Loues treasure" and treated her as a woman to be courted as it offered a blazon that praised her golden locks, twinkling eyes, heavenly face, and melodious voice.[5] When it compared her eyes to arrows that injure admirers, it lamented the melancholy of unrequited love. Songs and speeches about the imprisoning effect of being perpetually unfulfilled captured well the circumstances of a country house entertainment as a disenfranchised courtier might describe them: Elizabeth appeared more accessible and willing than she really was, but her suitors kept loving her despite this inherent futility. In the context of a royal performance, Petrarchan complaints became thinly veiled protests about the male courtier's lack of control and stymied attempts to gain power. Although such complaints were often self-deprecating and sometimes humorous, they also had the potential to be bold and contentious.

When Elizabeth visited Kenilworth Castle in 1575, Leicester adopted the stance of a Petrarchan lover through a character called Deep Desire. We have already seen that the entertainment began by presenting Leicester as Elizabeth's near equal as it tried to negotiate their authorities, and the concluding Deep Desire pageant, the one that began with hired writer George Gascoigne chasing Elizabeth's horse as she hunted in the forest, reformulated their relationship as that between a controlling mistress and her submissive but frustrated courtier. When Gascoigne adopted the persona of forest god Sylvanus in this pageant, he probably appeared according to conventional representations: wearing a loose tunic with a crown made of twigs and carrying fruit, pine cones, and a gardening sickle or tree branch.[6] He offered to serve as Elizabeth's footman and protector if she would simply listen to his story, and then he delivered a long speech about happenings in that very forest, especially the captivity of Deep Desire by his "courteous cruell" mistress (sig. c6r).[7] Her name was "Zabeta" or "Athebasile," both obvious monikers for Elizabeth. Sylvanus explained how Zabeta "so obstinatly and cruelly reiected" endless suitors and turned them into plants (sig. c5r). While Sylvanus acknowledged Zabeta's "iustice" toward some of them, his sympathies were clearly aligned with Deep Desire, whom

---

5 *The Speeches and Honorable Entertainment giuen to the Queenes Maiestie in Progresse, at Cowdrey in Sussex, by the right Honorable the Lord Montague. 1591* (London, 1591; *STC* 3907.7), sig. A4r–A4v.

6 See Peter F. Dorcey, *The Cult of Silvanus: A Study in Roman Folk Religion* (Leiden and New York: Brill, 1992).

7 "A Briefe Rehearsall, or Rather a True Copie of as Much as Was Presented before Her Maiesties at Kenelworth" in *The VVhole Woorkes of George Gascoigne Esquyre* (London, 1587; *STC* 11638).

he called "the worthiest that euer was condemned to wretched estate"
(sig. c6r). In fact, Sylvanus claimed such great distress at Deep Desire's
story that he was nearly unable to relay it: "the teares stande in mine eyes
(yea and my tongue trembleth and faltereth in my mouth)" (sig. c5r).

After this introduction, Sylvanus led Elizabeth to an arbor filled with
holly bushes, where she heard "straunge Musicke" and saw an actor playing
Deep Desire emerge from the largest bush – an action that, like most of
the pageant, was erotically charged. Sylvanus explained that Deep Desire
"was in this life and worlde continually full of compunccions, so is he now
furnished on euery side with sharpe pricking leaues, to proue the restlesse
prickes of his priuie thoughts" (sig. c6r). The "prickes" of his conscience
might have signaled regret or contrition, perhaps a meek apology for his
hot-headedness or assertions of authority earlier in her visit. The statement could have offered a witty comment on Leicester's frequent need to
apologize to Elizabeth, and in a more serious vein, it captured his position
as a lovelorn courtier whose cruel mistress repeatedly rebuked his earnest
advances. The repetition of "prick" highlighted a sexual undercurrent to all
of these interpretations. The *OED* traces the word's use as coarse slang for
penis to the mid-sixteenth century, and just in case this particular meaning
might be lost, Sylvanus added that unlike such "he Holly" as Deep Desire,
a "she Holly" would have "no prickes" (sig. c6r).[8] Deep Desire's own
speeches and song begged Elizabeth to stay. He called her "dame pleasure,"
warned that her departure would "breake in twaine this harmlesse heart of
mine," and exploited common poetic metaphors by saying he would "die
to see my deere delight go by" (sig. c7r). As in the later Cowdray entertainment, the word "die" captured both anguished longing and hope for
sexualized fulfillment, and the forest setting would have especially drawn
attention to the conventional analogy between "dear" and "deer." Deep
Desire characterized his beloved as both a hunted animal – an object for
the poet to possess and dominate – and a powerful force whose whim
controlled him.

Although it is likely that a professional actor took the part of Deep Desire,
the character clearly stood for Leicester and represented his frustrations.
The episode's metaphor is easy to unravel: the Queen had confined Leicester
to a painfully subservient role, and he begged for release. Some scholars
have taken his pleas at face value and argued that the entertainment staged
a marriage proposal, but this event was no proposal of marriage.[9] It was

---

[8] *OED*, "prick," *n.*, def. 12b.
[9] See, e.g., Jean Wilson, *Entertainments for Elizabeth I* (Woodbridge: D. S. Brewer, 1980), 119; Marie
Axton, "The Tudor Mask and Elizabethan Court Drama" in Marie Axton and Raymond Williams,

instead an erotically charged allegory for political ambition that revealed the difficulty of navigating the male courtier's role. Deep Desire expressed his dependence upon the Queen when he begged for her renewed favor ("O Queene commaund againe, / This Castle and the Knight") and when he spoke of his inability to survive without her (preparing to bid "farewell life" and "liue in darksome hell" once she left) (sig. c7v–c8v.) Yet the pageant also hinted at Deep Desire's unwillingness to surrender his own ambitions. Sylvanus described how Deep Desire never faltered despite intense pain: "he was such a one as neither any delay could daunt him: no disgrace could abate his passions, no tyme could tyre him, no water quench his flames: nor death it self could amasse him with terror" (sig. c6r). This emphasis on endurance could be interpreted as evidence of either steadfast royal allegiance or resolute political aspirations. Returning somewhat to the boldness of Leicester's welcoming pageants but with a more desperate tone, this episode's rhetoric hinted at the latter more than the former, especially when Sylvanus summarized Deep Desire's appeal as follows: "I do humbly crave in his behalfe, that you would either be a suter for him unto the heavenly powers, or else but onely to give your gracious consent that hee may be restored to his prystinate estate" (sig. c8v). Sylvanus pleaded with Elizabeth one final time to either endorse Leicester's agenda – in this case, a militant Protestant foreign policy and his own desire to lead a military campaign – or release her hold on him. The Deep Desire speech exemplified the vexed position of a male favorite at the Elizabethan court: he desired independence but could achieve it only with the Queen's permission.

When Leicester hosted Elizabeth at his estate at Wanstead three years later, a shepherd named Dorcas alluded to the Deep Desire episode as he spoke of the difference between his pastoral life and that of a courtier. He characterized a shepherd's life as follows:

> nether subiecte to violente oppression nor servile flattery how many courtiers (thincke you) I haue hard vnder our somer bushes make theire wofull complayntes some of the greatenes of theire mistris estate, which dazeled theire eyes and yet burned their hartes some of the extremytie of her beautie cupled wyth extreme creweltie some of to much witte which mad all these

eds., *English Drama: Forms and Development* (Cambridge University Press, 1977), 24–47; Ilana Nash, "'A Subject Without Subjection': Robert Dudley, Earl of Leicester, and *The Princely Pleasures at Kenelworth Castle*" in *Comitatus* 25 (1994): 81–102. Those who interpret the Petrarchan rhetoric metaphorically include Bates, *The Rhetoric of Courtship*, 55–61; Frye, *Elizabeth I*, 56–96; Diana E. Henderson, *Passion Made Public: Elizabethan Lyric, Gender, and Performance* (Urbana: University of Illinois Press, 1995), 68–79; Janette Dillon, *The Language of Space in Court Performance, 1400–1625* (Cambridge University Press, 2010), 49–75.

> theire Lovinge Labors folly O how often haue I hard one name sounde in
> many mouthes makinge our valleys wytnesses of theire dolefull Agonies so
> that with longe loste Labor fyndinge theyre thoughte bere no other wolle
> but Dispaire, of you courtiers they grewe owlde shepheardes.[10]

The entertainment elsewhere characterized Elizabeth as a powerful, unattainable woman who was deeply loved but capable of causing great pain in her devoted suitors. Characters repeatedly expressed fear and awe at the possibility of experiencing her physical presence and seeing her face, "where eares be burnte Eyes dazeled harte oppreste."[11] One character scurried away after delivering a petition because "the sighte of you is infectious," and another vowed not to "medle with her nor her eyes they saine in our Towne they are Daungerous both."[12] Although the Wanstead entertainment did so with more comic self-awareness, both it and the Kenilworth pageantry represented Elizabeth as a Petrarchan cruel mistress whose male subjects desired and clamored to influence her as they grappled for high standing at her court. Both entertainments emphasized the frustration male courtiers experienced within a patronage system that valued chastity but thrived on the language of erotic desire.

In Sir Henry Lee's 1575 and 1592 entertainments, he spoke with a more careful voice. Lee held lower ranking on the political hierarchy than did Leicester and was more cautious in his approach; as biographer E. K. Chambers has said, Lee was not one "to take any political risks."[13] His entertainments emphasized humility and lack of ambition as they proposed that courtiers should show absolute devotion to their monarch. In both performances, Lee played the part of Loricus, a wandering and lovesick knight who identified his own faults and desired only to prove himself worthy of serving a beautiful, chaste woman. The earlier entertainment, performed at Woodstock, built on Lee's new identity as court reveler. In the early 1570s, he established an annual tilt for Elizabeth and became her Champion of the Tilt. The later entertainment, performed at Woodstock and Ditchley, promised continued dedication to Elizabeth following his retirement from that role.[14] Neither performance mentioned Lee's own goals; instead they presented him as a loving attendant

---

[10] I quote from the manuscript copy of this entertainment, better known as Philip Sidney's "The Lady of May." This manuscript, often called the Helmingham Hall Manuscript, appends the entertainment to a copy of the *Old Arcadia*. BL, Additional MS 68121, f. 145r.

[11] Ibid., f. 142v.   [12] Ibid., f. 144v.

[13] E. K. Chambers, *Sir Henry Lee: An Elizabethan Portrait* (Oxford: Clarendon, 1936), 90.

[14] Gabriel Heaton argues persuasively, using accounts of the Treasurer of the Chamber, that the first day's entertainment took place at Woodstock and the second day's pageantry was performed at Ditchley. See his headnote to the entertainment in Elizabeth Goldring, et al. eds., *John Nichols's*

without political ambition.[15] The 1575 entertainment celebrated Lee's fairly recent appointment as keeper of the royal manor and advised Elizabeth on the marriage question by introducing a character who learns to surrender choice in marriage in favor of her country's good.[16] Yet the entertainment never insisted on Lee's authority, nor did it challenge Elizabeth's power or ask for more independence. This approach derived partially from the circumstances of her visit: she journeyed not to Lee's own estate, but to the royal manor where he was her lieutenant. In 1592, she visited both Woodstock and his own manor at Ditchley, but Lee maintained his dependence on Elizabeth by explicitly identifying her as his "Loue" and declaring that he spent his life "crauing no reward els but that he might loue, nor no reputation beside but that he might be knowne to loue" (3:698, 700).[17] Unlike Deep Desire, Loricus claimed contentedness with unrequited affection and presented himself as a courtier who knew his place in the political hierarchy.

On the first day of the 1575 Woodstock entertainment, the Queen stepped off her horse and stood in a bower covered with green ivy as Hemetes the hermit introduced her to Loricus, a knight who loved a "matchlesse" Lady. Despite Loricus' "vttermost deuotion" and many attempts to attain her favor, he remained unfulfilled (sig. B2r).[18] He eventually decided that "the want of his worth made his seruice vnaccepted" and that his Lady would never show the kind of love he desired (sig. B2v). He left his country in search of adventure, in the hopes that he might "deserue that reputation as this great and noble mistris woulde but thinke him worthy to be hers, though she would neuer bee none of his" (sig. B2v). The episode took a different approach from the Deep Desire pageant at Kenilworth, which never stopped begging for fulfillment. Hemetes, who

---

The Progresses and Public Processions of Queen Elizabeth I: A New Edition of the Early Modern Sources (Oxford University Press, 2014), 3:680–2.

[15] My analysis of Lee's image coincides with the portraits offered by Chambers, *Sir Henry Lee*; Gabriel Heaton, *Writing and Reading Royal Entertainments: From George Gascoigne to Ben Jonson* (Oxford University Press, 2010), 17–89; Tim Moylan, "From Queen's Champion to 'She Threatens a Progress': Sir Henry Lee and Elizabeth," an unpublished paper presented at the South-Central Renaissance Conference in March 2011. See also Sue Simpson, *Sir Henry Lee (1533–1611): Elizabethan Courtier* (Farnham: Ashgate, 2014), especially 72–93.

[16] Lee was appointed lieutenant of Woodstock manor in 1571.

[17] The Woodstock/Ditchley entertainment survives in the "Ditchley manuscript" (BL, Additional MS 41499A), a fascinating but occasionally illegible document that includes excerpts from various pageants and tilts. I quote from the edited version by Gabriel Heaton in Goldring, et al., eds., *John Nichols's The Progresses*, 3:680–703.

[18] I quote from the first printed edition, *STC* 7596. The original title page is missing and has been replaced by one that calls it *The Queenes Maiesties Entertainement at VVoodstock* (London, 1585).

was also reeling from a kind of lovesickness after loving a fickle
woman, advised Loricus that "nothing notable is woon without difficulty"
(sig. B4r). When we examine these lines in comparison to the entertainments at Kenilworth and Wanstead, we might notice the implication that
Lee was willing to work harder and with less reward than Leicester was.
The Woodstock entertainment also represented Loricus' mistress as less
cruel than Kenilworth's Zabeta. It emphasized not her maliciousness, but
the difficulty of knowing her true feelings: Loricus could not know "her
fancie" because she carried it "most closely" (sig. B2r).

Still, the entertainment complained about the powerlessness of his position. After his speech, Hemetes walked Elizabeth to the manor entrance,
where a large oak tree was covered with paintings of men in love and
accompanying poems. A singer sitting in the tree delivered a song of desire
and despair. Although its content remained generalized, we can identify
political allegory. The song included this verse:

> I am most sure that I shall not attaine,
> the onely good wherein the ioy doth lye.
> I haue no power my passions to refraine,
> but wayle the want which nought els may supply.
>
> (sig. C3r)

Through this song and the opening pageant at Woodstock, Lee offered the
same complaints as Leicester did at Kenilworth and Wanstead: powerlessness and the difficulty of gaining Elizabeth's favor. But the entertainment
in several places distinguished Lee from a character like Deep Desire by
identifying him as resolved to accept – even embrace – his subordinate
position because of his utter devotion to Elizabeth.

The Woodstock festivities ended with a lengthy pageant about Princess
Caudina, who started to elope with her chosen suitor Contarenus and
hence make a choice her father strongly opposed. She decided to end the
relationship in favor of prioritizing her country's needs instead of her own
preferences. This play advised Elizabeth to be cautious about marrying
for love or personal gain; she should instead seek counsel and marry only
if the match benefits England. At the end of this play, the dismissed
Contarenus lamented his "careful heart opprest with such desires" and
his intense "griefe" (sig. G2v). Contarenus sought comfort in the idea
that Caudina still loved him in an "honest sort," presumably the kind of
Platonic relationship Lee had with Elizabeth (sig. G3r). In fact, Contarenus
highlighted this parallel by wishing that Loricus would some day "find /

Reward for . . . his faithful seruice long" (sig. G2v). Finally, the song about Contarenus' grief ended with a warning against ambition:

> And you that looke aloft beyond degree,
> when fayrest wind doth fill your flying sayle,
> Hold fast for feare your footing ficklest bee,
> when hope wil seeme to helpe you to preuayle.
> So did she here with *Contarenus* play,
> from whom she fled when she made shew of stay.
>
> (sig. G2v)

This passage spoke to the audience directly. It informed social climbers that rises in station were built on fragile foundation, and it warned current and hopeful courtiers not to become too self-important. In this and other pageants, the Woodstock entertainment defined a good courtier as one who serves and is subordinate, not one who aggressively pursues his own agenda.

The later Woodstock/Ditchley entertainment continued this representation of courtiership, but with heightened language of love and despair that reflected Lee's new circumstances. He had retired as Champion of the Tilt in 1590 and had taken Anne Vavasour as his mistress.[19] The 1575 Woodstock pageantry did not mention Lee's wife Anne, who would have helped welcome Elizabeth to the estate, because it focused on Lee's role as Elizabeth's lieutenant and servant. The 1592 entertainment did not mention the new Anne, but it was her presence that gave Lee special reason to declare his love for Elizabeth. Many courtiers fell out of favor when they started romantic affairs, and Lee may have commissioned the Ditchley Portrait in 1592 to mark Elizabeth's forgiveness for directing his devotion elsewhere and his return to her favor (Figure 2.1).[20] The Woodstock/Ditchley performance certainly exhibited concern about inconstancy. It began at the entrance to a grove, where a knight stopped Elizabeth to recommend she not step inside this place filled with "sighes and mornfull songes / of hopeles people" (3:683). He identified the problem's source as inconstant women, who made the men despair and fade away. Especially when read alongside the earlier Kenilworth, Wanstead, and Woodstock entertainments, these complaints of "Despayer" about unrequited and inconstant love appear as a metaphor for frustrated courtiers desperately seeking preferment (3:684).

Once in the grove, Elizabeth found more thwarted lovers stuck in trees and heard a tale tinged with misogyny that celebrated her as an exception

---

[19] Chambers, *Sir Henry Lee*, 150–62.
[20] William Leahy, *Elizabethan Triumphal Processions* (Aldershot: Ashgate, 2005), 130–2.

2.1 The "Ditchley portrait" of Elizabeth I (*c.* 1592) by Marcus Gheeraerts the Younger, National Portrait Gallery, London.

to the natural faults of women. The knight leading Elizabeth gestured to the surrounding trees, which had ladies sitting on their branches and men dressed as knights standing at their trunks, and declared:

> we knights as trees whome roots of faith doe bynd
> our ladies Leaues who sometyme giue vs grace.
> but fall away with euerie blast of wynd
> our springe, our Autumne by ther loue is made
> as they affect we flourish and we fade.
>
> (3:684)

Although the women protested that "the fault is not in vs," the problem of their inconstancy was not wholly corrected by the end of the episode (3:684). When Elizabeth saved them from despair by virtue of her mere appearance, one of the imprisoned maids said, "Alas ther is but one of vs / A woman and she is not thus" (3:685). By emphasizing that Elizabeth was unlike these fickle women who caused their lovers so much pain, the pageant implied that women are naturally inconstant and represented Elizabeth as an exceptional mistress who would reward her courtiers more consistently. The trope of inconstancy justified Anne Vavasour's affair with Lee and revealed Lee's desire to make Elizabeth more constant in her favor. The entertainment then returned to Loricus. To mark his retirement but continue his life's work of proving his devotion, Loricus offered Elizabeth his full self and property in his "will," a short poem written down and handed to the Queen, in which he referred to himself as "Neuer crauing, euer seruing, / Little hauing, lesse deseruing" (3:700). As in the 1575 entertainment, Loricus claimed to focus all his energy on Elizabeth's wants and needs, although the 1592 performance placed slightly more emphasis on his desires and complaints. It continued to describe their relationship using Petrarchan imagery. Loricus' will and legacy included a conceit of courtiership as a manor whose features included "fearefull dispaire," "stolne delightes," "deepe sighes," and a "pittifull harte" (3:703). Even the humble, mostly compliant Lee relied on the language of love and courtship to describe his devotion to Elizabeth.

Alternate Kinds of Courtiership: Female Politicians at Bisham

Other entertainments performed during the 1592 progress that highlighted the contributions of female devisers implied that this kind of Petrarchan courtiership was outdated. When the widowed Elizabeth Russell hosted the Queen at Bisham on August 11, 1592, she wrote an entertainment in which her teenaged daughters Anne and Elizabeth played speaking roles.[21] The pageantry's structure centered on these women's performance of two shepherdesses who rejected the advances of Pan and argued for the superiority of women over men. Framing this pastoral play was an invocation by a "wild man" and a final pageant in which Ceres declared obedience to the Queen. These three episodes were performed in one day as the Queen progressed from the estate entrance at the top of a hill to Bisham manor at the bottom, and all were staged in the open landscape surrounding the house.

The visit gave the ambitious and resourceful Russell a public stage from which to decry injustices toward women, one of her favorite crusades. Never hesitating to exploit her family connections to the Cecils and other powerful men, Russell wielded an impressive amount of indirect influence on court politics before and after the Queen's 1592 visit.[22] In written correspondence she asked her brother-in-law William Cecil, Lord Burghley, and nephew Robert Cecil to appoint certain candidates for vacant posts at court and to pardon Calvinist dissenters, and because many of her letters thanked Robert for following her advice, she must have successfully influenced him. At the same time, her letters reveal great frustration with the indirect way she had to seek power. A 1597 letter expressed anger at a society that allowed women to gain prestige primarily through marriage: "as long as I can crawl, I will rather marry some one that shall want four of his five wits, rather than I will receive any indignity or disgrace by such base fellows for not being a wife to an earl or a baron."[23] The Queen's visit to Bisham offered Russell direct access to the social and political power she desired, and she used the opportunity to advertise her daughters as promising royal attendants.

[21] Although earlier literary critics attributed the Bisham entertainment to John Lyly or an anonymous male author, some recent scholars have begun identifying Elizabeth Russell as its author. Even if she hired a professional writer to help her, I am confident that Russell, who wrote epitaphs and religious translations, had control over the script. For more about her authorship, see Alexandra F. Johnston, "The 'Lady of the Farme': The Context of Lady Russell's Entertainment of Elizabeth at Bisham, 1592" in *Early Theatre* 5.2 (2002): 71–81; Jessica L. Malay, "Elizabeth Russell's Textual Performances of Self" in *Comitatus* 37 (2006): 146–68; Peter Davidson and Jane Stevenson, "Elizabeth I's Reception at Bisham (1592): Elite Women as Writers and Devisers" in Jayne Elisabeth Archer, Elizabeth Goldring, and Sarah Knight, eds., *The Progresses, Pageants, and Entertainments of Queen Elizabeth I* (Oxford University Press, 2007), 207–26; Elizabeth Cooke Hoby Russell, *The Writings of an English Sappho*, ed. Patricia Phillippy (University of Toronto Press, 2011), 147–57.

[22] For more on Russell's biography and use of kinship networks, see *English Sappho*, ed. Phillippy, 1–40; Chris Laoutaris, *Shakespeare and the Countess: The Battle that Gave Birth to the Globe* (London: Fig Tree, 2014); Gemma Allen, *The Cooke Sisters: Education, Piety, and Politics in Early Modern England* (Manchester University Press, 2013); Louise Schleiner, *Tudor and Stuart Women Writers* (Bloomington: Indiana University Press, 1994), 30–51.

[23] *English Sappho*, ed. Phillippy, 215.

Russell sought economic advantage for them at a time when she had been unsuccessfully fighting for their shares of the Russell estate for seven years, and court appointments would greatly increase their marriage prospects and the likelihood of financial stability.[24] As the Bisham performance spotlighted Russell's daughters in successful bids for positions at court, it offered an alternative to Petrarchan courtiership: a female courtier who modeled herself after the Queen.

The entertainment framed the young shepherdesses as teachers and counselors. In each of its three episodes, a misguided character expressed ambivalence or ignorance about the royal visitor's authority. Once these characters learned of Elizabeth's power, they offered their allegiance. By contrast, the Russell women recognized the Queen immediately and taught others how to praise her. The wild man's invocation implied subtle challenges to the Queen's authority and revealed some trepidation about female rule. When music signaled Elizabeth's arrival, the wild man asked, "who passed that way? what he or shee?" (sig. A2r).[25] By asking first for a "he" and wondering if the music accompanied male gods, he drew attention to Elizabeth's gender as unexpected. Once he realized that the visitor was the Queen, he spoke of attempts to represent her: "some saide your Pourtraiture might be drawen, other saide impossible: some thought your vertues might be numbred, most saide they were infinite" (sig. A2r). Using a popular trope in country house entertainment, these lines claimed that dramatic representations of the Queen would always be inadequate compared with Elizabeth herself. Even as the wild man apologized for shortcomings, he stated that some people identified Elizabeth's virtues as limited. The entertainment had Elizabeth's own presence decisively overcome such challenges by taming the wild man. He soon realized her identity and called himself "first in humility to salute you most happy I: my vntamed thoughts waxe gentle, and I feele in my selfe ciuility . . . Your Maiesty on my knees will I followe, bearing this Club, not as a Saluage, but to beate downe those that are" (sig. A2r–A2v). Although the wild man's desire to protect Elizabeth imagined her reception as potentially hostile by implying that she might need such protection, his posturing demonstrated deference and his words repeatedly emphasized her ability to tame his wildness. This opening episode established a pattern of misguided characters who caused trouble and needed to be disciplined or corrected by powerful women.

---

[24] Tim Stretton mentions Russell's involvement in her own legal affairs in *Women Waging Law in Elizabethan England* (Cambridge University Press, 1998), 55.

[25] The Bisham, Sudeley, and Rycote entertainment texts appear in *Speeches Delivered to Her Maiestie This Last Progresse* (Oxford, 1592; *STC* 7600).

When the Queen began walking down the hill from the estate entrance toward the manor, she encountered two shepherdesses named Sybil and Isabel, who sat in the grass sewing samplers. Their witty dialogue showed them resisting Pan's advances, disparaging men, and praising the Queen. As god of the wilderness, Pan was aligned with the wild man of the first episode, and the audience soon learned that he needed taming of his own. The play introduced him, in the words of the wild man, as "an eie-sore to chast Nymphes" and someone to be pitied rather than envied (sig. A2r). When Pan spoke, he delivered a long-winded monologue that further established him as a comic figure. He explained that he loved both shepherdesses and called them "more simple then the sheepe you keepe, but not so gentle" (sig. A2v). Scolding and mocking the women for refusing to submit to his desires, Pan said,

> Sure I am, that you are not so young as not to vnderstand loue, nor so wise as to withstand it, vnlesse you think your selues greater than gods, whereof I am one. . . . you are but the Farmers daughters of the Dale, I the god of the flocks that feede vpon the hils. Though I cannot force loue, I may obedience, or else sende your sheepe a wandring, with my fancies (sig. A2v).

He emphasized the women's lowly position within the social hierarchy, and in this context, their denial of him became a transgression against prescribed social roles. He then threatened their livelihood and emphasized that he possessed the power to force obedience.

At the same time, Pan's description of his rejection undermined any hazard he might have posed. He ended his speech with the following line: "Coynesse must be reuenged with curstnesse, but be not agaste sweet mice, my godhead cometh so fast vpon me, that Maiestye had almost ouerrun affection, Can you loue? Wil you?" (sig. A2v). As Pan moved from threats to desperate pleas, the moment during which he might have presented a serious sexual danger passed quickly. As we will see, a male god threatened a chaste woman's virtue in the Sudeley entertainment as well, but the Queen needed to rescue her. In the Bisham entertainment, Sybil and Isabel were able to resist male advances on their own.

Their responses diminished and ridiculed Pan. Sybil mocked him by claiming that he appeared more like a country laborer than an appropriate suitor: "Alas poore *Pan*, looke how he looketh Sister, fitter to drawe in a Haruest wayne, then talke of loue to chaste Virgins" (sig. A2v–A3r). In contemporary representations, Pan was typically depicted as part-human, part-goat, and the actor at Bisham probably wore goat-skin leggings and horns. Sybil interpreted this costume as ridiculous, and if it appeared comically rustic to the audience as well, it would have marked him visually as a figure not to be taken seriously. Sybil implied that she and her sister, as "chaste Virgins" who mirrored the Virgin Queen, belonged at court rather than in the country among incompetent wooers. Isabel also laughed away Pan's advances as she skewered men's inconstancy: "Men must haue as manie loues, as they haue hart-strings, and studie to make an ·Alphabet of mistresses, from A to Y which maketh them in the end crie, Ay. Against this, experience hath prouided vs a remedy, to laugh at them when they know not what to saie, and when they speake, not to beleeue them" (sig. A3r). This speech proposed female camaraderie as an antidote to male arrogance and deceit, and Isabel implied that the Queen was part of the "us" that learned to retaliate against men's advances by ignoring and ridiculing them. Sybil added: "weomens tongues are made of the same flesh that their harts are, and speake as they thinke: Mens harts of the flesh that their tongues, and both dissemble" (sig. A3r). She inverted contemporary rhetoric about insatiably lusty women with loose tongues, a stereotype supported by the Woodstock/Ditchley entertainment, and applied it to men instead. Her claim echoed and anticipated other literary attacks on men's false rhetoric of seduction in works such as *Endymion, Old Arcadia, Love's Labour's Lost,* and *Much Ado About Nothing,* pointing to a widespread desire among late Elizabethan writers to seek an alternative to the disingenuous rhetoric found in earlier chivalric literature.

In the context of an entertainment for the Queen, Sybil's lines also critiqued male courtiers' ubiquitous use of romantic language in political interactions with Elizabeth. When she insisted that men could not be trusted but that women were constant, she insinuated that pride interfered with men's ability to serve the Queen, while women were generally less aggressive, selfish, and competitive. The shepherdesses shared some features with the cruel mistresses of Leicester's and Lee's pageants, but they embraced these roles and proposed that a contemporary Laura would make a better courtier than would a desperate Petrarchan suitor. At the same time, the Bisham entertainment insisted that these young shepherdesses were never inconstant in love or politics, and it emphasized their status as "chaste Virgins" above all else (sig. A3r). Although Anne later used her status as a maid of honor to secure a husband, the Bisham entertainment smartly advertised her sister and her as disinterested in romantic courtship and solely concerned with serving the Queen.

The Russell women aligned themselves with the Queen in a variety of ways, one of which was the shared, typically feminine skill of needlework. When the text says they sat "sowing in their Samplers," it suggests that they were actively sewing, but it is likely that the samplers were pre-sewn (sig. A2v). Either way, the entertainment presented the Russell women as accomplished needleworkers. Like Elizabethan progresses, embroidery offered early modern women a pastime that was both domestic and political.[26] A young Elizabeth Tudor presented gifts of needlework to create and strengthen bonds with other women, including her stepmother, Katherine Parr, and she expected her maids of honor to be skilled in embroidery as well.[27] Other early modern women used embroidery to express their opinions on foreign affairs, especially England's relationship with Spain.[28] Ann Rosalind Jones and Peter Stallybrass have argued that early modern women viewed needlework as "evidence of quick understanding and aesthetic intelligence" and a way "to establish female bonds within doors, to create material histories, and to transgress domestic boundaries through the 'publication' and transmission of their work."[29] The Bisham entertainment supports these claims, although it reminds us that embroidery was an activity not only for women stuck "within doors." The Russell daughters represented the outdoor landscape at Bisham as a liberating space where women could commune together, not unlike Aemilia Lanyer's later description of Cookham in her country house poem, and, through their stitching, Anne and Elizabeth Russell demonstrated their ability to emulate the Queen in using domestic skills to gain political influence outside the home.[30]

They also demonstrated their wit. When Pan asked them to read their samplers, the shepherdesses revealed that their embroidered phrases appropriately reiterated the entertainment's criticism of men and celebration of single women. They identified the Queen's stitch as "all right," which signified accuracy and truthfulness, as opposed to "Mens tongues, wrought all with double stitch but not one true" (sig. A3r). Another sampler read, "The honour of Virgins who became Goddesses, for their chastity"

---

[26] On the political value of needlework, see especially Susan Frye, *Pens and Needles: Women's Textualities in Early Modern England* (Philadelphia: University of Pennsylvania Press, 2010).

[27] Frye, *Pens and Needles*, 31–45; Lisa Klein, "Your Humble Handmaid: Elizabethan Gifts of Needlework" in *Renaissance Quarterly* 50 (1997): 459–93; Violet A. Wilson, *Queen Elizabeth's Maids of Honour and Ladies of the Privy Chamber* (London: John Lane, 1922), 5–6. See also Clare McManus' discussion of the value of needlework at Queen Anna's court in *Women on the Renaissance Stage: Anna of Denmark and Female Masquing in the Stuart Court* (Manchester University Press, 2002), 188–95.

[28] Ann Rosalind Jones and Peter Stallybrass, *Renaissance Clothing and the Materials of Memory* (Cambridge University Press, 2000), 162.

[29] Ibid., 145, 158.

[30] Similarly, Alison Findlay argues that the Bisham entertainment "casts the landscape as women's terrain" to be controlled by Russell, her daughters, and the Queen in *Playing Spaces in Early Women's Drama* (Cambridge University Press, 2006), 80.

(sig. A3r), a reference to the Queen and a nod to the Russell daughters' desire to become maids of honor. The suggestion that multiple virgins could become goddesses had the potential to shore up competition between Elizabeth and her ladies, especially because Elizabeth had notoriously tumultuous relationships with some of her Privy Chamber women. Those who flirted shamelessly with courtly men or married in secret tended to enrage her.[31] However, the entertainment encouraged its audience to understand "goddesses" as a metaphor for movement into court positions, and because it explained that chastity elevated women, the sampler suggested that women could earn higher status and craft more productive alliances by following Elizabeth's chaste model. The concept of multiple virgins' achievement revealed the opportunity for multiple women's simultaneous, allied political power.

Following the discussion of needlework, Sybil ended the entertainment's second episode with praise of the Queen. This part again emphasized that Sybil and Isabel applauded her virtues better than the entertainment's male figures did. Sybil said, "But prythy *Pan* be packing, thy words are as odious as thy sight, and we attend a sight which is more glorious, then the sunne rising" (sig. A3r–A3v). When Pan asked if she spoke of Jupiter, she replied, "No, but one that will make *Iupiter* blush as guilty of his vnchast iugglings" (sig. A3v). She explained that the Queen's virtues, about which "our mother hath often tolde vs," could not be long concealed from Pan (sig. A3v). Sybil described the male figures of Pan, the sun, and the king of the gods as "odious" compared to the "more glorious" feminine power of Queen Elizabeth. Like the wild man in the first episode, Pan misunderstood and needed to learn this lesson. By contrast, the two young women, tutored by their mother, were already poised to serve as loyal subjects who "attend" the Queen and teach others to praise her.

The Bisham entertainment represented these young women not simply as skilled domestic workers and devoted companions, but also as budding diplomats who were knowledgeable about England's economy and international relations. At the end of the second pageant, Sybil delivered a long prophetic speech in which she represented Elizabeth as a virtuous Protestant monarch and encouraged her to offer military support to France and the

---

[31] Karen Robertson suggests that secret marriages in the Privy Chamber challenged Elizabeth's representation of virginity as ideal and "made only too apparent the discrepancy between the mask of the ever youthful virgin Queen and the ageing body beneath" in "Negotiating Favour: The Letters of Lady Ralegh" in James Daybell, ed., *Women and Politics in Early Modern England, 1450–1700* (Aldershot: Ashgate, 2004), 101. See also Charlotte Merton, "The Women Who Served Queen Mary and Queen Elizabeth: Ladies, Gentlewomen, and Maids of the Privy Chamber, 1553–1603" (PhD diss., University of Cambridge, 1992).

Low Countries.[32] She called Elizabeth "natures glory, leading affections in fetters, Virginities slaues" (sig. A3v). Caroline McManus interprets this line, and the entertainment as a whole, as suggesting that the Queen's virginity enslaved young women to its service along with lustful men.[33] However, the entertainment resisted this implication by maintaining that the shared concerns of chastity and gender politics united the Russell women and the Queen for mutual benefit. This particular line came directly after Sybil told Pan that an explanation of the Queen's merits "may hereafter make thee surcease thy suite, for feare of her displeasure, and honour virginitye, by wondering at her vertues" (sig. A3v). Indeed, after Sybil's speech, Pan yielded his flocks and dedicated his service to Elizabeth. When read in its context, Sybil's line about "Virginities slaues" claimed that the Queen could control passionate men, just as the shepherdesses easily resisted Pan's advances. Sybil continued to describe Elizabeth as a ruler "In whom nature hath imprinted beauty, not art paynted it; in whome wit hath bred learning, but not without labour; labour brought forth wisdome, but not without wonder" (sig. A3v). Sybil complimented the Queen's natural beauty and her hard-earned wisdom and wit, which was appropriate praise coming from Russell, whose father especially valued women's education. The entertainment represented the Queen as a strong, educated leader who was well able to defend herself against unwelcome male advances. The Russell women fashioned themselves similarly and implied that they would help the Queen counter male criticisms of her rule and person. By placing the Queen firmly at the center of their descriptions of England's success, the Russell women celebrated her authority as they aimed to elevate themselves through her example.

Sybil taught Pan about the Queen's effective leadership as she defined England as peaceful and fruitful. She explained, "By her it is (*Pan*) that all our Carttes that thou seest, are laden vvith Corne, when in other countries they are filled vvith Harneys" (sig. A3v). This line alluded to Elizabeth's controversial inclusion of corn in her list of contraband goods in the early 1590s. This policy blocked Catholic Spain's imports of corn at a time when Spain saw a decline in its own cereal production, and the Low Countries, although fighting the Spanish Empire, protested this policy because they relied on profits from grain exports to Spain.[34] Sybil's speech demonstrated

---

[32] I analyze this aspect of the entertainment in greater detail in Chapter 4.

[33] Caroline McManus, "Reading the Margins: Female Courtiers in the Portraits of Elizabeth I" in *The Ben Jonson Journal* 2 (1995): 50–1.

[34] R. B. Wernham, *After the Armada: Elizabethan England and the Struggle for Western Europe 1588–1595* (Oxford: Clarendon Press, 1984), 250–7.

an excellent example of mutually beneficial politics. The Russell women would encourage their network to support the Queen's export ban, and she would continue to implement a Protestant policy they endorsed. The entertainment suggested that the Queen's virtues extended beyond chastity to godliness when Sybil later called the Queen a leader "on whom God hath laide all his blessinges" (sig. A3v). As part of a speech that praised Elizabeth's support of Protestants abroad, this reference implied that her religious leanings had led to peace and prosperity for England.

By demonstrating their knowledge of international politics, the Russell women presented themselves as capable political advisors. Sybil delivered the following line: "Daunger looketh pale to beholde her Maiesty; and tyranny blusheth to heare of her mercy" (sig. A3v). This line stressed the Queen's ability to keep England safe, perhaps especially from Catholic threats, the specific "Daunger" and "tyranny" at the forefront of policy discussions. Debates about royal marriage had certainly died down by the 1590s, but some noblemen still questioned a female leader's ability to command an army successfully.[35] The Russell women responded to such challenges and to the factional politics consuming Elizabeth's male advisors by representing the Queen as a shrewd ruler and by highlighting her and their own knowledge about foreign affairs. When Sybil concluded by wishing "to her enemies, as many troubles, as the Wood hath leaues" (sig. A4r), she alluded to Elizabeth's Catholic rivals and male opposition: both enemies that the Russell women encouraged her to obliterate through firm leadership. Sybil urged the Queen to maintain the Protestant cause and recommended that she employ knowledgeable female courtiers who could better assist her in religious and gender battles than could her male advisors.

At the end of their dialogue, the shepherdesses invited Elizabeth to walk downhill toward the manor, and near the house she saw an actor wearing a "Crowne of wheat-ears with a Iewell" standing on a grain cart (sig. A4r). Because there is no evidence that a member of the household or a female country reveler performed this role, soon revealed to be the goddess Ceres, it seems likely to have been played by a hired actor who was male and cross-dressed. This final pageant followed the pattern established by the wild man: Ceres initially challenged Elizabeth's authority and then yielded to her. Ceres declared herself the most superior of gods, the "only Queene of heauen," and claimed she had greater power than Cynthia, a stand-in

---

[35] Paul E. J. Hammer, *Elizabeth's Wars: War, Government and Society in Tudor England 1544–1604* (Basingstoke: Palgrave, 2003), 4.

for Elizabeth: "Cynthia that shineth, / Is not so cleare, / Cynthia declineth, / When I appeere" (sig. A4r–A4v). As a goddess associated with fertility and motherly love, Ceres potentially called into question Elizabeth's decision not to marry and produce an heir. The popular comparison of Elizabeth and the lunar goddess Cynthia also carried negative connotations: womanly changeability and a secondary status to the sun that could verify female inferiority. Ceres explained that she heard of Elizabeth-as-Cynthia's "blessed" reign and wide-reaching fame but would only acknowledge that "Cynthia shalbe Ceres Mistres" if her cart collapsed (sig. A4v). It immediately did. When the goddess of agriculture and grain then surrendered to Queen Elizabeth, "accounting nothing ours but what comes from you" (sig. A4v), the entertainment advanced Sybil's previous claim that Elizabeth was responsible for England's bountiful grains and other countries' lack of corn. Although entertainments often exaggerated England's glories and advantages, this claim about an excellent harvest was somewhat historically accurate. England experienced recurrent crop failures in the late 1590s, but the years 1591–92 yielded especially good harvests.[36] Ceres' submission also depicted Elizabeth as superior to the model of an ideal queen as fertile and child-bearing, extending the entertainment's earlier emphasis on chastity. In the Ceres episode and elsewhere, the Bisham pageantry did not deny the tensions that emerge when a single female monarch heads a patriarchal society, but it maintained that Elizabeth could continue to overcome such challenges.

The entertainment further implied that alliances with capable female advisors would help her do so, especially when it ended with a direct reference to Elizabeth Russell's desire to please the Queen. Addressing the Queen, Ceres said that "this muche dare we promise for the Lady of the farme, that your presence hath added many daies to her life," and she described the entertainment as a "short praier, poured from her hart" (sig. A4v). The notions expressed here, along with Sybil's earlier statement, "We upon our knees, wil entreat her to come into the valley, that our houses may be blessed with her presence, whose hartes are filled with quietnes by her gouernement" (sig. A3v), somewhat echoed a letter the Queen sent Russell following her first husband's death in September 1566.[37] After praising her "sober, wise and discreet behaviour" and "testimony of virtue in such hard times of adversity," the letter ends, "And so we would have you to rest

---

[36] Jim Sharpe, "Social Strain and Social Dislocation, 1585–1603" in John Guy, ed., *The Reign of Elizabeth I: Court and Culture in the Last Decade* (Cambridge University Press, 1995), 192–211.

[37] Malay, "Elizabeth Russell's Textual Performances of Self," 149–54, proposes that Russell's verses on her husband's tomb also imitate the rhetoric of this letter.

yourself in quietness, with a firm opinion of our especial favour towards you."[38] The Bisham entertainment evoked and reinforced a long-standing alliance between its host and guest, who each aided the other's political agenda.[39] It built upon the Queen's praise of Russell's ability to remain virtuous in difficult times to argue that she and her daughters would help the Queen overcome adversity as well. The performance at Bisham did not exclude men; many male courtiers accompanied the Queen on progress, some men acted in the entertainment, and Russell hosted the Queen at an estate that legally belonged to her son Edward. But the entertainment presented itself as Russell's gift to the Queen and argued for the ability of an alliance of women to succeed socially and politically without men.

At Bisham, the Russell women rewrote Elizabethan courtiership as less about pride or competition between genders and more about mutual benefit and cooperation between like-minded women with corresponding goals. They urged Elizabeth to employ and trust skilled female advisors rather than flawed male ones, and because they used their performance to advise the Queen on foreign policy, their entertainment suggested that courtly women could offer diplomatic advice as well as companionship and household service. The Queen's actions in the next few years demonstrated a positive response to these ideas about female courtiership. She invited them to be her maids of honor in 1594 and 1595, as their performances lobbied for her to do. The younger Elizabeth Russell died in July 1600, but Anne married well and remained active at court. Although Queen Elizabeth often disapproved of her maids' marriages, she accepted Anne's marriage to Lord Herbert on June 8, 1600, attended the wedding, and danced in the masque that followed.[40] But despite this apparent success, the elder Elizabeth Russell did not remain satisfied with her relationship with the Queen. She complained to Robert Cecil in a 1601 letter that her daughters' five- and six-year services to the Queen caused "no small charge to my purse" and did not bring enough benefit in terms of money or social honor. She explained, "Since my farewell from court hath been every way so uncomfortable, it hath killed a courtier and parliament woman of me."[41] She used

---

[38] Qtd. in J. H. Wiffen, *Historical Memoirs of the House of Russell* (London, 1833), 2:501.

[39] Russell had hosted the Queen once already at Bisham in December 1569. Additionally, the Queen had agreed to be her daughter Elizabeth's godmother and had granted her the custodianship of Donnington Castle in 1589 – a title much disputed because several nobles thought it should be held only by men.

[40] Rowland Whyte describes the wedding masque in a letter to Robert Sidney quoted in John Nichols, *The Progresses and Public Processions of Queen Elizabeth* (London, 1823), 3:489–99.

[41] *English Sappho*, ed. Phillippy, 289–90.

the oxymoron "parliament woman" and the appropriate label "courtier" to describe herself as a qualified politician who deserved adequate reward. By assigning herself roles usually occupied by men, she underscored her continuing desire to engage directly in court politics and governing despite her gender.

Alternate Kinds of Courtiership: Sudeley's Female Servant

When Elizabeth visited Sudeley Castle on September 9–11, 1592, the Brydges family devised expensive spectacles that secured their position as one of the wealthiest and most powerful families in the area. An old shepherd welcomed her with a short speech that introduced the pageantry as her gift from "the honorable Lord and Lady of the Castle" (sig. B1r). When the shepherd emphasized the serenity of the "healthy, and harmeles" locale and praised the people of the Cotswolds (sig. B1r), he indirectly celebrated the local leadership of Giles Brydges, Lord Chandos, and his role in maintaining peace in this province. Chandos had been active in local government since 1572, and as Lord Lieutenant of Gloucestershire in 1587–88 he secured and maintained a trained militia to protect the region from Spanish invasion.[42] When he and his wife hosted the Queen in 1592, the lavish display of fireworks, feasts, jousts, and bear- and bull-baiting that followed the shepherd's invocation would have highlighted his family's affluence.[43] These extravagant spectacles, combined with the shepherd's emphasis on regional pride and authority, exposed subtle friction between local and royal patriotism, as Chapter 4 explains in greater detail. This chapter will focus on the second and longest pageant, which turned to matters of gender and courtiership. It was performed the day after the Queen's arrival in the "pleasance," the enclosed garden behind the castle's Great Hall with a fountain in the center and pebbled walkways stretching in four directions (see Figure 2.2). In this pageant, a shepherd and Apollo both professed unrequited love for the chaste Daphne, whom Apollo had turned into a tree for refusing him, and Queen Elizabeth's presence as a protector of female chastity brought about Daphne's release.[44]

---

[42] Brydges' correspondence with the Queen and her top advisors between March 1587 and July 1588 reveals his responsibilities as Lord Lieutenant of Gloucestershire, which Elizabeth identified as one of her countries "most subiect to . . . invasion" in a March 1587 letter (SP Domestic, Elizabeth I, 12/199/11).

[43] My descriptions of the performance are indebted to Emma Dent's *Annals of Winchcombe and Sudeley* (London, 1877), which contains the only known details of the progress visit besides those in *Speeches Delivered*.

[44] The printed book includes a third pageant, planned but not performed due to "vnfit" weather, in which the shepherds choose a festival King and Queen who engage in a pastoral debate about gender roles and courtship. I discuss this pageant in Chapter 4.

2.2 The old "pleasance," the earliest trace of formal gardens at Sudeley, was discovered in the middle of the nineteenth century. This spacious area is now called "the Queen's Garden." Photograph by the author, 2008.

The only known text of the entertainment does not identify who performed Daphne, but its language suggests that the role served as a vehicle for a young woman of the household to advertise her suitability for a court position. Following a handful of earlier scholars, I posit that Elizabeth Brydges played the part.[45] In 1592, she was about seventeen, and her sister Katherine, probably between the ages of nine and eleven, was slightly too young to pursue a court appointment or marriage prospects. However, her parents were actively seeking both for their eldest daughter. A portrait of Elizabeth Brydges painted a few years earlier signals her marriageability (see Figure 2.3). It represents her as poised, virtuous, and a gentlewoman of means. She wears fashionable attire and exquisite gold jewelry that mark her as the daughter of a wealthy aristocrat, and she gazes to the side demurely. Her averted gaze, her stiff and upright posture, and her clasped hands held close to her body all signify virtue. The lap dog beside her may

---

[45] Wilson, *Queen Elizabeth's Maids of Honour*, 219; Caroline McManus, "Reading the Margins," 50; Alison Findlay, Stephanie Hodgson-Wright, and Gweno Williams, *Women and Dramatic Production 1550–1700* (Harlow: Pearson, 2000), 61.

2.3 This portrait of Elizabeth Brydges, signed by Hieronimo Custodis and dated 1589, is now at Woburn Abbey, Bedfordshire.

symbolize refinement or fidelity, and the painting overall creates an image of a genteel and virtuous young woman ready for marriage. Like Elizabeth Russell and other noble parents, Frances and Giles Brydges sought a financially stable future for their daughter. The 1592 progress visit gave them an excellent opportunity to present their eldest daughter as a dedicated, skilled attendant for the Queen. Because the remaining speaking parts were probably performed by hired players, perhaps from her father's own company, the pageantry would have showcased Elizabeth Brydges as the only non-professional actor.[46] As it advertised her as a model royal servant to advance her personal goals, it identified education and disinterest in romantic courtship as desirable traits for a female courtier. Compared to the Bisham entertainment, the Daphne pageant constructed the role of female courtier as even more dependent upon the Queen's rule and example.

The Sudeley performance presented Daphne as a virtuous young woman uninterested in love or marriage. As a shepherd and Apollo professed their love for her, the entertainment emphatically illustrated their undesirability. The shepherd condemned Apollo's quick transition from flattery and gifts to attempted rape: "her he woed; with faire wordes, the flatteries of men, with great gifts, the sorceries of gods, with cruell threates, the terrefiing of weake damosels" (sig. B1v). The Sudeley entertainment represented Apollo as a serious sexual threat, unlike Bisham's Pan. Apollo then mocked the shepherd's lowliness in a revolting description of an imagined sexual encounter between Daphne and the shepherd: "When broomy bearde, to sweepe thy lips perfume, / When on thy necke, his rough hewen armes shall moue" and "When that his toothlesse mouth shall call thee loue, / Noght will I saie of him, but pittie thee" (sig. B2v). While the shepherd emphasized Apollo's disregard for Daphne's own desires that left her "twixt feare and vertue," Apollo insisted that the shepherd was not worthy of Daphne (sig. B1v). At first neither suitor respected Daphne's devotion to chastity and rejection of marriage. The shepherd learned to do so first. He identified chastity as "immortall" and described Apollo's desire to take Daphne's maidenhead as "treason," a metaphor that linked chastity to political authority (sig. B1v). Eventually Apollo conceded that "chastety shalbe Apolloes Queene," a phrase that alluded to the example set by Queen Elizabeth (sig. B2r). The entertainment suggested that women's virtues could overpower men's wills, especially when Apollo admitted that "neither men nor gods, can force affection" (sig. B2r).

---

[46] The surviving record attributes no court poet to this entertainment. If Robert Armin had joined the company by this time, he might have had a hand in the entertainment. For more on the Lord Chandos' Men, see *REED (Records of Early English Drama): Cumberland, Westmoreland, Gloucestershire*, ed. Audrey Douglas and Peter Greenfield (University of Toronto Press, 1986), 259; John Tucker Murray, *English Dramatic Companies 1558–1642* (Boston and New York: Houghton, 1910), 2:28–32.

When Daphne spoke, she revealed herself to be an educated courtier poet ready to serve the Queen. Despite her strong virtue, she depended on her royal mistress to serve as her role model and protector. When rescued, she explained that she would not have escaped without the Queen's assistance: "I stay, whether should chastity fly for succour, but to the Queene of chastity, by thee [Apollo] was I enterred in a tree [. . .] by your highnes restored" (sig. B2v). Daphne represented the Queen not only as chaste herself, but also as a guardian of female chastity. The Woodstock/Ditchley entertainment placed Elizabeth in a similar role, but unlike its erring ladies, Daphne already led a chaste life and simply needed help fending off aggressive suitors. Daphne used her few lines to advertise herself as an ideal Privy Chamber servant: well educated, articulate, humble, loyal, and chaste. When Daphne delivered written verses to the Queen, she said, "I humbly present to your Maiesty, not thinking, that your vertues can be deciphered in so slight a volume, but noted; the whole world is drawn in a small mappe, *Homers Illiades* in a nutshel" (sig. B2v). She revealed her worldly and scholarly knowledge, as well as her understanding of the limitations of panegyric as she attempted to praise the Queen satisfactorily. Queen Elizabeth was often represented as a learned queen whose quick wit was a key aspect of her image, and the Sudeley entertainment likewise presented Daphne as a writer familiar with classical literature and geography, whether or not she actually penned the verses.[47] Daphne did not promote herself at the Queen's expense or present herself as a rival. Instead, she desired to elevate her status through the Queen's power.

Like the Bisham entertainment but with more subtlety, the Sudeley pageantry argued for the suitability of female leaders and identified the limitations of male ones. The commendatory verses Daphne gave Elizabeth applauded characteristics commonly praised in poems to female patrons: reputation, beauty, affection, and virtue. The verses read:

> Let fame describe your rare perfection,
> Let nature paint your beuties glory,
> Let loue engraue your true affection,
> Let wonder write your vertues story,
> By them and Gods must you be blazed
> Sufficeth men they stand amazed.
>
> (sig. B3r)

---

[47] On Elizabeth's representation as an educated queen, see Linda Shenk, *Learned Queen: The Image of Elizabeth I in Politics and Poetry* (Basingstoke: Palgrave, 2010); Mary Thomas Crane, "'Video et Taceo': Elizabeth I and the Rhetoric of Counsel" in *SEL: Studies in English Literature 1500–1900* 28.1 (1988): 1–15.

These lines represented Elizabeth as a warm, loving monarch who exemplified feminine beauty. As the poem revered the Queen as a model woman, it aligned her with Daphne and with Elizabeth Brydges, whose portrait and role in the performance similarly emphasized ideal feminine traits. These verses advised the Queen to "let" others represent her through poetry and portraiture so that her reputation might be made more widely known. Because the entertainment presented them as the work of Daphne, it positioned Daphne as ready to offer Elizabeth counsel. The word "men" in the final line may have referred to all mortals, but its position within a scene about male lust called attention to its gendered use and implied that the Queen's presence especially affected men. The word "amaze" connotes bewilderment, panic, and infatuation – all apt descriptions of Petrarchan suitors in Leicester's entertainments and the wild men at Bisham and elsewhere. When read alongside other country house entertainments, these aspects of the Sudeley performance hinted that the Queen's presence tended to leave men dumbfounded, while Daphne appeared poised, knowledgeable, and loyal.

The entertainment also juxtaposed Daphne's voice with several male ones striving unsuccessfully for unattainable women. The two men who pursued Daphne professed love both undying and unrequited, and the entertainment ended with a Petrarchan song in the voice of a frustrated male suitor who described his failed attempts at wooing. He concluded in exasperation: "O sacred loue if thou haue any Godhead, / Teach other rules to winne a maidenhead" (sig. B4r). Daphne understood what these male suitors did not: the desire to "winne a maidenhead" was inappropriate in a political climate that valued female chastity. With Petrarchan lyrics framing Daphne's presentation, the Sudeley pageantry insinuated that female courtiers were more cautious, loyal, and chaste than their male counterparts, who used rhetoric of romantic love for political ends. Through Daphne, the entertainment suggested that an ideal female courtier was a humble servant who followed Elizabeth's example. Daphne (and by extension, Elizabeth Brydges) was ready to serve and support her royal mistress, and she ended her speech by explaining her "poore virgins wish, that often wish for good husbands, mine, only for the endlesse prosperity of my soueraigne" (sig. B3r). Even more explicitly than the shepherdesses at Bisham, she rejected marriage in favor of serving the Queen and implied that cooperative, unmarried female courtiers made ideal royal servants. The argument must have succeeded because the Queen invited Elizabeth Brydges to court two years later, although Brydges ended her time at court in

disgrace.[48] The Sudeley performance carved out space for female courtiership as it advertised Brydges' virtues. It identified chastity, education, and
eloquent speech as crucial elements of female courtiership, and together
with the Bisham entertainment, it implied that successful female servants
had to promise to forgo marriage as they dedicated themselves completely
to the monarch whose image and orders they followed.

Alternate Kinds of Courtiership: Absent Military Men at Rycote

The Queen's visit to Rycote Park in late September and early October
1592 offered Henry and Margery Norreys an ideal opportunity to lobby
for financial assistance and their sons' career advancement during a time
of hardship. The entertainment foregrounded Margery's long-time friendship with Elizabeth – one that predated Elizabeth's queenship.[49] Margery
played an active role in court affairs from the beginning of the reign
until her death in 1599, and her political activism and alliance with the
Queen were primarily responsible for her husband's and sons' successful
careers.[50] The Norreys family was especially reliant upon Elizabeth's help
in 1592 because they had run into debt supporting their sons' military
exploits, and their land holdings were "engaged in the Queen's hands"
and not available for sale.[51] At the Queen's arrival at Rycote Park, Henry
Norreys delivered a welcoming speech that introduced the entertainment's
personalized military and religious themes. The next day, Henry greeted

---

[48] Dent, *Annals*, 240–1. Once at court, Elizabeth Brydges did not fulfill her promise to reject marriage
and obey the Queen. She faced royal displeasure for disobedience and flirting with male courtiers,
especially Essex. In 1603 she married Sir John Kennedy, a member of King James' Scottish household,
and it ended badly. He depleted her fortune, and when she discovered he had another wife in
Scotland and ordered him to leave their house, he and about twenty men threw her and a male
companion into the cold half-naked. She died in poverty.

[49] Margery's father, Sir John Williams, was appointed as one of Elizabeth's guardians while she was
imprisoned during Mary's reign. He took her to his family's primary residence, Rycote, in May
1554 and July 1555 during her journeys to and from Woodstock. She met Margery there. By 1592,
Elizabeth had stayed at Rycote at least five times previously, including these two early visits and
three more times during her royal progresses (1566, 1568, 1570).

[50] The family's Oxfordshire holdings were always listed in Margery's name as well as her husband's,
as John S. Nolan points out in *Sir John Norreys and the Elizabethan Military World* (University of
Exeter Press, 1997), 10. When Henry served as ambassador in Paris from 1567 to 1571, Margery took
part in state business and sometimes acted as messenger for his reports to Elizabeth. He endorsed
his May 22, 1567 letter to the Queen "By my wife" and later referred to Margery's delivery of it (BL,
Stowe MS 147). In the 1590s, Margery wrote a series of letters to Robert Cecil that requested help
securing military appointments and leaves for her sons, sought advice about her sons' careers, and
advocated her nephew for a political position.

[51] The quote comes from Margery's letter to Robert Cecil in 1593, quoted in Historical Manuscripts
Commission, *Calendar of the Manuscripts of the Most Honourable the Marquess of Salisbury*, 24 vols.
(London, 1883–1976), 4:376–7.

Elizabeth in the estate gardens with a short speech accompanied by music, as well as a pageant uniquely structured around the letters of absent family members. Three messengers, probably played by professional actors, read aloud five letters with accompanying jewels, one from each of the four living Norreys sons to the Queen and an additional letter from a soldier to his mistress. The eldest son, William, had already died in battle. The youngest son, Maximilian, also died in military service, and although the date of his death is less certain, language in the entertainment suggests that he was no longer living in 1592.[52] The other four sons – John, Edward, Henry, and Thomas – had been engaged in military action in such places as Ireland, the Low Countries, Spain, and France. On the final day, a fourth messenger stopped Elizabeth to deliver greetings from Henry's absent daughter Catherine as a farewell gift. In all of its episodes, the Rycote entertainment identified soldiers who take action on behalf of Protestant principles, not courtiers who use flattering rhetoric, as the Queen's ideal servants. While the Bisham and Sudeley entertainments aimed to align young women with the Queen, the Rycote performance drew on the Queen's long-standing alliance with the estate's mistress Margery to ask for her help.

The entertainment repeatedly emphasized the Norreys sons' willingness to sacrifice their lives in the line of duty as it lobbied for their continued, lucrative employment. While welcoming Elizabeth to Rycote, Henry Norreys referred to his horse, armor, shield, and sword as "the riches of a young souldier, and an olde souldiers reliques" and explained "my foure boies haue stollen them from me, vowing themselues to armes, and leauing mee to my prayers, fortune giueth successe, fidelitye courage, chance cannot blemish faith, nor trueth preuent destinye, whateuer happen, this is their resolution, and my desire, that their liues maye, be imployed wholy in your seruice, and their deathes, bee their vowes sacrifice" (sig. CIV). Henry advertised their determination and reliability, as well as his expectation that they would be "wholy" dedicated and "wholy" employed. He underscored the Protestant mission behind the family's service when he represented himself as devout and used the words "faith" and "devotion." He emphasized chance and fate to illustrate his sons' bravery and willingness to encounter whatever lay ahead.

In the letters, each son wished he could be at Rycote to show his duty, but remained dedicated to his military responsibilities. The final letter, written

---

[52] In the entertainment's introductory speech (cited below), Norreys refers to his "foure boies" (sig. CIV). See also Sarah Ross' headnote to the entertainment in Goldring, et al., eds., *John Nichols's The Progresses*, 3:616–17.

from the perspective of John Norreys, exemplified this inner conflict: "the same time that I receiued letters that her Maiesty would be at Ricort, the winde serued for Britaigne, I was ouer ioied with both, yet stoode in a mannering whether I should take the opportunity of the winde, which I long expected or ride poste to do my duetie, which I most desired, necessitye controlled affection, that bid me vnlesse I could kepe the winde in a bagge, to vse the windes when they blew" (sig. c3v).[53] The entertainment's recurring metaphor of wind, which another letter called "vnconstant," represented the Norreys men as submissive to orders and ready to go wherever their ships sailed (sig. c2r). They recognized that Elizabeth was always at the helm. When Edward's letter admitted he nearly shipped himself to England at the news of Elizabeth's visit, he added, "to come without leaue, might be to returne without welcome" (sig. c2v). The pageantry stressed that soldiers could not control their locations or destinies.

Yet the letters revealed little resistance to this lack of control and insisted that the Norreys men desired no other kind of life. John's letter suggested that he was "ouer ioied" with the prospect of being carried off into the wind, and other letters revealed similar excitement. A recurring emphasis on sacrifice depicted the Norreys sons as dedicated soldiers who were willing to forfeit their lives for Elizabeth and England. One read, "With this protestation pourde from my hart, that in her seruice, I will spende the bloud of my hart" (sig. c3v), and another wished "that what my toung deliuers, my bloud may seale, the end of my seruice, that in her seruice, my life may end" (sig. c2v). Many of these promises would prove prophetic because all the remaining sons but Edward would die within the next seven years. Each letter included a motto that declared absolute loyalty to the Queen, such as "I flye onely for my soueraigne" or "I doe not commande but under you" (sig. c2r–c3r). These mottoes represented the Norreys sons as obedient servants who acted only in accordance with Elizabeth's orders – a crucial, though dubious, claim for a group of soldiers who often

---

[53] The entertainment text does not explicitly identify which son each letter represented. The first letter's delivery by an Irish footman pointed to Thomas, currently in Ireland. The second represented Edward, Governor of Ostend, because it was delivered from Flanders. A French page delivered the final three together: a soldier's to his mistress, probably meant to be written by either Henry or John; one with a French motto from the younger Henry Norreys; and a final letter with a Spanish motto representing John. My assessment of these letters' implied authorship aligns with that of Ross in Goldring, et al., eds., *John Nichols's The Progresses* (3:618–19) and differs from that of Wilson in *Entertainments for Elizabeth I* (150–1, n. 149–54), who proposes that John Norreys was present during the Queen's visit and not a letter-writer. However, evidence suggests that he was in Southampton at the time, and the last letter claimed to come from the sea coast. Its motto, reference to Brittany, and insistence upon commanding only at the Queen's request implied John's perspective. On his whereabouts during this time, see Nolan, *Sir John*, 196–9.

walked a fine line between favor and disfavor. Thomas seems to have been even-tempered and reliable, but John, Edward, and the younger Henry all periodically angered Elizabeth with their short tempers and moments of insubordination.[54] Because the entertainment defined duty to Elizabeth as international military service, the letters underscored that the sons' absence best demonstrated their loyalty.

As the Rycote pageantry pursued the Norreys family's personal aims by presenting the sons as deserving of favor, it also promoted an alternative kind of courtiership, one that treated the Queen as a martial commander rather than as a Petrarchan mistress. In his opening speech, the elder Henry asked Elizabeth "to heare a rough hewen tale of a souldier, wee vse not with wordes... but by deedes, to shew the loyalty of our harts, and to make it good with our liues" (sig. c1v). Although the appearance of a humble figure who claimed to be rustic and untamed was familiar within the genre, Henry distinguished himself and his sons from conventional courtiers as he dismissed the rhetoric of wooing and emphasized the significance of action. At every turn, the pageantry insisted that military service better demonstrated allegiance than did panegyric verses. The letter by the younger Henry Norreys exemplified this trope when it said, "Eloquence and I, am vowde enemies, loialty and I, sworne brothers, what my words cannot effect, my sworde shall" (sig. c3v). When it set "eloquence" and "loialty" in opposition, it identified flattering rhetoric as meaningless and not proof of fidelity. "Eloquence" is the purview of the courtier poet, and the Rycote entertainment argued that the deeds of a dedicated soldier serving abroad would better serve the Queen than would the empty, self-serving words of a courtier in close proximity. The pageantry ironically used words to make these claims, but its language differed from the professions of undying love and pained yearning that Elizabeth encountered at Kenilworth, at Woodstock and Ditchley, and in several other country house entertainments. The Norreys sons did not profess unrequited love for a cruel mistress; instead they bolstered a mutually beneficial alliance with their military leader.

A comic letter to a soldier's mistress, positioned in the middle of the letters to the Queen, sustained the entertainment's promotion of an alternative to political Petrarchism and continued to espouse the virtues of action rather than rhetoric when it came to serving Elizabeth. The addressee,

---

[54] For examples, see Nolan, *Sir John*, 59–61, 204–6; Elizabeth's letter to Francis Drake and John Norreys, 20 May 1589 in SP Domestic, Elizabeth I, 12/224/53; D. J. B. Trim, "Norris, Sir Edward (*c.* 1550–1603)," in *Oxford Dictionary of National Biography*, ed. H. C. G. Matthew and Brian Harrison (Oxford University Press, 2004); online edn., ed. Lawrence Goldman, January 2008.

Lady Squeamish, was by her name a coy, prudish woman averse to the soldier's advances, and the letter playfully used and mocked Petrarchan conventions to describe romantic courtship. It was filled with witty retorts, such as the comment that love makes "the vaines shrinke and the purse to" (sig. C3r). It insisted, as did the rest of the entertainment, that soldiers are not conventional wooers when it explained that "we proue it by the sword, others, by their Sonets" and "I meane not, to haue my tongue ringed at my Mistris eare like a Iewel, alwaies whispering of loue" (sig. C3r). Whereas the other letters declared absolute loyalty to Elizabeth, this one claimed that dedicated soldiers show "inconstancy" in love (sig. C3r). Its witty, flippant attitude toward romantic love contrasted with the other letters' simply stated devotion to Elizabeth. Together they underscored the difference between romantic courtship and political service as they repeatedly distinguished active soldiers from verbose lovers. The letter to Lady Squeamish described lovers as flatterers, parasites, and papists. It said, for example, "I cannot be so superstitious as these nice louers, who make the pax of their mistris hands, tis flat popery" (sig. C3r). As the letter identified an inherent difference between a soldier (whose heart and mind are focused on his military duties) and a lover (who worships his beloved like an idol), it insinuated that romantic devotion to a mistress would be wrongly placed. The letter ended with this line: "I cannot be patient, the winde calls me away, and with the winde, awaie shall my affections" (sig. C3r). Because the metaphor of wind elsewhere signified Elizabeth's directives, this line vowed that a soldier's duty is to his country and sovereign. Together with the other letters, it claimed that a dedicated soldier is willing to sacrifice love, family, home, and life for that duty. The word "wind" is a particularly clever one because it also connoted empty or vain speech, which all of the soldiers' letters decried as the hallmark of the ineffectual courtly lover. The Rycote entertainment treated courtly love not as an appropriate metaphor for interactions with Elizabeth, but as a needless distraction from the serious business at hand.

This model of royal service made Elizabeth's gender surprisingly immaterial because its representation of her as a Protestant military leader implicitly validated her role as a female ruler. Yet its definition of allegiance as military duty left little room for female courtiership, even though women would serve crucial roles as mothers of warriors under this model. After the soldiers' letters were read aloud, Henry Norreys knelt and delivered his final words, which boasted about his sons' performance of their "fidelitie" and spotless "faithes" that should make Elizabeth "confident" in their devotion (sig. C3v–C4r). He claimed he had one grief, that his daughter

Catherine Poulett forgot her duty and failed to write. He said, "I doubt not her excuse, because shee is a woman, but feare the truth of it, because it must be to her soueraigne" (sig. C3r). This moment offered Henry a courtly way both to invoke the ideal of feminine silence and to honor the Queen as an unusual woman. Catherine's hesitancy to express herself in a public setting corresponded to early modern depictions of women as ideally silent and obedient, yet Elizabeth would have illustrated that not all women emulated that standard. When a messenger arrived from Catherine's home in Jersey the next morning to present Elizabeth a gift, he did not deliver a letter. Instead he spoke on Catherine's behalf, emphasizing her humility and virtue, and explained that "her hart [had] no tongue, but infinite affections" (sig. C4r). Catherine's mother Margery was present, but she did not speak for herself in the pageantry. The printed text represents the two female members of this family as literally silent in the performance. If ideal service to the Queen was male military duty, then courtier women must exert influence indirectly and through men – exactly what Elizabeth Russell bemoaned in her letters.

Still, Margery's influence over the entertainment and family status is apparent. The entertainment valued female intimacy with the Queen as a fruitful means to power, as it underscored how Margery's enduring alliance with Elizabeth made possible the family's social, financial, and political privilege. It showcased the Norreys family's familiarity with the Queen and her image, and it relied on personal connection rather than extravagant spectacle.[55] It also relied less on the pastoral mode than did the shows at Bisham and Sudeley. The Norreys family might have been less interested in presenting Rycote as an idyllic space because the Queen already identified it as a familiar escape from court. She stayed there when Margery's father served as her guardian, and she visited several times as queen. Because the estate was Margery's inheritance and the place where she first befriended Elizabeth, the performance's setting would have called attention to Margery's key role in securing the family's status.

In the opening pageant, Henry foregrounded his wife's intimacy with the Queen by referring to her using only the Queen's nickname for her, "Crow," and working it into an extended metaphor.[56] The rumor of their sons' deaths, he said, "hath so often affrighted the Crowe my wife, that her hart, hath bene as blacke as her feathers . . . And although, nothing be more

---

[55] The performance would have required only three or four professional actors and a few musicians, and there is no evidence that Henry and Margery Norreys renovated Rycote prior to the visit.

[56] Elizabeth used this nickname in a letter dated September 22, 1597 (BL, Additional MS 38137, f. 130); the Rycote entertainment reveals that she called Margery her "crow" earlier than that.

vnfit to lodge your Maiestye, then a crowes neste, yet shall it be most happy to vs, that it is by your highnesse, made a Phoenix neste" (sig. CIV). This passage wove a personal touch into standard motifs. It apologized for unfit lodgings, as was typical in the genre, and it employed yet another popular metaphor for Elizabeth. The phoenix, which had been associated with the Virgin Mary in medieval literature, was part of a cluster of images including the moon, roses, and pearls that Protestants attached to Elizabeth.[57] It symbolized a variety of aspects of the Queen's reign, including her status as an icon of embattled, prevailing Protestantism. Additionally, the phoenix symbolized transformative rejuvenation and thus Elizabeth's ability to transform this "crowes neste" and the other houses she visited into centers of political action. The Rycote entertainment cleverly aligned Elizabeth with Margery using bird imagery that was at once conventional and personalized. It suggested that their alliance would continue to bring about positive results for all involved.

Both women indeed recognized their friendship's political worth. Although it is unclear whether Margery lobbied for Elizabeth to visit Rycote in 1592, a 1582 letter from Leicester to Christopher Hatton makes apparent her strong desire to host the Queen then. Margery had expected Elizabeth but received Leicester instead. He wrote:

> I met with a piece of cold entertainment at the Lady's hands of the house here; and so had you done too, if you had been in my place; for she was well informed ere I came that I and you were the chief hinderers of her Majesty's coming hither [. . .] Well, I did, I trust, satisfy my Lady, albeit she saith she cannot be quiet till you have part of her little stomach too. Trust me, if it had not been so late, I think I should have sought me another lodging, my welcome awhile was so ill; and almost no reason could persuade but that it was some device to keep her Highness from her own gracious disposition to come hither. But I dealt plainly with her, that I knew she would have been sorry afterwards to have had her Majesty come at this time of the year to this place. I assure you, you should find it winter already. Thus much I thought good to tell you, that, when my Lady comes thither, you may satisfy her, as I hope I have done; but her Majesty must especially help somewhat, or else have we more than half lost this lady.[58]

---

[57] Literature and paintings used the phoenix to represent Elizabeth during and after her life. Some examples include the "Phoenix Portrait" (1575), attributed to Nicholas Hilliard; Thomas Churchyard, *A Handeful of Gladsome Verses, Giuen to the Queenes Maiesty at Woodstocke this Prograce* (1592), which repeatedly refers to Elizabeth as a phoenix; the miscellany *The Phoenix Nest* (1593); and Shakespeare's "The Phoenix and The Turtle" (1601).

[58] Qtd. in Norreys Jephson O'Conor, *Godes Peace and the Queenes: Vicissitudes of a House, 1539–1615* (Cambridge: Harvard University Press, 1934), 31–2.

This passage reveals that Margery desired Elizabeth's visit, and Leicester's final line, which emphasizes his need for "this lady" to maintain their alliance, underscores Margery's social clout and engagement in courtly affairs. Like Margery, Elizabeth felt physical proximity to be a key element of their friendship. John Norreys wrote his mother a letter in 1590 that began with these lines: "Ryght Honorable my very good Lady and Mother, her Maiestye the same nyght that I arryved heer intertayned me uery kyndly, and the next morninge lykewyse; asked often for your Ladyship and wyshed her self at Rycott."[59] Elizabeth's rhetorical desire to be at Rycote underscores that she valued and wished to maintain her social-political bond with Margery. Both women conceptualized royal visits as mutually advantageous occasions during which they could display and strengthen their valuable alliance. The 1592 pageantry represented the occasion similarly. As it argued for a kind of courtiership in which absent military leaders prove their loyalty better than those in attendance at court, it celebrated the female alliance underpinning those between the Norreys men and their monarch. Although the pageantry text offered only silent roles for the Norreys women, the event would have implicitly defined a female courtier as one whose long-standing friendship with the Queen brought about sustained political favor for her entire family.

Our surviving accounts of country house entertainments reveal that both favored and hopeful courtiers were actively, repeatedly rethinking how to define their roles in late Elizabethan England, and gender was an essential component of their relationships with the Queen. At Kenilworth, where a group of male devisers jockeyed for favor, the position of courtier was presented as a masculine one. Although the entertainment featured performances by lower-class women in rustic pageants, it nowhere claimed these women could offer Elizabeth advice or serve her as attendants. Leicester's later entertainment at Wanstead and Lee's pageantry at Woodstock and Ditchley followed suit, as they relied on erotic language to describe the courtier–monarch relationship. Diana Henderson has proposed that Elizabeth's gender might have emboldened male devisers to offer unsolicited advice.[60] When combined with the country house entertainment's circumstances of place and ownership, her gender indeed made men more audacious in offering advice, but it also opened up opportunities for other women to engage in political alliances. Although the genre involved female devisers throughout its brief existence, women made their contributions

---

[59] BL, Additional MS 11342(B).
[60] Henderson, *Passion Made Public*, 71.

more visible starting with the 1592 progress. These women did not rely on older models of praise, but redefined royal service and revealed a range of ways women could play the role of "courtier." As the performances at Bisham, Sudeley, and Rycote urged Elizabeth to look beyond the London court and beyond conventional rhetoric for good servants and advisors, they reimagined the Elizabethan system of courtiership and women's roles within it.

CHAPTER 3

An *"abundance of dainties"*
Hospitality and Housewifery at Elvetham,
Mitcham, and Harefield

In Elizabethan England the term "hospitality," which referred to the ide-ology of receiving guests with liberality, captured a range of practices: the Christian virtue of charity for the poor, the social practice of treating guests properly, and the act of providing luxury accommodations to the most elite visitors. As Felicity Heal has shown, Tudor England understood hospital-ity as the foundation of a moral society and a uniquely English virtue.[1] Country estates were ideally open and generous in the entertainment of the rich and the poor, friends and strangers alike. A country house embodied the qualities of its owner – good housekeeping marked true gentility and cleanliness of character – and households served as stages on which to display personal virtues and power.[2] Hospitality was therefore an integral part of the genre of country house entertainment, which revolved around the opening of a home, the welcoming of guests, and the generous offering of food and shelter. One of Elizabeth's advisors summarized the genre's main challenges when he advised a householder to "see euery thinge well ordered, and your house kept sweete and cleane, to receaue her hyghnes whensoeuer she shalbe pleased to see it."[3] Every host needed to demonstrate effective hospitality, often with little advance notice. The performances analyzed in this chapter – those at Elvetham (1591), Mitcham (1598), and Harefield (1602) – especially highlighted hospitality as they publicized new marriages and new estates to claim increased status. Unlike the top advisors and long-held friends who entertained Elizabeth at Theobalds, Kenilworth, and Rycote, these particular hosts believed they had to prove themselves because they felt undervalued or had only recently risen to power. They

---

[1] Felicity Heal, *Hospitality in Early Modern England* (Oxford: Clarendon Press, 1990), 1–10.

[2] Heal, *Hospitality*, 23; Mark Girouard, *Life in the English Country House: A Social and Architectural History* (New Haven: Yale University Press, 1978), 2–5; Alice T. Friedman, *House and Household in Elizabethan England: Wollaton Hall and the Willoughby Family* (University of Chicago Press, 1989), 33–7.

[3] Christopher Hatton to William More, 1583, Woking, Surrey History Centre, MS 6729/6/52.

used hospitality to establish their new homes as political centers and themselves as legitimate members of the most elite ranks.

They also engaged in a conversation about shifting attitudes toward hospitality, which many writers identified as dying among the nobility by the end of Elizabeth's reign. Several families were starting to break up their country households to move to London, which increasingly was becoming the center of English life, and for some late Elizabethans, the concepts of moderation and the kind of "civility" that separated the cultured classes from the poor were starting to become more desirable than open generosity.[4] But for those who still believed that hospitality was a crucial aspect of noble identity, its decline would signify the deterioration of England's nobility.[5] A royal proclamation on November 2, 1596, which aimed to correct what the Crown identified as the nobility's neglect of this feudal tradition, emphasized the ritual's local and national functions:

> . . . her majesty is particularly informed of some intentions of sundry persons, of ability to keep hospitality in their countries, to leave their said hospitalities and to come to the city of London and other cities and towns corporate, thereby leaving the relief of their poor neighbors as well for food as for good rule, and with covetous minds to live in London and about the city privately and so also in other towns corporate, without charge of company. For withstanding whereof her majesty chargeth all manner of persons that shall have any such intention during the time of this dearth not to break up their households nor come to the said city or other towns corporate; and all others that have of late time broken up their households to return to their houses without delay. And whilst her majesty had thus determined for relief of her people to stay all good householders in their countries, there in charitable sort to keep hospitality, her majesty hath had an instant occasion given her to extend her commandment even for the necessary defense of her realm.[6]

This proclamation defined hospitality as assistance to the poor offered by country householders, and it identified elite generosity as the groundwork for effective local governance and economies. It revealed that the Crown depended upon elite households to protect the realm in uneasy times

---

[4] This gradual process of moving from provincial to urban estates began at the end of Elizabeth's reign and continued into the Stuart period. See Heal, *Hospitality*, 91–140; Girouard, *Life in the English Country House*, 84–5. On the emerging emphasis on civility, see Anna Bryson, *From Courtesy to Civility: Changing Codes of Conduct in Early Modern England* (Oxford: Clarendon, 1998), esp. 107–50.

[5] Daryl W. Palmer, *Hospitable Performances: Dramatic Genre and Cultural Practices in Early Modern England* (West Lafayette: Purdue University Press, 1992), 27.

[6] Qtd. in Paul L. Hughes and James F. Larkin, eds., *Tudor Royal Proclamations* (New Haven and London: Yale University Press, 1969), 3:171–2.

by feeding, housing, and caring for poor neighbors whose hunger might inspire rebellions. The Crown issued this proclamation at a time when Elizabeth's government feared another Spanish invasion, when poverty was widespread, when food riots during harvest failures were fairly common, and when Parliament worried about increased numbers of the wandering and potentially violent poor. In fact, two weeks later, a group of servants at Rycote staged a failed uprising to protest food shortage.[7] This particular definition of hospitality informs our interpretation of entertainments that claim to demonstrate the ritual before the Queen.

The notion of reciprocity, which underlies the Elizabethan concepts of hospitality and modern theories of the gift, is also crucial to understanding the politics of country house performance.[8] Entertainments presented themselves as part of an ongoing cycle of giving and receiving. Hosts gave Elizabeth tangible gifts of jewels and gowns, and rhetoric in their pageants represented the entire event as a grand gesture. The Kenilworth entertainment spoke of Leicester as a "worthy gift," and the 1571 Theobalds entertainment offered to "give" Elizabeth the house, its master, and his family.[9] Hosts hoped these events would build enduring alliances and encourage the Queen to reciprocate in the form of intangible gifts such as favor and privilege.[10] A focus on gift-giving and hospitality reveals what all country house entertainment meant beyond the individualized rhetoric in performed dialogue. Elizabeth's hosts implicitly made a case for their ability to serve the Crown, and successful entertainment of the Queen marked a household as elite and morally sound. Likewise, as country house entertainments provide examples of Elizabethan hospitality in actual practice,

---

[7] William Leahy, *Elizabethan Triumphal Processions* (Aldershot: Ashgate, 2005), 89–91.

[8] Modern gift theory is indebted to anthropologist Marcel Mauss, who argues that gifts are theoretically voluntary but actually "given and repaid under obligation." *The Gift: Forms and Functions of Exchange in Archaic Societies*, translated by Ian Cunnison (Glencoe, Ill.: Free Press, 1954), 1. Especially relevant to my project are three studies that apply Mauss' theories to early modern culture: Natalie Zemon Davis, *The Gift in Sixteenth-Century France* (Madison: University of Wisconsin Press, 2000); Ilana Krausman Ben-Amos, *The Culture of Giving: Informal Support and Gift-Exchange in Early Modern England* (Cambridge University Press, 2008); and Felicity Heal, *The Power of Gifts: Gift Exchange in Early Modern England* (Oxford University Press, 2014).

[9] "A Briefe Rehearsall, or Rather a True Copie of as Much as Was Presented before Her Maiesties at Kenelworth" in *The VVhole Woorkes of George Gascoigne Esquyre* (London, 1587; *STC* 11638), sig. A6r. For a translated text of the 1571 entertainment, see Appendix 2.

[10] Felicity Heal, "Giving and Receiving on Royal Progress" in Jayne Elisabeth Archer, Elizabeth Goldring, and Sarah Knight, eds., *The Progresses, Pageants, and Entertainments of Queen Elizabeth I* (Oxford University Press, 2007), 46–6; Heal, *Power of Gifts*, 103–11. For more on the centrality of gift exchange to Elizabethan court culture and literature, see Louis Adrian Montrose, "Gifts and Reasons: The Contexts of Peele's *Araygnement of Paris*" in *ELH* 47.3 (1980): 433–61; Alison V. Scott, *Selfish Gifts: The Politics of Exchange and English Courtly Literature, 1580–1628* (Madison and Teaneck: Fairleigh Dickinson University Press, 2006), 47–82.

they reveal various discourses about hospitality and giving. The practices Ben Jonson would later criticize in "To Penshurst" – ostentatious excess in new construction, offering different kinds of hospitality to guests of different ranks – were alive and well in some late Elizabethan circles, yet other elite householders worried about the pitfalls of open hospitality and extravagant liberality.

When the Queen visited the country houses at Elvetham, Mitcham, and Harefield late in her reign, her hosts opened their doors to her entourage and their neighbors as they staged manufactured displays of hospitality on a grand scale. The manors at Elvetham and Harefield in particular became visible arguments for the preservation of aristocratic hospitality. Both underwent extensive renovations prior to the royal visit to make them more accommodating and aesthetically pleasing. The Elvetham entertainment anticipated the Crown's concern about the aristocracy's growing lack of social consciousness, and it assured Elizabeth that Edward and Frances Seymour, Lord and Lady Hertford, had together made Elvetham estate a regional center of power and support for the Elizabethan government. This argument was crucial to the goals of Lord Hertford, who sought Elizabeth's forgiveness for his past transgressions. His relatively new marriage to one of her former maids of honor provided an excellent opportunity to present his estate and himself as reborn. The Mitcham and Harefield entertainments also showcased recent marital alliances that made Sir Julius Caesar and Thomas Egerton the heads of new households. The performance at Harefield emphasized that its hosts had not broken up their household to move to the city, as had many of their peers, but had instead established a new country residence poised to serve the Queen. The Mitcham entertainment partially made a similar argument, but it also demonstrated movement away from hospitality and toward the ideology of civility by promoting the idea that proper gentlemen would not consort with those of lower ranks. While the Seymours and Egertons demonstrated their legitimacy by claiming that they upheld a key English tradition, the Caesars' entertainment combined aspects of the older custom of hospitality and emerging theories of civility to present themselves as a new kind of gentry that was simultaneously urban and rural. Yet none of these entertainments genuinely followed the Crown's definition of hospitality because they focused more on showing off than on providing charitable service. Together they identified hospitality not only as an elite virtue, but also as a privilege for those who deserve it.

Gender has not been a central focus of scholarship on hospitality, although a few studies identify it as the purview of men. Kari Boyd McBride argues that an English country house displayed the status only of its male owner and that the discourse surrounding such houses reveals that female authority was confined to domestic spaces and private life.[11] Lisa Celovsky determines in her examination of "To Penshurst" that hospitality was tied to cultural expectations for masculinity and that feminine hospitality was "more the exception than the rule."[12] Country house entertainments encourage us to look anew at gender expectations and authorities within country houses. As the genre reveals, hospitality was a crucial part of the expected social role of the mistress of a country estate. Some women who co-hosted with their husbands took a supporting role and helped advance men's ambitions within their household, while others cultivated their own authority and honor. Early modern conduct books urged women to perform good housewifery, a term that denoted the quality of managing a household efficiently and encapsulated a range of daily activities.[13] In her 1599–1605 diary, Margaret Hoby describes her daily household labor, which includes overseeing workmen and maids, supervising the harvest, paying bills, collecting rent, cooking, doing needlework, preserving fruit, making candles, gardening, performing midwife duties, and taking responsibility for the religious instruction of her servants.[14] At Harefield, Alice Egerton, Countess of Derby, supervised 120 servants, arranged the educations and marriages of her three daughters, oversaw tenants as landlord of several of her late husband's estates, used letter-writing to connect her household to larger social and political networks, and received guests with and without her husband.[15] When the Queen visited a country manor on progress, an elite housewife's regular administrative duties would become politically valuable as the foundation of her desired alliance with the Queen. Country

---

[11] Kari Boyd McBride, *Country House Discourse in Early Modern England: A Cultural Study of Landscape and Legitimacy* (Aldershot: Ashgate, 2001), 3–5. See also Friedman, *House and Household*, 46–9.

[12] Lisa Celovsky, "Ben Jonson and Sidneian Legacies of Hospitality" in *Studies in Philology* 106.72 (2009): 178–206, esp. 190. In *Hospitality*, Heal provides several examples of women practicing hospitality, but she speaks of the custom in gendered terms as "the practice of Englishmen" (2).

[13] See especially John Fitzherbert, *The Boke of Hvsbandry* (London, 1533; *STC* 10995.5); Thomas Tusser, *Fiue Hundred Pointes of Good Husbandrie* (London, 1580; *STC* 24380); John Dod and Robert Cleaver, *A Godlie Forme of Hovseholde Government* (London, 1598; *STC* 5383).

[14] Joanna Moody, ed., *The Private Life of an Elizabethan Lady: The Diary of Lady Margaret Hoby, 1599–1605* (Stroud: Sutton, 1998), xxxiv–xxxvi; Sharon Cadman Seeling, *Autobiography and Gender in Early Modern Literature: Reading Women's Lives, 1600–1680* (Cambridge University Press, 2006), 25–8.

[15] Alice's letters engage in what we might call outreach activities: pursuing legal cases, serving as a literary patron, and offering advice and support to men seeking political appointments. Several are extant in collections at HEH, BL, LPL, and Hatfield House. For evidence of her servant supervision and landlord duties, see, e.g., HEH, Ellesmere MS 285; Northampton, Northamptonshire Record Office, Ellesmere (Brackley) MS 173, 181.

house entertainments represented hospitality as an elite but not necessarily masculine virtue. Especially when the guest of honor was England's highest-ranking woman, hospitality could be women's work too.

Seeking Forgiveness through Hospitality at Elvetham

For the Queen's four-day visit in late September 1591, the Seymours presented at Elvetham estate in Hampshire the grandest country house entertainment since Kenilworth in 1575. An especially detailed account of the event was printed shortly after the performance and then revised and reprinted later in the year; no known manuscript accounts survive.[16] When Elizabeth arrived at Elvetham in the late afternoon of Monday, September 20, a group of at least two hundred men met her two miles outside the park and led her to the estate entrance, where she was greeted by a Latin oration, singing, and supper. The second day featured a visually stunning water pageant staged in a large man-made pond. In this pageant, sea-god Nereus and his train of Tritons, along with the landed Sylvanus and his followers, all arrived to honor Elizabeth. They got into a skirmish after Nereus pushed Sylvanus into the water to keep him from lusting after sea-nymph Neaera. The final two days brought more music, tennis playing, fireworks, an elaborate banquet, a Fairy Queen pageant, and a speech on Elizabeth's departure. Every aspect was characterized by excess, and the especially eager Seymours tried to outshine or "overgo" all others as they struggled to rewrite Hertford's reputation and mark the beginning of a new era.[17]

Hertford had involved himself in intense personal drama and disputes with the Queen from the beginning of the reign, and he had established a reputation as an outsider whom Elizabeth found unreliable and untrustworthy. Her visit gave him the chance to stage an ostentatious public apology. Curtis Breight has analyzed the entertainment in the context of Hertford's secret marriage to Catherine Grey in 1560, and certainly this context is important.[18] As sister to Jane Grey and great-granddaughter of Henry VII, Catherine was a potential heir to the throne, and her marriage

---

[16] See Chapter 5. In this chapter I cite the second edition of the printed book, unless otherwise noted: *The Honorable Entertainement Geuen to the Queenes Maiestie in Progresse, at Eluetham in Hampshire, by the Right Honorable the Earle of Hertford. 1591* (London, 1591). Held at the Royal Collection, Windsor Castle (shelf mark RCIN 1024755), it has not been assigned an *STC* number.

[17] See Chapter 6 for further discussion of this kind of poetic imitation.

[18] Curtis Breight, "Realpolitik and Elizabethan Ceremony: The Earl of Hertford's Entertainment of Elizabeth at Elvetham, 1591" in *Renaissance Quarterly* 45.1 (1992): 20–48.

and resulting pregnancy posed a risk to Elizabeth. When Elizabeth discovered the secret, she sent the couple to the Tower and charged Hertford with rape. Catherine died shortly after they were released, and Hertford was left with a hefty fine and two sons who were declared bastards. This event haunted Hertford for the rest of the reign as he worked to legitimize his sons, to pay off his fine, and to regain favor slowly.[19] Breight interprets the 1591 performance as a covert assertion that Hertford's relationship with Catherine was consensual, but what I find striking about the Elvetham pageantry is its lack of references to Hertford's first marriage.[20] Although Hertford still desired forgiveness and sought legitimacy for his sons in 1591, his entertainment aimed to move past the secret nuptials and announce his improved status following his marriage to Frances Howard, a well-connected former maid of honor in Elizabeth's favor.[21] The two had received Elizabeth's consent in 1585, and when she traveled to Elvetham six years later, they displayed their marriage as a public one sanctioned by her. Their match offered Hertford a new chance to represent himself as the Queen's ally and as a social and political insider.

The Elvetham performance emphasized hospitality both to impress Elizabeth and to claim status for Hertford. The Seymours did not invite Elizabeth to Elvetham, but heard of her plans secondhand. When they saw in the "Gesse" ("gest") and heard from "friends in the Court" that the progress route included a visit to their their relatively small house at Elvetham, which was unprepared to accommodate such an event, they might have interpreted this choice as a burden rather than as a favor (sig. A2r). In response, they made a supreme effort to show that they could meet this challenge and exceed Elizabeth's expectations. They ordered

---

[19] Besides the major conflict surrounding his first marriage, Hertford also argued with the Queen about what to do when his eldest son married without their consent in 1581. A series of letters in the Seymour Papers outlines these events: Longleat House, Archives of the Marquis of Bath, Seymour MS, vol. 5, ff. 118–19, 130, 136, 144–5, 152–7, 168.

[20] Breight, "Realpolitik," 20–48.

[21] Two recent essays by H. Neville Davies and Sarah Crover also argue that Hertford used the entertainment to pronounce his loyalty to Elizabeth and present an improved version of Elvetham that would please her, although neither discusses the importance of his recent marriage to this project. Additionally, I disagree with Davies that attempts to find political allusions in country house entertainments are "misdirected" (238). While the Elvetham entertainment is exceptionally cautious and conservative in its approach, several other examples are quite bold and transparent in their agendas. H. Neville Davies, "Looking Again at Elvetham: An Elizabethan Entertainment Revisited" in Margaret Shewring, ed., *Waterborne Pageants and Festivities in the Renaissance: Essays in Honour of J. R. Mulryne* (Farnham and Burlington, VT: Ashgate, 2013), 211–42; Sarah Crover, "A Taste of High Life at Elvetham: Elizabethan Progresses and the Rural Consumption of Royal Neverwheres" in Susan Bennett and Mary Polito, eds., *Performing Environments: Site-Specificity in Medieval and Early Modern English Drama* (Basingstoke: Palgrave, 2014), 180–98.

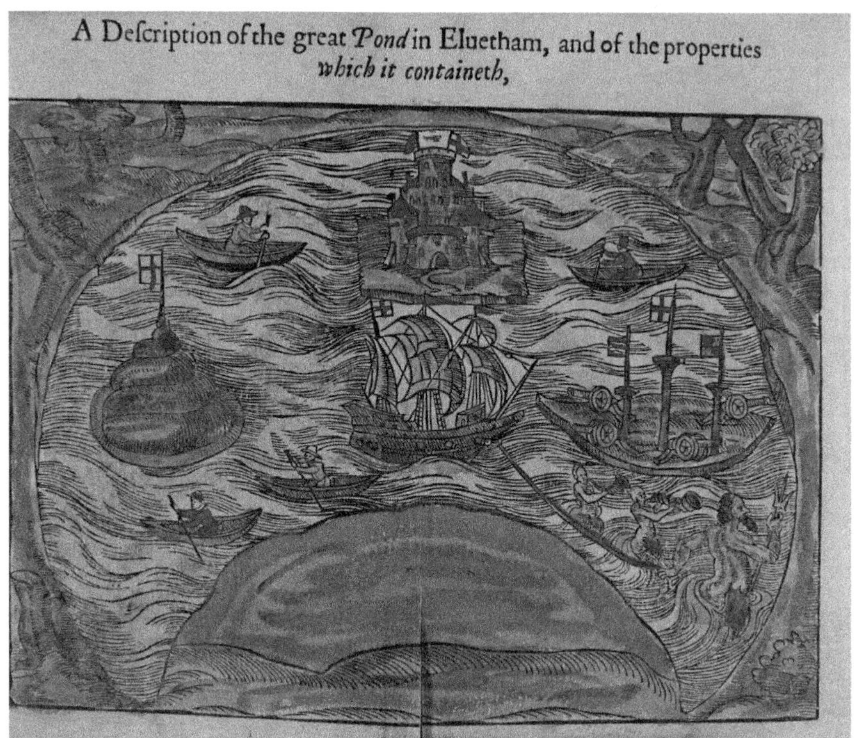

3.1 Hand-colored drawing of the water-pageant scenery at Elvetham, enclosed in the first
quarto. LPL, shelf mark (zz)1593.28.07.

extensive renovations, including the construction of more than twenty new
rooms and spaces, so that they could turn a modest house into a grand center of hospitality. They covered the floors with green rushes, the Elizabethan
symbol of hospitality, to indicate visually the convivial openness of the
estate (sig. A2v). They altered the landscape and added a crescent-shaped
pond, a fort, and a twenty-foot man-made mountain shaped like a snail – all
of which would form the scenery for the water pageant (see Figures 3.1 and
3.2). Many other country house entertainments represented themselves as
spontaneous displays of hospitality and therefore implied that their estates
could welcome strangers at a moment's notice, but the Elvetham pageantry
included none of this language. The Seymours chose to highlight rather
than mask their preparations – which went above and beyond what most
hosts undertook – to demonstrate their successful navigation of the circumstances surrounding Elizabeth's visit. As they introduced the improved
Elvetham to Elizabeth and the public, they also introduced a new version

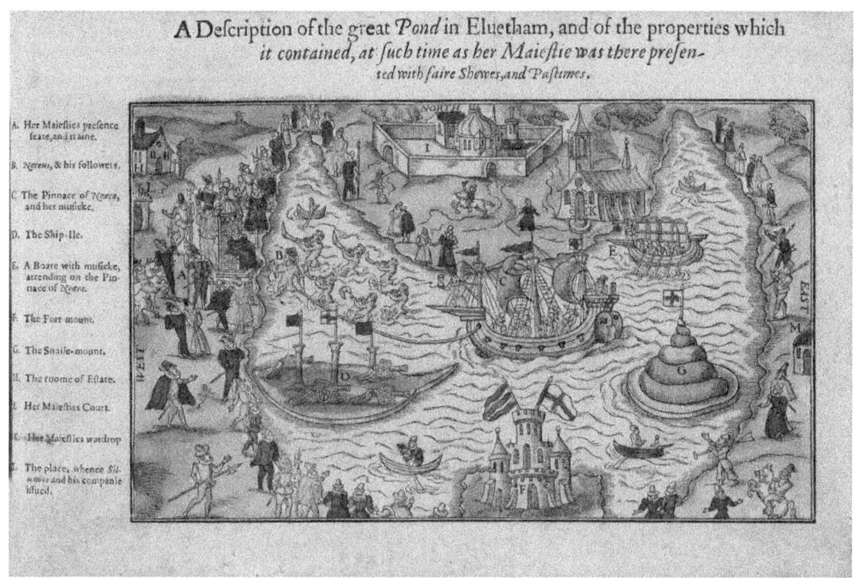

3.2 Hand-colored revised drawing of the water-pageant scenery at Elvetham, enclosed in the second quarto. Royal Collection Trust at Windsor Castle, shelf mark RCIN 1024755.

of Hertford – one who would spare no cost or inconvenience to prove his loyalty to the Queen.

The renovations and costly festivities flaunted Hertford's resources, as did the pageantry's performance by his own company.[22] The opening speech, which insisted that a stronger alliance with Hertford would benefit Elizabeth, was performed in Latin and marked Hertford and his household as learned and elite. As the performance celebrated the Seymours' standing and influence, it threatened in subtle ways to undercut its message of deference to Elizabeth's authority. When the band of two hundred men greeted her, they were led by Hertford and dressed uniformly, with gold chains around their necks and yellow and black feathers in their hats.[23] This ceremonial display signified Hertford's readiness to entertain Elizabeth to the fullest extent, but it also allowed him to declare his own importance by leading an entourage that might nearly rival the size of hers. The entertainment's principal claim that Elvetham served as a regional center could

[22] Professional players performed the speaking parts, as evidenced by Elizabeth's payments to them (sig. D1r, D3r). For the argument that Hertford's company played these roles, see the Introduction.

[23] The costumes are described in the book's first edition, *The Honorable Entertainement Gieuen to the Queenes Maiestie in Progresse, at Eluetham in Hampshire by the Right Honorable the Earle of Hertford. 1591* (London, 1591; *STC* 7583), sig. A4r.

have undermined Elizabeth's jurisdiction, and when the pageantry records
boast about bombarding her with entertainment, they reveal a subtle version of something we see often in the genre: the desire to control the royal
guest. After Elizabeth entered the house on the first day, "she had not
rested hir a quarter of an houre" before more festivities occurred, and on
the last day, "hir Maiestie was no sooner readie, and at hir Gallerie window, looking into the Garden, but there began three Cornets to play certaine fantastike dances" (sig. B4r, D2v). Such moments, in which Elizabeth
seems unable to escape the festivities, help show that Hertford dedicated
substantial resources to his liberal entertaining, but they also reminded
Elizabeth that she was his guest. Above all, Hertford rested his hopes on
the idea that especially abundant entertainment would yield substantial
reciprocation.

The Elvetham entertainment seems to have taken fewer risks than many
other country house entertainments.[24] Its moments of potential subversion
were slight, and its opening speech overstated Hertford's loyalty as it invited
Elizabeth to command all inside. It humbly welcomed her to "Semers
fraudlesse house" and described her host in these terms:

> His mouth yeeldes pray'rs, his eye the Oliue branch;
> His praiers betoken duetie, th'Oliue peace;
> His duetie argues loue, his peace faire rest;
> His loue will smooth your minde, faire rest your bodie.
> This is your *Semers* heart and qualitie:
> To whom all things are ioyes while thou art present,
> To whom nothing is pleasing in thine absence.
>
> (sig. B2v).

These lines depict Elvetham as a peaceful respite for the Queen and the
reformed Hertford as completely under her control. Besides the gift of
the entertainment, Hertford gave Elizabeth his loyalty and insisted it was
exactly what she needed – yet another strategy to make her feel indebted
to him. The welcoming speech carefully represented the estate as owned
by Elizabeth and kept for her by Hertford, to whom it later referred as
"him, that vnder you doth hold this place" (sig. C2r). As the actor ushered Elizabeth toward the house, he invited her to "commaund what it
containes: / For all is thine: each part obeys thy will" (sig. B3r). The song

---

[24] Its apparently conservative approach to entertaining the Queen might be attributed to Hertford's
use of the performance as an apology, or it might suggest that Hertford had some control over our
surviving record. I discuss the second possibility in Chapter 5.

that followed repeatedly asked Elizabeth to "Accept of our vnfeined ioy," a phrase that insisted on the sincerity of the excessive praise (sig. B3v). Linda A. Pollock advocates studying generosity in elite social life with a focus on kindness and human interaction rather than approaching hospitality as a selfish exchange. She complains that the latter provides "a coldly functional approach to relationships."[25] But even though the Elvetham entertainment and others in its genre spoke of heightened emotions – such as joy, excitement, gratitude, and love – it is difficult not to see them as calculated, selfish requests for favor because they made these underlying motivations so apparent. Some entertainments were infused with warmth, and many desired to build something like friendship or intimacy with the Queen. But country house entertainments were primarily driven by the desire for political exchange – a point made with special clarity by the Elvetham entertainment.

It placed Elizabeth firmly at its center, suggesting spatially and verbally that all activity revolved around her.[26] During the performance, she was seated or elevated to declare her superior position. She arrived on horseback and did not alight her horse until after the welcoming pageant. She watched several devices from above the action out of her window. When it came time for the water show, she expected "the issue of some deuise" because it had been "aduertised that there was some such thing towards" (sig. C1r). Four knights held up an exquisite canopy made of luxury fabrics, and she sat under it and waited for the performance to begin (sig. C1r). All of these moments demonstrate something unusual for a country house performance: instead of being surprised by spontaneous pageants, Elizabeth was made to appear in control of her surroundings. All of the characters came simply to entertain and worship her; none ever posed a threat to her security or authority. As we have seen, wild men and versions of the rowdy Sylvanus frequently appeared in country house performances, but unlike the others, Elvetham's Sylvanus emerged already tamed by Elizabeth's arrival. He stepped forward from the trees carrying an olive branch, and his first words declared his deference: "*Siluanus* comes from out the leauie groues, / To honor her whom all the world adores" (sig. C3v). The rest of his twenty-line speech heaped praise after praise upon Elizabeth and stated directly her power: "More learned then our

---

[25] Linda A. Pollock, "The Practice of Kindness in Early Modern Elite Society" in *Past and Present* 211.1 (2011): 121–58.

[26] Michael Leslie makes a similar point in "'Something Nasty in the Wilderness': Entertaining Queen Elizabeth on Her Progresses" in *Medieval and Renaissance Drama in England* 10 (1998): 58–60.

selues, she ruleth vs" (sig. B2r). The entertainment still relied on her inter-action with performers; the water pageant, for example, asked her to name the ship at its center. However, the distance between Elizabeth and the per-formers illustrated the rift between Hertford and the Queen as it enabled Elizabeth to appear especially powerful. Many aspects of the entertain-ment sent the same messages: Elizabeth deserved exceptional hospitality, and Elvetham was an important political center constructed to serve her purposes.

The performance represented the new Elvetham as a center of social gathering for those of multiple ranks, but it paid careful attention to social hierarchy and offered different hospitalities based on rank. Its exam-ple demonstrates that the Elizabethan practice of open hospitality, or the offering of food and shelter at country estates, highlighted inequality and affirmed economic and political hierarchies. The Elvetham entertainment embraced this emphasis on class difference in its own definition of hos-pitability as segregated, enviable display. A printed text claims that "neer tenne thousand people, from sundrie places" gathered to watch Elizabeth arrive at Elvetham, and even if this is an exaggerated estimate, it is likely that a large crowd was present (sig. A4r). This audience alone made the case for the newly renovated Elvetham as a pillar of the region. When Elizabeth ate dinner on the second day, she sat with top-ranking nobles in a room at the top of a hill, and the commoners were allowed to gaze at her from a distance through an open door. They were also able to watch at least some of the pageantry, and the printed text celebrates how Hertford's "louing entertainment" included the Queen, nobility, and "all other, frends, or strangers," which suggests that all audience members partook in some way (sig. B4r). It is unclear whether commoners received any of the estate's "liberall bountie" or "plentifull abundance" (sig. B4r). One account of the Sudeley entertainment describes how the hosts provided commoners free ale and bread, and it is likely that the Elvetham performance also offered a chance for country folk to receive charity.[27] But the Seymours mostly directed their supplies where they focused their energies: toward the Queen and the most elite.

Whereas the commoners stood on the outskirts and might have received meager charitable offerings, the guests of highest status were treated to formal banquets that offered an "abundance of dainties" (sig. B4v). One particularly elaborate banquet was staged in a low gallery in the Queen's privy garden, a space created just for this event. Our surviving description

----

[27] Emma Dent, *Annals of Winchcombe and Sudeley* (London, 1877), 228.

of the banquet exemplifies food historian Ken Albala's claim that early modern banquets were theatrical performances: "there was a banket serued all in glasse and siluer, into the low Gallerie in the Garden, from a hill side foureteene score off, by two hundred of my Lord of Hertfordes Gentlemen, euerie one carrying so many dishes, that the whole number amounted to a thousand: and there were to light them in their way, a hundred torch-bearers."[28] These thousand dishes included a first course of dishes "in sugar-work" and later courses of fruits, jellies, and seafood consisted mostly of delicate items: oysters, mussels, cockles, periwinkles, crabs, and lobsters. All of these foods were associated with high status and cultural refinement. The hosts' ability to procure such a variety, including seafood when Elvetham was not near the sea, further attested to their wealth, and the seafood complemented the water show and therefore highlighted the hosts' innovative renovations. The entire banquet performance would have validated social position and power in its hosts and consumers.

The banquet's show-piece was an enormous selection of sculptures made of sugar, some standing upright and others flat against the table. The intricate designs, meant to impress the guests, showed off the great effort that went into the banquet's preparation, and they signified power in design and ingredient. The sculptures presented a hierarchy in the order they were delivered: the Queen's arms; "the seuerall Armes of all our Nobilitie"; common men and women; symbols of war (forts, drummers, soldiers); and many animals.[29] The household's access to enormous quantities of sugar pointed to their affluence.[30] In the 1590s, England aimed to acquire colonies that could produce this luxury commodity, but Spain and the Netherlands were still leading importers.[31] Large amounts of sugar shaped into little soldiers and other symbols of war therefore signified England's emerging colonial impulse. During the banquet, a fireworks display over the pond further alluded to England's military prowess. Shots and rockets were fired from each of the three islands, and following were a "castle of fire-works of all sorts," "a Globe of all maner of fire-workes, as big as a barrell," and "many fire wheeles, pikes of pleasure, and balles of wild-fire, which burned

---

[28] Ken Albala, *The Banquet: Dining in the Great Courts of Late Renaissance Europe* (Urbana: University of Illinois Press, 2007), 1–26. I cite the first edition of *The Honorable Entertainement*, sig. D4r.

[29] *The Honorable Entertainement*, sig. D4r.

[30] Sugar was starting to become more widely available, but not in these quantities. For more on the history and cultural significance of sugar, see Sidney W. Mintz, *Sweetness and Power: The Place of Sugar in Modern History* (New York: Penguin, 1985), esp. 89–91; Kim F. Hall, "Sugar, Gender, and the Cirum-Atlantic Performance of Class" in Rebecca Ann Bach and Gwynne Kennedy, eds., *Feminisms and Early Modern Texts: Essays for Phyllis Rackin* (Cranbury, NJ: Associated University Press, 2010), 66–8.

[31] Mintz, *Sweetness and Power*, 29–38.

in the water" (sig. D2r). This display must have been spectacular, and it claimed power for Hertford as it celebrated Elizabeth as the military and political leader of a prosperous nation with growing international prestige.

Additionally, the banquet's emphasis on sugar may have alluded to Frances Seymour's domestic labor. Kim F. Hall suggests that confectionary was a gentlewoman's art and that "the language of sugar itself is connected with the feminine" in the late sixteenth and seventeenth centuries.[32] Although Frances would not have prepared the sculptures herself, they could have connoted her influence and supervision, which were crucial to the event. When Elizabeth arrived at Elvetham and then at the manor, "hir maiesty alighted from horsbacke at the hall dore, the Countesse of Hertford, accompanied with diuers honourable Ladies and Gentlewomen, moste humbly on hir knees welcomed hir highnesse to that place: who most graciously imbracing hir, tooke hir vp, and kissed hir, vsing manie comfortable and princely speeches, as wel to hir, as to the Earle of Hertford standing hard by, to the great reioysing of manie beholders" (sig. B3v). Elizabeth had watched the opening pageantry from an elevated position on her horse, but to greet Frances, she stepped off the horse and interacted more familiarly with her former companion. This description represents the two women as intimate friends, which is especially striking within an entertainment that otherwise lacks intimacy. In a public performance of their alliance, Frances played the role of hospitable host and humble servant as she kneeled before the Queen, and Elizabeth acted in accordance with her high position by delivering "princely speeches." Female co-hosts at Mitcham, Cowdray, and Rycote performed similar roles; their husbands met Elizabeth first and they greeted her more intimately at the house. These moments, although not the genre's only model of welcoming Elizabeth, might be interpreted as illustrating a division of hospitality along gender lines in which the woman's space is in the household but not beyond. At the same time, each entertainment underscored the crucial role of women's work in the event and in their family's standing. When Frances greeted the Queen, this moment emphasized both her supervisory role over hospitality at Elvetham and her existing alliance with Elizabeth.

A letter written by Frances several years earlier highlights Elizabeth's dissatisfaction with Hertford and reveals Frances' role as their mediator. Hertford obtained the Queen's permission to marry Frances, but only

---

[32] Kim F. Hall, "Culinary Spaces, Colonial Spaces: The Gendering of Sugar in the Seventeenth Century" in Valerie Traub, M. Lindsay Kaplan, and Dympna Callaghan, eds., *Feminist Readings of Early Modern Culture: Emerging Subjects* (Cambridge University Press, 1996), 168–90.

after some convincing and probably after the fact. Archival evidence indicates that they may have married as early as a decade before Elizabeth consented.[33] In a 1585 letter to Hertford, Frances describes conversations in which Elizabeth argued forcefully against marriage: "many persawasons che vsed agaynst maryge and the inconvenyenses thereof and how lettell you wolde care for me tellyng me how well I was here and how muche che cared for me."[34] In Frances' retelling, Elizabeth's resistance to the match was founded not only on her own troubled history with Hertford, but equally on her desire to keep Frances in her household. Elizabeth eventually relented, declaring she would not stand in the way of a mutually desired marriage.[35] Elizabeth's reluctance left open the possibility that this marriage might further damage her relationship with Hertford, but Frances was confident that she had played her role as intermediary well. She assured Hertford at the end of her letter, "truste me siwet Lorde the worste is paste and I warrant you che will neuer speake one angery worde to you."[36] When Hertford hoped to launch a new era through his country house entertainment, Frances' alliance with Elizabeth offered his best chance for redemption, and as his co-host, Frances again lobbied on his behalf. When she greeted Elizabeth at Elvetham and Elizabeth raised her to her feet so that they stood on equal footing, this moment underscored that Elizabeth had the power to elevate Frances and, by extension, Hertford. Elizabeth symbolically accepted Frances' new role as mistress of Elvetham, and she extended her long-standing alliance with Frances to include Hertford.

Our records of the performance claim that Elizabeth was pleased with the entertainment; she showed her satisfaction by paying players generously, commanding encores of songs and pageants she liked, and stating as she left that she had thoroughly enjoyed the event (sig. D3r–D4v). Hertford's company of players performed at court on Twelfth Night 1592, which may have been a reward for their performance at Elvetham, but Hertford himself seems not to have gained any specific reward or favor as a result of the entertainment. He and his sons continued to fight for their legitimacy, and when the Queen and her advisors feared repercussions, Hertford

---

[33] In a 1582 letter, Hertford's son addressed Frances as mother. Seymour Papers, Longleat House collection, vol. 5, ff. 118–19, Microfilm Reel 4, Institute of Historical Research. See also Susan Doran, "Seymour, Edward, First Earl of Hertford (1539?–1621)" in H. C. G. Matthew and Brian Harrison, eds., *Oxford Dictionary of National Biography* (Oxford University Press, 2004), online edn., ed. Lawrence Goldman, May 2010.

[34] Seymour Papers, Longleat House collection, vol. 5, f. 164v, Microfilm Reel 4, Institute of Historical Research.

[35] Ibid., f. 164v.   [36] Ibid., f. 164v.

was once again imprisoned in the Tower from November 1595 to January 1596. During this imprisonment, Elizabeth wrote to Frances to express her sympathy, and her letter reveals that she continued to identify her alliance with Frances as important to maintain.[37] Yet Elizabeth's relationship with Hertford remained tenuous. Even if the Elvetham entertainment provided a temporary claim to insider status, it seems not to have achieved the long-term goals Hertford sought. He learned a difficult lesson about attempting to engage in a reciprocal exchange with the Queen: gifts and hospitality encouraged but could not guarantee reciprocity, and if the Queen chose to reciprocate, she also chose how she did so.[38]

The Elvetham entertainment emphasized the host family's extensive preparations and primary goal of indulging the most elite guests. There were traces of the kind of hospitality later advocated by the Crown: Elvetham's war symbols and minor inclusion of those of lower ranks indicated that Hertford could serve the Queen by protecting and keeping order in the region. But as the entertainment represented Hertford as a generous country house owner, its definition of hospitality retained only some of the traditional emphasis on the aristocracy's social obligation to provide food and shelter for needy travelers and poor neighbors. It did not advocate moderation, but it did argue for mindful hospitality that took into account rank, what kind of treatment a guest deserved, and what the host desired in return. It made transparent the Elizabethan approach to gift-giving as a way to gain political advantage and the dependence of all forms of hospitality on social standing.

Hospitality and Elite Civility at Mitcham

Sir Julius Caesar's entertainment at Mitcham, Surrey, did not stage an apology, but it did present its host in a new light. This was Elizabeth's first visit since Caesar married Alice, the widow of alderman John Dent, two years earlier and took possession of the house as a result. As a Londoner, Caesar had no experience with country living or progress hosting, and as the son of an Italian physician, he felt insecure about his status in English society. His September 1598 entertainment, a text of which survives in manuscript in his personal papers, legitimized his new role as a member

---

[37] SP Domestic, Elizabeth I, 12/254.

[38] Lisa Klein similarly highlights the inequality involved in gift exchange with the Queen and the Queen's adeptness at manipulating that inequality in "Your Humble Handmaid: Elizabethan Gifts of Needlework" in *Renaissance Quarterly* 50.2 (1997): 459–93.

of the country gentry.[39] It did so by demonstrating a more exclusive kind of hospitality, which it defined as a tradition both maintained and enjoyed by the upper classes, that hinted at a discourse of civility. This discourse advocated a refined elite that congregated in small exclusive communities set apart from those of the lower ranks. It emphasized good breeding, polite society, and proper behavior instead of open generosity.[40] By employing the somewhat conflicting ideologies of hospitality and civility, the Mitcham entertainment was at the forefront of shifting attitudes about the country gentry in the late Elizabethan period.

From its first lines, Caesar's entertainment represented him using a series of paradoxes that captured a conflicted attitude toward hospitality, giving, and access. It asserted his power within Elizabeth's patronage system and England's legal order but alternately decried and embraced his lack of authority under Elizabeth's governance. It presented him as effecting justice for those of the lower ranks but marked him as detached from the poor. The opening speech, in which an actor delivered a written petition to Elizabeth, introduced Caesar by his position as Master of Requests and reminded Elizabeth of the important service he performed by hearing civil petitions from the poor and others. Yet the entertainment suggested that his most helpful service might be keeping the poor away from Elizabeth. The actor greeted Elizabeth with these lines:

> Greate Ladye, Your maister of Requestes, either with melancholie, with ioye, or busynes, is growen so peremptorie, that hee hath layd penalties vpon all such as shall delyver petitions. I, more confident of your gracious aspect then fearefull of his commaund, haue secretely conveyed my self into this honorable troupe; in all humilitie offering these fewe lynes, with a wish that you would bee pleased to reade them er you sleepe, and ever to conceale them from him they most concearne.[41]

The speech characterized Caesar as stern, commanding, and protective of Elizabeth, and it offered multiple potential reasons for his decision to limit access to her: he was too busy preparing his home for her visit, he was too overcome with happiness at her arrival, or he had grown despondent. The entertainment later revealed the source of his "melancholie" as poverty and personal hardships, but perhaps Caesar desired respite for the Queen and himself from the nuisance of the poor and their petitions. The opening speech both touted and undercut Caesar's authority as Master of Requests;

---

[39] BL, Additional MS 12497, ff. 233, 253–262v.   [40] Bryson, *Courtesy to Civility*, 107–50.
[41] I quote this speech and the pageant that follows from Leslie Hotson's edited version in *Queen Elizabeth's Entertainment at Mitcham: Poet, Painter, and Musician* (New Haven: Yale University Press, 1953), 19. The original is BL, Additional MS 12497, f. 253–262v.

he was strict, but his orders were ignored. Likewise, it made access to Elizabeth appear both limited and open. Caesar wanted to shield her from petitioners, but he took the opportunity of a progress visit – a time at which petitioners could circumnavigate the formalized receiving of petitions at Elizabeth's court – to present one himself. Because his petition was delivered by someone acting "secretely" without his knowledge, the entertainment enabled Caesar to appear selflessly generous.

The actor then handed Elizabeth a written petition that praised Caesar in a humble, self-deprecating fashion. Elizabeth might have read it later in private – the actor encouraged her to peruse it "er you sleepe" – but it is more likely that she or someone else read it aloud during the performance. The petition described Caesar as "nowe in your realme the eldest Iudge the youngest and the poorest, the first a riddle, the last a wonder, for that in all adges, it hathe ben thought rare for Iudges and executors to be begers."[42] This riddle emphasized that Caesar had long served Elizabeth even though he was rather young, and it highlighted his aspiration for greater reward for his service. In letters in the late 1580s and 1590s, Caesar represented himself as a judge who spent more than he made in public service, and he complained that he had received too little favor from Elizabeth. He petitioned Sir Francis Walsingham; Anne Russell; William Cecil, Lord Burghley; Robert Devereux, Earl of Essex; and others for money or to lobby Elizabeth on his behalf.[43] Although Caesar had been appointed to a new office and had finally been granted an audience with Elizabeth by 1598, the entertainment reveals that he was still not content with his status. He had spent a substantial amount of money securing the Dent daughters' wardships, and, according to his household records, he also spent £700 plus his own provisions on Elizabeth's progress visit, including the expenses associated with multiple postponements.[44] The supplication's reference to Caesar's poverty might even have implied protest about Elizabeth's tendency to reroute progresses, which cost her hosts a great deal.

To improve his circumstances, Caesar hoped to prove himself vital to Elizabeth's success and England's governance. The supplication strategically mentioned Caesar's father, who had served as royal physician: "his father *Physition* to your highness was as *Martha* carefull for your body, hym selfe haueing the better parte, soliciter of your mynde, most happy in bothe

---

[42] I quote this supplication from the original manuscript, BL, Additional MS 12497, f. 233.

[43] See Edmund Lodge, *Life of Sir Julius Caesar Knt* (London, 1827), 14–18 and the collection of Caesar's letters at the BL, especially Lansdowne MS 155.49, 155.19, 155.35, and 155.9.

[44] Caesar was appointed to the office of Master of Requests in the early 1590s and had his first audience with Elizabeth in 1595. For a record of his entertainment costs, see BL, Sloane MS 4160, f. 20.

that your Maiestie hath in your tyme reposed a trust, in them of body and mynd."[45] This passage claimed that Caesar, like his father, had been a crucial contributor to Elizabeth's reign, and it emphasized the trust she placed in these two men, whom it represented both as servants and as powerful sources of influence over the Queen. The word "soliciter" could have referred to an officer of the law in court; alternately, it could have denoted someone who urges or prompts. The term therefore encapsulated two possibilities: Caesar acted on behalf of Elizabeth's wishes or he influenced her mind. The comparison of Caesar's father and Martha is a fascinating choice as well. In the Bible, Martha effectively managed the home of her brother Lazarus, and as an exemplary hostess, she embodied Christian hospitality. The analogy suggested that Caesar's father cared for Elizabeth's body as Martha cared for her brother's home, and it imagined his father's job as a kind of hospitality.

The Mitcham petition employed rhetoric of gift-giving to encourage a reciprocal exchange with Elizabeth, like the Elvetham entertainment, but it also used language of surprise and spontaneity to represent Mitcham as always open to visitors. It described Elizabeth's visit as a gift when it said that Caesar joyed at "this vnexpected fauoure, that your highnes vouchsafeth to viset his Cell."[46] Any surprise would have been manufactured because Caesar had expected Elizabeth for some time, although after several cancellations he might have grown doubtful that she would ever visit. Her gift pleased Caesar greatly; the petition claimed that his joy at Elizabeth's arrival had caused him almost to lose the ability to think or speak.[47] As the petition pledged Caesar's home and heart to Elizabeth in a grand gesture of hospitality, it had him both yield and showcase his authority. Neither the supplication nor the petition directly ceded ownership to Elizabeth or acknowledged her as the estate's true owner. The supplication called Caesar "the owner of this howse" and emphasized the "authoritie he hathe" within the household and over the performance.[48] These lines had the potential to displease the monarch who firmly believed she owned all of England, but it was crucial to Caesar's attempts to present himself as a country householder. Furthermore, because the house, performance, and hospitality were his own, they reflected him and demonstrated his desire to please Elizabeth: "He presentes his harte, his large and wyde harte, wherein all the roomes are onlie taken vp for your maiestie furnisht with noe other Tapistrie then truthe."[49] Using one of the genre's most prevalent motifs,

---

45 BL, Additional MS 12497, f. 233.   46 Ibid., f. 233.
47 Ibid., f. 233.   48 Ibid., f. 233.   49 Ibid., f. 233.

the petition argued that Caesar's house and heart were equally open to Elizabeth. The opening speech defined hospitality as protecting the Queen, and the petition imagined it as a gift in return for the favor of her arrival. By separating Caesar's petition from the welcoming speech and claiming that he did not want to present it, the entertainment crafted a fictional view of his hospitality as motivated by his love for her instead of by a specific request.

Even as the entertainment declared Caesar the "owner" of Mitcham, it revealed that his hopes rested on the status and experience of his new wife.[50] Caesar married Alice in April 1596, and this match brought him the lucrative wardships of her daughters along with properties including Mitcham estate.[51] Although the supplication began with Caesar, it ended with Alice:

> As for your ould hostesse ioye hath ouertaken her with a straing accident silence, the tong which is the hartes herralde, is nowe becom Embassader to the hart where receauing impressions not to be expressed, it selfe is torned into harte, soe that whensoeuer hereafter she shall speake there is noe worde that proceadeth out of her mouth that shall not be growing fast to the hart, soe shall you haue her hartes bottome at her tonges ende, and in the meane tyme her eyes, and handes must supply the want of her tongue, till she recouer this happie traunce.[52]

The passage represented Alice as normally outspoken but currently awestruck in Elizabeth's presence. It underscored her honesty and loyalty. Alice served as Elizabeth's host and faithful ally, and, like Frances Seymour at Elvetham, she was poised to welcome Elizabeth with a warm embrace. The phrase "your ould hostesse" suggested familiarly and fondness as it presented Alice as an experienced progress host. Elizabeth had visited Mitcham several times before Alice married Caesar, and the supplication implied that the two women shared a certain intimacy based on that experience.[53] The Mitcham entertainment relied on Alice's alliance with Elizabeth to encourage greater favor for her husband, who believed that his good deeds should be better rewarded. Before Elizabeth and her court, Caesar hoped to mark himself as country gentry, an identity rendered

---

[50] Ibid., f. 233.
[51] L. M. Hill, *Bench and Bureaucracy: The Public Career of Sir Julius Caesar, 1580–1636* (Stanford University Press, 1988), 89–92.
[52] BL, Additional MS 12497, f. 233.
[53] See Mary Hill Cole, *The Portable Queen: Elizabeth I and the Politics of Ceremony* (Amherst: University of Massachusetts Press, 1999), 197–9. In her table of Elizabeth's progress visits, she identifies stays at Mitcham in July 1592, August 1595, and October 1596.

possible only because of his marriage to Alice. Although the entertainment silenced Alice, it revealed her importance behind the scenes as co-host.

The Mitcham entertainment shared motivations with the Elvetham one but presented a slightly different approach to elite hospitality. The Elvetham performance was at least partially open to neighboring commoners, and Hertford relied on their presence to bolster his honor as a country house owner. The Mitcham entertainment instead represented access to the Queen as a guarded privilege. There is no indication in our surviving records or the pageantry text that the Caesars fed a large crowd or that any commoners attended. Household expense records show that they ordered enormous portions of food, wine, and beer for a select few visitors: the Queen, members of her Privy Chamber and Privy Council, and a small number of lords and ladies.[54] The banqueting highlighted the Caesars' elite status and perhaps conservative approach to hosting by offering an array of domestic and wild game often enjoyed in Elizabethan feasts: partridges, quail, capons, mutton, salmon, sturgeon, and pheasants.[55] If the supplies Caesar ordered were meant for a fairly small crowd as household records imply, they offered his guests the opportunity to imbibe an extravagant quantity of food and drink. The entertainment represented itself as an intimate, exclusive experience shared by a select few members of the civilized elite, and our surviving text of the event implies the same. It exists in two parts in Caesar's papers: the supplication on a single broadsheet and the two speeches on quarto-sized pages bound together as a small book. An inscription on this book identifies the speeches as delivered to Elizabeth "at my house at Mitcham."[56] It contains no narrative, only the script. These records were intended not for the masses, but to commemorate an important event in Caesar's life as a privileged insider.

An emphasis on status continued in the final pageant, which featured a dialogue between a Poet, Painter, and Musician. These characters debated whose art could best capture the Queen's beauty and power. They praised Elizabeth in conventional terms as they emphasized that no one could adequately represent her: "her perfection admitteth no coloring" and "I cannot express all her worth."[57] After concluding that "Witt, colors, nor ayres can express that which wee most covet, her perfection," they decided that their arts better applied to lower-ranking subjects.[58] The Poet said, "I'le keepe my sonetting for semsters to sing over their idle lazy

---

[54] BL, Additional MS 12497, ff. 237–41.　　[55] Ibid., ff. 237–41.　　[56] Ibid., f. 237.
[57] Hotson, *Queen Elizabeth's Entertainment*, 24–5.　　[58] Ibid., 26.

stitches," and the Musician replied, "And I my notes for Contry tunes and London cryes."[59] The Painter responded as follows:

> And I this bord for a contrye mistres, who cares not howe she be paynted, so she be paynted. Our art growes stale; for where in elder ages, none were colored but memorable for their vertues to paynt out imitation to posterity, nowe every Citizens wife that weares a taffata kirtle and a velvet hatt, and every gentlewoman that can boord a paire of borders must have her picture in the parlour. And if hereafter aske, who was this? It was one of the companies of such a trade, or a Justice of the peace his wife, of such a shire. But it is not in vs only, but in mocking of auncyent monumentes; for now, if one dye riche, he must have a toumbe and an epitaphe, when nothing remayneth for memory, but that he dyed so much worth; so that heretofore vertue was interred in toumbes of gold; now gold is buryed with vertues.[60]

There is no better way to prove oneself as "old money" than to decry the damaging influence of "new money" on English culture and elite values. The passage insisted that wealth and virtue were not necessarily linked and that true gentility involved cultural refinement and respectable behavior or noble deeds. Building on the kind of hospitality offered at Elvetham and other country estates on progress, the Mitcham entertainment represented its brand of hospitality not as charity but as generosity to fellow elite insiders who deserved it. In this new figuring, the English country house was crucial to maintaining the values and traditions of high society not because it functioned as a communal gathering place like Elvetham, but because it differentiated those with power from those without.

This perspective stemmed from Caesar's attempt to distinguish his wife and himself from citizens or those claiming gentle status undeservedly. Unlike the Seymours at Elvetham, the Caesars were not aristocratic. As the Mitcham entertainment outlined Caesar's rise from his father's position to his new marital alliance, it nonetheless aspired to present him as a settled member of the country gentry. The playful tone of the Painter's speech might have enabled audience members to laugh with Caesar at its irony, but it still angled for an elevated position. One of Caesar's letters distinguished status from wealth in a way that might further illuminate his entertainment's references to money. He wrote Anne Russell, Countess of Warwick, in 1589 that he did not achieve his position "by corruption," as had been rumored. He added, "neither ambition moveth me to desire it, for I list not to climbe; neither covetousnes causeth me to sue for it, so vile and base a thing I esteeme money; but the necessitie of her

---

[59] Ibid., 27.　　　[60] Ibid., 27.

Maiestie's favourable aspect to the place wherein I am, for the furtherance of her Maiestie's service, and doing of justice to poore straungers."[61] He described the judicial profession as a hospitable practice, and his language exemplified that of an elite suitor to the Queen who claimed to desire only her approval. Although money could enable a rise in status and although Caesar's entertainment flaunted his wealth, his entertainment maintained that money alone did not determine rank. Instead, elite status implied moral virtue, productive political alliances, and behavior befitting a member of the gentry.

The Mitcham entertainment performed the rural tradition of hospitality by welcoming guests with language of spontaneous openness and expecting political reward in return, but it also included a more contemporary, urban emphasis on civility. As a response to Elizabeth's call for provincial hospitality, it presented Caesar as poised to serve her in a common law court and as a new country householder. It stressed his role in keeping order, rewrote his father's and his positions as gestures of hospitality rather than employment, and in some ways implied that he would carry on the tradition of hospitality that the Crown sought to preserve. But the entertainment did not suggest that Caesar was invested in providing poor relief, and it stressed the undesirability of consorting with those of the lower ranks. As it represented Caesar paradoxically as both new and settled gentry, it implicitly questioned whether country hospitality was the best approach to achieving honor. Caesar seems not to have received any immediate reward following the Mitcham pageantry, but his own memoranda states that Elizabeth left "with exceeding good contentment" and appointed him as senior Master of Requests two years later.[62] This eventual promotion might even imply that the definition of hospitality performed at Mitcham met with Elizabeth's approval. Despite her proclamation's insistence that country hospitality meant aid for the poor, Elizabeth expected extravagant entertainment on progress, and as her hosts tried to please the most difficult of guests, they increasingly identified hospitality as an elite privilege.

The Politics of Housewifery and Exclusivity at Harefield

Elizabeth's final summer entertainment further developed the notion that hospitality was an exclusive ritual, but it claimed to exemplify traditional aristocratic hospitality. Staged at Harefield estate in Middlesex in 1602,

---

[61] Qtd. in Lodge, *Life of Sir Julius Caesar*, 15–6. The original is BL, Lansdowne MS 155, f. 19.
[62] BL, Sloane MS 4160, f. 20.

it was co-hosted by Alice, Countess of Derby, and her second husband, Thomas Egerton. While the entertainments at Elvetham and Mitcham revealed that household women's alliances and liberality were crucial to their husbands' agendas, the Harefield entertainment more explicitly identified hospitality as women's work. It presented the country house as a microcosm for England, in which high-ranking housewives ran households just as Elizabeth governed the nation. In doing so, it argued that elite women like Alice Egerton were as crucial to the late Elizabethan court as they were to country estates.

The Harefield event was nearly as grand as the one at Elvetham, and it began with a dialogue between domestic workers that foregrounded the issue of hospitality. A Bailiff and a Dairymaid greeted Elizabeth at the estate entrance with a comic debate. She then walked to a chair a few steps from the house, where she listened to a dialogue between the personified characters Place and Time. During the next two days, she encountered three further devices: the "Petition of St. Swithin," which apologized for rainy weather, a mariner's song and lottery in which women in the audience received poems and gifts, and a final speech by Place dressed as a widow to mourn the Queen's departure. Like others in its genre, this entertainment was the collaborative effort of its hosts and their hired writers and performers, but it was in many ways Alice's event.[63] Her husband later wrote that the Queen's entertainment "cost me more then I will remember," and when he blamed this incredible cost on his wife's misspending, he revealed that she played a central role in planning and financing the performance.[64] The pageantry's language also rendered the event a gift from Alice to the Queen. Together these factors encourage us to consider Alice its lead patron and deviser.[65]

Alice's surviving letters and household documents reveal that she seized the opportunity of the Queen's visit to pursue several specific goals. In 1602, she already occupied a high social status and served as a powerful political and literary patron, and the Harefield entertainment advertised and expanded her patronage. Her letters used familial ties to leading courtiers to offer petitioners political and legal advice; she and her first husband,

---

[63] John Davies wrote at least some of the script. See Gabriel Heaton, *Writing and Reading Royal Entertainments From George Gascoigne to Ben Jonson* (Oxford University Press, 2010), 100–2.

[64] See Thomas Egerton's 1603 petition to King James (HEH, Ellesmere MS 163) and his manuscript entitled, "An Unpleasant Declaracion of Thinges Passed betwene Countese of Derby and Me since Our Marriage" (HEH, Ellesmere MS 213).

[65] My analysis of Alice's role builds on two earlier essays that identify her agency more briefly or hesitantly: Jean Wilson, "The Harefield Entertainment and the Cult of Elizabeth I" in *The Antiquaries Journal* 66.2 (1986): 315–29 and Sara Mueller, "Domestic Work in Progress Entertainments" in Michelle M. Dowd and Natasha Korda, eds., *Working Subjects in Early Modern English Drama* (Aldershot: Ashgate, 2011), 145–60.

Ferdinando Stanley, were well-known patrons of drama and other literature; and she is the dedicatee of many religious and secular texts in the late sixteenth and early seventeenth centuries.[66] Writers sought her patronage because her reputation and connections could bring them fame as well. Because Alice had moved to Middlesex from northern England just eight months earlier, her entertainment aimed to impress her new neighbors and to represent her as a pillar of her new community.

Alice sought patronage as well, and her entertainment highlighted numerous expensive gifts to Elizabeth and smaller gifts in the lottery pageant to about thirty women, including Privy Chamber ladies and high-ranking patrons. According to Harefield records, the Queen's four-day visit cost at least £2,084 – £134 more than the estimated yearly household expenses.[67] This extravagant display of wealth reveals that the Egertons were anxious to prove themselves as established members of the aristocracy. Thomas held a high-ranking position at Elizabeth's court, but he was also an illegitimate son and self-made man. Although he had already earned the Queen's favor, his wife had not, and her overspending suggests she was eager to do so. She had married twice without Elizabeth's permission and probably sought approval for her current marriage retrospectively. Her husband later intimated that the Queen advised against their coupling. While writing that his unhappy marriage must be "a punishment inflected vpon me by almighte God," Thomas added that he "haue often tyme had cause to remember, what my Late gracious Soueraigne Quene Elizabeth sayed vnto me, when she first spake with me of This Mariage."[68] Alice's pursuit of Elizabeth's acceptance, which may have been an uphill battle, underlay every section of the entertainment.

---

[66] She probably inspired Edmund Spenser's mourning widow Amaryllis in *Colin Clovts Come Home Againe* (London, 1595; *STC* 23077), and John Harington praises her marriages and virtuous reputation in *The Most Elegant and Witty Epigrams of Sir Iohn Harrington, Knight* (London, 1618; *STC* 12776). Dedications include John Davies, *Yehovah Summa Totalis* (London, 1607; *STC* 6337); Davies, *The Holy Roode, or Christs Crosse Containing Christ Crucified* (London, 1609; *STC* 6330); Henry Lok, *Svndry Christian Passions Contained in Two Hundred Sonnets* (London, 1593; *STC* 16697); Barnabe Barnes, *Parthenophil and Parthenophe* (London, 1593; *STC* 1469); and Spenser, *Complaints* (London, 1591; *STC* 23078). For more on Alice's patronage, see French R. Fogle, "'Such a Rural Queen': The Countess Dowager of Derby as Patron" in French R. Fogle and Louis A. Knafla, eds., *Patronage in Late Renaissance England: Papers Read at a Clark Library Seminar, 14 May 1977* (Los Angeles: Clark Library, 1983), 3–29. For more on her extended family, see J. J. Bagley, *The Earls of Derby 1485–1985* (London: Sidgwick, 1985); Mary E. Finch, *The Wealth of Five Northamptonshire Families 1540–1640* (Oxford University Press, 1956), 38–65.

[67] I take these figures from household accounts in the Ellesmere collection at HEH, especially MS 285. Some expense records were famously forged by J. P. Collier, but this one appears legitimate, especially because Thomas Egerton's later complaints about Alice's spending offer corroborating evidence. The cost includes construction, gifts, rewards for servants, and large quantities of food.

[68] HEH, Ellesmere MS 213.

An alliance with the Queen and other powerful patrons could also help Alice with her legal affairs, especially an ongoing battle over her three daughters' inheritance with the current Earl of Derby, William Stanley. Stanley rested his claim on the first Earl's decree that his title and estate should transfer only to male heirs, while Alice claimed the inheritance for her daughters based on her late husband's death-bed revision of his will.[69] They reached a tentative settlement in 1600 that divided the inheritance between Stanley and the three co-heiresses, but the agreement was not legally solidified until 1606, and the lucrative and politically valuable title to the Isle of Man, temporarily in the Crown's possession, would not have its ownership resolved until 1609.[70] Furthermore, although Alice's late husband left an impressive number of estate holdings in several counties, he died in debt, and his creditors continued to sue her daughters and her until 1619.[71] In the Harefield lottery, Alice received a particularly apt fortune: "Yowe thriue, or woulde, or may, your lotts a purse / Fill yt with goulde and you arre nere the worse."[72] This verse highlighted her attempt, through hosting the monarch, both to flaunt and to increase her wealth. Her gift-giving and entertaining encouraged Elizabeth to reciprocate with valuable gifts such as royal favor, land, avenues to social advancement, and support for her legal pursuits.

As the Harefield performance served Alice's interests, it claimed to serve the Queen's even more. Like the earlier entertainments at Elvetham and Mitcham, it carefully balanced petition with praise, and self-promotion with celebration of Elizabeth's authority. It represented a reciprocal relationship between loyal subjects and a loving monarch in the way it represented its location. When the character Place first appeared, she wore a robe colored "lyke the brickes of the howse" and drew attention to Harefield manor, a visible symbol of Alice's status and desire to solidify the 1600 inheritance settlement (4:182). In December 1601, her trustees bought Harefield on her behalf with money earned from the settlement. Even though her husband

---

[69] The legal documents detailing this case are preserved in the Ellesmere (Brackley) collection at the Northamptonshire Record Office. On the origins of the dispute, see especially MSS 27, 47.

[70] A. W. Moore, *A History of the Isle of Man* (London: Unwin, 1900), 1:223–5; Northampton, Northamptonshire Record Office, Ellesmere (Brackley) MS 53, 55a. The sheer size (seventy-two folios) of the Act of Parliament about the long-standing lawsuit illustrates the massive amount of land and money at stake.

[71] For evidence of Ferdinando Stanley's continuing debts, see Hertford, Hertfordshire Archives, Ashridge II MS 912d; HEH, Ellesmere MS 880.

[72] I cite the Harefield entertainment from Gabriel Heaton's edited version in Elizabeth Goldring, et al., eds., *John Nichols's The Progresses and Public Processions of Queen Elizabeth I: A New Edition of the Early Modern Sources* (Oxford University Press, 2014), 4:174–95. I thank Heaton for kindly supplying me with a copy in advance of its publication. For this particular quote, see 4:188.

may have had legal ownership by virtue of their marriage, the indenture detailing this sale neglects to mention him and specifies Harefield manor as Alice's possession.[73] During the first summer she owned Harefield, the 1602 progress offered her the chance to show off her new estate and renovations and to present the manor as belonging to her.[74] Because a bald claim to ownership would not have been prudent, the pageantry employed well-worn conventions to applaud Elizabeth's governance: the notion that "no place is greate enoughe" to receive the Queen, the popular fantasy that Elizabeth's "daies haue bene most cleere" and that she ruled over a unified England, and the heart–home analogy we saw in the Mitcham entertainment (4:182–5). Fashioning the Egertons and Elizabeth as loving allies, Place said, "were I as large as theire hartes that arre my owners, I shoulde bee the fairest pallace in the worlde: and were I agreeable to the wishes of theire hartes, I should in somme measure resemble her sacred self, and bee in the outwarde fronte exceedinge faire, and in the inwarde furniture exceedinge riche" (4:184). This pageant further attributed Harefield's transformation to the royal presence when Place asked, "dothe not the presence of a Prince make a Cottage a Courte?" (4:183). By highlighting the transformative effect of royal visits, the entertainment revealed Alice's hope that proximity to the Queen would bring her increased fame and influence. More importantly, if Harefield appeared as grand and extravagant as Alice hoped it would, the entertainment instructed the Queen to interpret that excess as a commendatory salute to her visit rather than a selfishly showy display.

Some aspects of the performance demonstrated that Alice and her household upheld aristocratic hospitality as defined by the Crown. Instead of the retired shepherd, wild man, or poet who typically opened country house entertainments, the Queen was greeted by two domestic servants. Even though neither the Dairymaid nor the Bailiff recognized the royal entourage, both immediately offered to host the travelers. The Bailiff began to lead the group toward the main manor "without any comission" (4:180). The Dairymaid claimed her dreams of green rushes had predicted the arrival of strangers in need of accommodation, and she excitedly invited them to her much smaller dairy house. She represented even this house,

---

[73] Northampton, Northamptonshire Record Office, Ellesmere (Brackley) MS 55a.

[74] Evidence for the renovations can be found in the household records printed in *The Egerton Papers*, which show payments for several household laborers. See J. Payne Collier, ed., *The Egerton Papers: A Collection of Public and Private Documents, Chiefly Illustrative of the Times of Elizabeth and James I* (London, 1840), 340–57. As mentioned above (in note 67), Collier's tendency to forge early documents makes all his transcriptions suspect, but this particular section is taken from manuscripts that appear to be legitimate.

presumably the estate's most meager lodging, as perpetually welcoming and able to supply at a moment's notice an abundance of fresh dairy products – cow's milk, cheese, syllabub (a curdled drink), and posset (a hot liqueur drink) – along with other English farm goods, such as various kinds of apples and plums (4:180–1). Her long list of provisions emphasized the prosperity of England under Elizabeth's rule, as well as the household's readiness for guests. This opening used rhetoric of infinite and altruistic generosity that harkened back to an older ritual of country houses offering food and shelter to passersby.

Harefield manor would itself have been a visible argument for the preservation of that tradition. At a time when many elite owners streamlined the staff in their country homes, the Egertons instead ran Harefield more along the lines of medieval models.[75] Thomas Egerton affirmed the royal position on hospitality at the end of the 1601 Parliament session when he commanded MPs to return to their country estates to prepare for a defense of the realm.[76] The Egertons' entertainment the following summer represented the couple as leaders of a select group dedicated to obeying royal commands and preserving tradition. The manor would have especially advertised Alice's pedigree. She spent her childhood traveling among her father's three large manors in Northampton, Warwickshire, and London; she was the mistress of estates in nearly half of England's shires during her first marriage; and she learned about hospitality on a particularly grand scale from her first father-in-law, Henry Stanley, Earl of Derby, who was one of the most influential householders in Elizabethan England.[77] By using language and imagery associated with country hospitality, the Harefield performance emphasized Alice's influence and demonstrated the Egertons' legitimacy as true members of the English aristocracy.

Despite the entertainment's apparent attachment to tradition, it actually revealed a definition of hospitality that privileged promotional display rather than charity for the poor. As the Dairymaid encouraged Elizabeth and her retinue to choose the dairy house, she joked about the main manor's insufficiencies:

---

[75] Lodge, *Life of Sir Julius Caesar*, 82–5.

[76] HEH, Ellesmere MS 488; John Earnest Neale, *Elizabeth I and Her Parliaments: 1584–1601* (London: Cape, 1953), 2:425–6.

[77] Fogle, "Such a Rural Queen," 8; Cynthia B. Herrup, *A House in Gross Disorder: Sex, Law, and the 2nd Earl of Castlehaven* (Oxford University Press, 1999), 12; William Ffarington, *The Derby Household Books*, ed. F. R. Raines (London, 1853), 13–90. Henry Stanley's 1586–90 household records demonstrate his constant reception of guests and Alice's frequent visits.

> I pray yow hartely forsooth come neare the house, and take a simple lodginge
> with vs to night; for I can assuere yow that yonder house that he talkes of, is
> but a pigeon house which is very little, if it weere finishte, and yet very little
> of is finishte, and yow will beleeue mee vpon my life Lady; I saw Carpenters
> and bricklayers and other workemen about it within lesse then these two
> howers, besides I doubt my Master and Mistress are not at home, or if they
> be yow must make your owne prouision, for they haue noe prouision for
> such strangers: yow shoulde seeme to be Ladies. (4:180)

Although the Dairymaid advocated "simple" accommodations and represented the estate as warmly open to unexpected strangers, her speech
emphasized the Egertons' extensive preparations for the occasion. She
worried that Harefield was not ready to offer provisions to such a large
group of distinguished guests, and she asked pardon for any possible inadequacies by dismissing the great house as miniscule. She continued not to
recognize the Queen, an ongoing joke in the pageant, and added, "I know
not what yow are, nether am I acquainted with your dyet; but if yow will
goe with me, yow shall haue cheare for a Lady" (4:180). The Dairymaid
described Harefield as so well stocked that it could accommodate those of
high rank, even "the Queene her selfe" (4:180). These lines suggested even
more directly than did the Elvetham and Mitcham entertainments that
different guests deserved different levels of hospitality. This entertainment
did not advocate civility as parts of the Mitcham one did; it simply exposed
the hierarchy and self-promotion behind aristocratic hospitality.

It further defined hospitality as rooted in exclusivity when the Bailiff
offered to accommodate the group not because Harefield estate routinely
provided shelter for passersby, but because he understood that these particular visitors were high-ranking and thus Harefield was privileged to host
them. He noted of the company's leader, "though she know the way to all
mens harts, yet she knowes the way but to few mens howses, except she
loue them very well I can tell yow" (4:180). These lines stress the significance of the Queen's stay and the favor she bestowed upon the Egertons
by virtue of her rare visit. The Bailiff and Dairymaid both indicated that
Alice instructed them to pay close attention to strangers, but they disagreed
as to what that meant. The Bailiff insisted that they cater generously to
high-ranking guests when he noted that Alice would scold them if they
failed to bring "so faire a flight" to the main house (4:181). The Dairymaid
instead thought they should put strangers to work; she added, "my Mistress charged me earnestly to retaine all idele hearuest folkes that past this
way" (4:181). The word "retain" conveyed multiple meanings: to receive

as a guest, to employ in service, or to hinder or restrain. These disparate meanings overlapped for comic effect: the pageant encouraged the audience to assume that Alice instructed her servants to harbor those in need, just as the Crown asked of aristocratic householders, but the Dairymaid instead thought she was to hire them as laborers. Her line also implied that the servants might have stood not as a welcoming committee, but as estate guards charged with keeping out the poor.

In reality, the entertainment would have been an exclusive event. Access to the Queen was a particularly well-guarded privilege after a 1601 royal proclamation declared that all masterless men and families "of the inferior sorte" must avoid the Queen and her court on progress.[78] Some anecdotes survive about threats to the Queen's person on progress, and, as she got older, she and her advisors must have felt she was increasingly vulnerable.[79] According to the proclamation, those who opened their homes to banned commoners during a royal visit would face three hours in the stocks and the temporary closure of their households.[80] This decree reveals a conflict between the Queen's rhetorical confidence in her subjects' love and her actual practice, as well as a striking disparity between what Elizabeth expected of her aristocrats and what she did herself. It also helps explain why records of commoners at Elizabethan country house entertainments are so sparse at the end of the reign.[81] Although the Harefield entertainment claimed to maintain an older tradition, in which estates remained open to strangers in need, the type of hospitality it performed was mindfully planned and in accordance with Elizabeth's desires to avoid the poor. The elated participation of local commoners at Elvetham became a key part of the entertainment's argument that Hertford was a valuable asset to Elizabeth, but, unless they were employed as servants, the non-elite had no place at Harefield.

The Harefield performance's exclusion of commoners was a practical one, enforced by a royal order, but the entertainment's emphasis on status also helped develop its analogies between Alice and the Queen. The welcoming pageant characterized the members of the estate as cordial and hard-working, which would have reflected well upon the household mistress. When the Bailiff belittled the Dairymaid's plan by saying, "if my Mistress should heare of this, I faith shee would giue yow little thankes I can tell yow," he depicted Alice as a firm supervisor who valued hospitality (4:181). The Dairymaid retorted:

---

[78] Qtd. in Cole, *Portable Queen*, 164.　　　[79] Ibid., 167–8.　　　[80] Ibid., 164.
[81] Leahy, *Elizabethan Triumphal Processions*, 81–3 notes that records of Elizabeth's progresses rarely refer directly to the presence of common people.

> I dare say she would giue me great thankes for yow know my Mistress
> charged me earnestly to retaine all idele hearuest folkes that past this way:
> and my meaning was, that if I could hold them al this night and to morrow
> on munday morning to cary them into the feilds and make them earne
> there entertainment well and thriftily and to that end I haue heere a rake
> and forke to deliuer to the best huswife in all this company. (4:181)

She then identified the Queen as the "best huswife" and presented her
a jeweled rake and fork (4:181). As the Dairymaid endorsed the pastoral
assumption that rustic simplicity was far favorable to courtly pretension,
she also advocated physical work. As royal pageantry, the entertainment
necessarily condoned the idle pleasures of courtly shows in practice, but,
unlike much pastoral literature, it foregrounded the importance of a well-
run estate and the domestic labor that enabled such pleasures. Although
the joke was that the Dairymaid's homely English rural values were incom-
patible with the royal agenda, her continued insistence that the dairy house
would best receive the Queen implied that Elizabeth should value the practical labor of estate maintenance, just as Alice did. The gift of ornamental
rather than useful tools emphasized that Elizabeth's appropriate role, like
that of Alice, was not field laborer, but supervisor.

By calling Elizabeth a "huswife" here and "mistress" elsewhere, the entertainment aligned her with Alice, its own effective household mistress. When
the Bailiff first saw the Queen, he identified her as "the Mistress of this faire
company," giving her the same title he assigned Alice (4:180). No other
country house entertainment named Elizabeth "Mistress." Some called
her "Lady" or "Madame"; most referred to her as "Majesty," "Sovereign,"
"Highness," and "Queen." Because the word "mistress" could signify a
female governor as well as a housewife, it began to establish an analogy
between managing a household and ruling a state, which was solidified
when the Dairymaid and Bailiff both called the Queen "the best huswife
in all this company" (4:181). The entertainment represented both Alice and
the Queen as proficient household managers to build an alliance between
them, and, although housewifery could privilege wives over maids and
critique the Queen's singlehood, the entertainment insisted on solidarity
among these women. It also implied that Alice and Elizabeth shared authority over the estate and occasion. By labeling Elizabeth a model housewife,
the entertainment alluded to the daily labor all aristocratic housewives
performed in order to run households effectively. Alice, after all, strengthened her relationship with Elizabeth by fulfilling her domestic duties as
a housewife and offering hospitality to visitors. By drawing attention to
her effective housekeeping during the entertainment, Alice not only aimed

to please Elizabeth and represent herself positively, but also claimed to resemble the Queen as manager of a huge household.

As the metaphor of Queen-as-housewife reflected Alice's personal agenda, it carried larger political implications. Jean Wilson has suggested that this metaphor domesticated the Queen "to a position of power accepted as legitimate for women by her contemporaries."[82] Instead of reading the analogy as commenting on the limited power of women, however, I suggest that it reveals housewifery as a socially and politically crucial job. Social historians alternately highlight the power within housewifery or argue that the Tudor–Stuart household was a restrictive space for women, and the Harefield entertainment argued for the former.[83] As the queen–housewife analogy praised Elizabeth as the hard-working, efficient manager of England's largest household, it represented country houses as places in which women held power. It also verified their work as politically important. Elizabeth may have called herself an exception to her sex, but the Harefield entertainment insisted that women could learn to govern themselves, their households, and their communities from the Queen's example. Instead of comparing rulers to fathers, as patriarchal political theory would do, the entertainment identified women's domestic labor as a more appropriate metaphor for Elizabeth's long-term rule.[84] The entertainment presented this labor and alliances between women as integral to the governing of late Elizabethan England.

There is little proof that Alice Egerton earned any specific reward for her part in entertaining the Queen. This lack of reciprocation can be attributed partially to circumstance because Elizabeth died less than a year after she visited Harefield. But the entertainment may also have failed to please her. Eyewitness accounts suggest that the entertainment's representation of Elizabeth as a symbol of harmony may have contrasted with actual discord at the event. One observer, using the name Anthony Rivers, reported the following in a letter:

> [The Queen] being at the Lord Keeper's, in her merriest vein, the Countess of Derby (his wife) moved that it would please her to accept of the Lady Strange [Anne Stanley] and her sister [Frances Stanley] to wait on her in her privy chamber, and to bestow them in marriage where she thought fit, or at least to give her leave to bestow them: at which motion the Queen was

82 Wilson, "The Harefield Entertainment," 326.
83 Friedman, *House and Household*, 46–9; Heal, *Hospitality*, 182–3; McBride, *Country House Discourse*.
84 Susan Amussen has pointed out that patriarchal theory was not fully articulated in England until after Elizabeth's reign. Amussen, "Gender, Family and the Social Order, 1560–1725" in Anthony J. Fletcher and John Stevenson, eds., *Order and Disorder in Early Modern England* (Cambridge University Press, 1985), 196–217.

> exceedingly passionate and commanded silence on that behalf. The younger,
> as is supposed, is contracted to the Keeper's son, and the parents hoped the
> Queen would have approved it, and made him knight. Now they are at a
> nonplus, and know not how to proceed.[85]

His description reveals Alice's hope that this visit would ensure the social advancement of her daughters, and it shows the Queen's resistance to approving Frances' marriage retrospectively. There is no evidence that Elizabeth looked any more favorably upon the marriage between Alice and Thomas Egerton, although Thomas Gainsford rewrote Alice's relationship with Elizabeth fourteen years later. In a dedication to Alice in *The Historie of Trebizond*, Gainsford praises her for being "so farre beholding to Fortune, that shee sheltred vnder the couert of the greatest and magnificenst Prince in the World Q. Elizabeth; and shee so ouermantled her with Fauour, that King Iames kept her still glorious vnder the same."[86] This image of Elizabeth as Alice's protector may not accurately describe their relationship, but it certainly captures Alice's desires for their alliance.

Alice did enjoy a certain degree of notoriety through the entertainment's afterlife. Fragmented records of the performance survive in twelve contemporary sources, many of which circulated well into James' reign, and the entertainment was a popular source of gossip among letter-writers.[87] The printing of excerpts six years after the performance suggests that the event reached a new audience interested in its aesthetic quality. Robert Jones' songbook 1605 includes the music for the mariner's song, and the text of the lottery pageant is printed in the second edition of *A Poetical Rapsodie* (1608).[88] The entertainment became available for political appropriation in manuscript as well. A manuscript that belonged to members of the Newdigate family – former owners of Harefield – includes the full Dairymaid and Bailiff skit, several other pageantry fragments, and an additional lyric that appears in no other early modern sources.[89] These texts were enclosed in a letter that probably came from sources within or closely connected to the Egerton household, but their authors are unknown. It is also unclear whether the lyric, a complaint of the satyrs against the nymphs, was performed at Harefield in 1602, but at least some readers experienced it as part of the entertainment.[90]

---

[85] Qtd. in Heaton, *Writing and Reading*, 106.

[86] Thomas Gainsford, *The Historie of Trebizond in Foure Bookes* (London, 1616; *STC* 11521.3), sig. A3v.

[87] Heaton, *Writing and Reading*, 102.

[88] Robert Jones, *Vltimvm Vale* (London, 1605; *STC* 14738); *A Poetical Rapsodie* (London, 1608; *STC* 6374). Mary Sidney's 1599 unperformed entertainment also appears in the latter; see Chapter 6.

[89] Heaton, *Writing and Reading*, 109.

[90] Nichols, *Progresses* attributes it to the Harefield entertainment based on the manuscript's own attribution, written in a later hand, to "the Countess of Derby's entertainment" in 1602. In his

Read in this context, the lyric reveals male anxiety about female communities. The satyrs pursue women who shun them. In protest, they identify
their own faults – rough beards, hairy bodies, and unappealing feet – and
praise a series of mythological women who honored their husbands and
sons despite the same imperfections. The complaint ends with two stanzas
in which the satyrs argue that their own bestiality is no worse than the
nymphs' commodification of desire:

> Breefly if by nature we,
> But imperfect creatures be
> Thinks not our defects so much
> since Celestiall powres be such
> But yow Nymphes whose veniall loue
> Loue of gold alone doth moue
> Though yow scorne vs, yet for gold
> Your base loue is bought and sold.
>
> (4:195)

The description of the nymphs' love as "venial" and "base" represents them
as ambitious, fiercely chaste, and money-seeking, and the lines suggest that
the nymphs prostitute themselves to satisfy their desire for wealth. As a
response to the Harefield entertainment, the lyric implies similar motivations for Alice Egerton, who receives a purse in the ladies' lottery, whose
wealth is highlighted throughout, and who made transparent her desire to
exchange gifts for favor. As it neatly turns the table on her self-representation
as a politically powerful aristocratic housewife, the lyric imagines love as a
commodity and calls into question the avenue to social advancement most
often available to Elizabethan women: marrying multiple rich men. This
strategy poses quite a contrast to Elizabeth's lauded virginity.

The archival evidence therefore suggests that the 1602 entertainment
received mixed reviews. Although the performance may not have achieved
all that Alice desired, two seventeenth-century household entertainments
revealed the lasting influence of the Harefield pageantry, at least for a specific aristocratic network, as they highlighted Alice's roles as a patron of
drama and a household queen. A 1607 performance at her daughter and
son-in-law's estate at Ashby, written by John Marston, celebrated Alice as its
honored guest and modeled its tribute to her on the 1602 entertainment's
celebration of Elizabeth.[91] In the early 1630s, Alice's family performed

---

edition of the entertainment (4:194), Heaton notes that he doubts the performance included it
because of its inappropriate tone and because no other manuscript refers to it.

[91] HEH, Ellesmere MS 34/B/9. See James Knowles, "Marston, Skipwith, and *The Entertainment at
Ashby*" in *English Manuscript Studies 1100–1700* 3 (1992): 137–92, esp. 173; Mary C. Erler, "'Chaste

another entertainment to thank her for her hospitality, which it defined as sheltering displaced family members.[92] During this entertainment, Milton's *Arcades*, Alice sat in a "radiant" throne at Harefield and played the role occupied by Queen Elizabeth about thirty years earlier.[93] Employing language that recalled the 1602 entertainment, *Arcades* praised Alice as "the great Mistres of yon princely shrine" and "a rural Queen."[94] Fittingly, her hospitality and housewifery earned her the title of "Queen" within her household. The entertainment also moved hospitality from the public to the private realm, as something more like civility that is shared among a select few.

The three Elizabethan entertainments at Elvetham, Mitcham, and Harefield reveal that their genre played an important role in the beginnings of a shift from hospitality to civility in late sixteenth- and seventeenth-century England. The genre necessitated hospitality but provided a space in which country house owners reimagined practical applications of the ideology. Although the concept of civility was only beginning to emerge, the Mitcham entertainment illustrated its appeal, especially to those straddling the worlds of the city and the country. The Elvetham and Harefield entertainments instead argued for the preservation of more traditional hospitality – a ritual they revealed always affirmed class hierarchies but did not necessarily uphold gendered ones. While all three entertainments upheld an ancient tradition in part, their manors embodied a new movement toward the "proud, ambitious heaps" that Ben Jonson would later criticize for being "built to envious show."[95] To the Seymours, Caesars, and Egertons, rank mattered a great deal in terms of what accommodations would be available to guests – unlike Jonson's praise of an idealized Penshurst that offered similarly "liberal" hospitality to King James and

Sports, Juste Prayses, and all Softe Delight': Harefield 1602 and Ashby 1607, Two Female Entertainments" in A. L. Magnuson and C. E. McGee, eds., *The Elizabethan Theatre: XIV* (Toronto: Meany, 1991), 1–25.

92 Cedric C. Brown, *John Milton's Aristocratic Entertainments* (Cambridge University Press, 1985), 20–6; Mary Ann McGuire, "Milton's Arcades and the Entertainment Tradition" in *Studies in Philology* 75.4 (1978): 451–71.

93 *Poems of Mr. John Milton Both English and Latin* (London, 1645), sig. D2v. The text of *Arcades* identifies itself as part of an entertainment presented to Alice at Harefield. It does not include a date, and scholars have speculated that it was performed between 1631 and 1634. Cedric C. Brown dates it to the late summer of 1632, while William B. Hunter, Jr., suggests that it celebrated Alice's birthday in May 1634. Brown, *John Milton's Aristocratic Entertainments* (Cambridge University Press, 1985), 26–47; Hunter, *Milton's Comus: Family Piece* (Troy, NY: Whitston, 1983), 20.

94 *Poems of Mr. John Millton*, sig. D3r, D4v.

95 Ben Jonson, "To Penshurst" (1616) lines 1 and 101. I cite from M. H. Abrams and Stephen Greenblatt, eds., *The Norton Anthology of English Literature*, 9th edn. (New York: Norton, 2012), 1B: 1546–8.

the poor.[96] Although Elizabethans might never have practiced hospitality quite like Jonson imagines, discourses surrounding the concept – at least for some late Elizabethan country householders – were shifting from a focus on social obligation to an emphasis on elite privilege.

96 Ibid., line 59.

PART II

Print

CHAPTER 4

"Pleasures by a profitable publication"
Publishers and Readers of Printed Entertainment

Of the seventeen known Elizabethan country house entertainments, eleven were printed in fragments or fuller records. Each book was crafted by multiple hands: the writers and hosts who planned and performed the pageantry, the audience members and scribes who recorded elements of the event, and the publishers who brought it to print. Printed entertainments offer crucial insights into ephemeral events, but they also cultivate new meanings in new contexts. This chapter argues that publishers were the controlling agents, or lead "devisers," who shaped these books and our interpretations of them. By paying close attention to these controlling agents, we can ascertain why country house entertainments might have reached print, how contemporary readers might have responded to them, and how the same entertainment can produce a range of meanings depending on the context.

An engaged publisher who helped shape the printed text is part of the story of all printed country house entertainment books, even those that may have been co-financed by hosts. We have only two surviving prefaces written by publishers of Elizabethan country house entertainment, which I analyze below, and both claim that the publishers chose to collect and finance these texts because they identified an existing readership. Although Elizabethans did not typically use the modern term "publisher," it allows us to designate the agent behind a publication, or the stationer who is financially and conceptually responsible for a book's publishing.[1] By studying publishers and their aims in printing Elizabethan pageantry, we can understand better the value and functions of printed entertainment. In his study of printed commercial plays, Zachary Lesser has demonstrated that early modern publishers were readers: when considering whether to invest in a certain book, "a publisher had to understand the book, using his or her critical skills

---

[1] On the distinction between publishers, printers, and booksellers, see Peter Blayney, "The Publication of Playbooks" in John D. Cox and David Scott Kastan, eds., *A New History of Early English Drama* (New York: Columbia University Press, 1997), 389–92.

to judge the book's potential appeal and possible consumers, a judgment that depended on making meaning of the text of the book."[2] Because early publishers tended to specialize in certain kinds of books, we can analyze an entertainment within the context of its publisher's career to understand why it might have reached print.[3] Because little evidence survives of those who owned and read these texts in the sixteenth century, their publishers often serve as our earliest readers. Their catalogs and our two printers' notes offer the best available evidence about why and how these texts were distributed and interpreted.

Some publishers also served as editors. No text describes all aspects of a performance; instead, each offers selective details gathered from eyewitness accounts or from those involved behind the scenes. The narrator of *The Princelye Pleasures, at the Courte at Kenelwoorth* (1576) illustrates a common trope when he adds the parenthetical statements "as I remember" and "as I haue heard credibly reported."[4] In *The Queenes Maiesties Entertainment at VVoodstocke* (1585), the narrator reveals that he has made conscious choices about what matters when he says in the middle of one episode: "Heere the Pages abiding, vse a prety act of sport, but because the matter wilbe full without it, I haue thought good not to trouble you with suche Parenthesis, but making their speeches ended I wil only recite the introduction to their comming in."[5] These texts do not simply report a performance, but shape its meanings according to the aims of the book's writers and publishers.

Both *Princelye Pleasures* and *The Queenes Maiesties Entertainment at VVoodstocke* were small books of individual entertainments, the most common type of printed country house pageantry and the kind on which this chapter focuses. The stationers responsible for publishing the known country house pamphlets specialized in either current events or courtly literature, and the texts themselves alternately emphasize both functions. Chapter 5 will examine how printed accounts of performances at Cowdray (1591)

---

[2] Zachary Lesser, *Renaissance Drama and the Politics of Publication: Readings in the English Book Trade* (Cambridge University Press, 2004), 35.

[3] Ibid., 26–51.

[4] I quote from the transcription of the original printed text in *Kenilworth Illustrated; or, The History of the Castle, Priory, and Church of Kenilworth* (Chiswick, 1821), 52–80 in the appendix, because the 1576 edition is now lost. For these particular quotes, see 53, 60. See also the second edition, "A Briefe Rehearsall, or Rather a True Copie of as Much as Was Presented before Her Maiesties at Kenelworth" in *The VVhole Woorkes of George Gascoigne Esquyre* (London, 1587; STC 11638), sig. AIr, A7v. Its running header is "The princely pleasures at Kenelworth Castle." The two editions are very similar except there might have been some spelling variants (or else the nineteenth-century publications altered the spelling), and the first edition included the prefatory note and a few marginal comments that do not appear in the second.

[5] *The Queenes Maiesties Entertainement at VVoodstock* (London, 1585; STC 7596), sig. F2r.

and Elvetham (1591) served as news books; here I contend that small books of the entertainments at Kenilworth (1575) and Woodstock (1575) published by Richard Jones and Thomas Cadman functioned primarily as literature valued as pleasurable and instructive reading beyond the events they describe. After examining the circumstances surrounding the publication of Elizabethan country house entertainment and especially the precedents set by the Kenilworth and Woodstock books, this chapter analyzes a particularly interesting case: a pamphlet of three entertainments performed in 1592. Publisher Joseph Barnes marketed this book as masculine, elite, and local – an interpretation that runs counter to the politics of the entertainments in performance but that would have appealed to Barnes' established readership.

The Literary Value of Printed Pageantry: Kenilworth and Woodstock

The best evidence of a publisher's aims in printing pageantry comes from a preface to a now-lost book about the entertainment performed at Kenilworth Castle in 1575. *The Princelye Pleasures, at the Courte at Kenelwoorth* was published by Richard Jones in London and dated March 26, 1576. Although the last remaining copy was destroyed in a fire in 1879, transcripts and descriptions of the original material book survive in nineteenth-century publications.[6] We can use these descriptions alongside the surviving second edition to recreate several aspects of the lost one. Besides *Princelye Pleasures*, two books probably published in late 1575 or early 1576 capitalized on interest in the same performance: an account of the court's travels that summer called *The Pastime of the Progresse*, which is also lost, and the informal letter about the Kenilworth festivities titled *A Letter: Whearin, Part of the Entertainment vntoo the Queenz Maiesty, at Killingwoorth Castl, in Warwik Sheer, in This Soomerz Progress. 1575. Is Signified.*[7] A decade later, *Princelye Pleasures* was republished as part of the 1587 posthumous collection of Gascoigne's works.[8] As this collection of books demonstrates,

---

[6] Besides *Kenilworth Illustrated*, see also John Nichols, ed., *The Progresses and Public Processions of Queen Elizabeth* (London, 1823), 1:486.

[7] Robert Langham, *A Letter* (London, n.d.; *STC* 15190.5). For Langham's authorship, see Chapter 1, n. 16. Court official William Patten seems to have had a hand in the publication of this book, but we do not know precisely when, how, or by whom it was published. The book bears no publisher's name, date, or place of publication.

[8] Although the book appeared after Gascoigne's death, it is generally thought to be edited by him. It was published with two different title pages: *The VVhole Woorkes of George Gascoigne Esquyre* (*STC* 11638) and *The Pleasauntest Workes of George Gascoigne Esquyre* (*STC* 11639). Bookseller Abel Jeffes published both in 1587, and both contain the same material after the title page.

the popular Kenilworth entertainment had a rich afterlife in print. Each text warrants substantial analysis on its own, and Langham's *Letter* and the second edition of *Princelye Pleasures* have received a fair amount of attention already.[9] But the original *Princelye Pleasures* was most influential in establishing a market for printed country house entertainment, as well as shaping scholarly conceptions of the Kenilworth performance and its genre for centuries.

Because the second edition of *Princelye Pleasures* appears in a collection of Gascoigne's works, the Kenilworth entertainment has generally been seen as his text.[10] We know little about how *Princelye Pleasures* came to print, but Gascoigne surely had a hand in its construction. It included the lengthy script of an unperformed device he wrote, and it marked the beginning of a partnership between Gascoigne and Jones that produced two further works, probably following the success of the first.[11] Gascoigne's contributions to the performance promoted his ambitions to become a courtier and an author, and *Princelye Pleasures* continues to advance these goals, which are apparent in many of Gascoigne's works. Just two months earlier, he had given Elizabeth a meticulously crafted presentation manuscript of the tale of Hemetes the hermit, a pageant performed at Woodstock in 1575. When Elizabeth requested a copy, Gascoigne jumped at the chance, even though he did not write the device himself.[12] The manuscript showed off

---

[9] Several scholars who discuss the Kenilworth performance draw evidence from both texts, but those who consider the texts as separate projects include Sandra Logan, *Text/Events in Early Modern England: Poetics of History* (Aldershot: Ashgate, 2007), 93–183; Wendy Wall, *The Imprint of Gender: Authorship and Publication in the English Renaissance* (Ithaca: Cornell University Press, 1993), 111–67; Elizabeth Goldring, "'A mercer ye wot az we be': The Authorship of the Kenilworth Letter Reconsidered" in *English Literary Renaissance* 38.2 (2008): 245–69; David Scott, "William Patten and the Authorship of 'Robert Laneham's Letter' (1575)" in *English Literary Renaissance* 7 (1977): 297–306; Janette Dillon, "Pageants and Propaganda: Robert Langham's Letter and George Gascoigne's *Princely Pleasures at Kenilworth*" in Mike Pincombe and Cathy Shrank, eds., *The Oxford Handbook of Tudor Literature 1485–1603* (Oxford University Press, 2009), 623–36; Susan Anderson, "'A True Copie': Gascoigne's *Princely Pleasures* and the Textual Representation of Courtly Performance" in *Early Modern Literary Studies* 14.1 (2008): n.p.; Alex Davis, *Chivalry and Romance in the English Renaissance* (Cambridge: D. S. Brewer, 2003), 73–98.

[10] For a recent example, see Gillian Austen, *George Gascoigne* (Cambridge: D. S. Brewer, 2008), 115–32. Based on her biographical knowledge of Gascoigne and the inclusion of *Princelye Pleasures* in his collected works, Austen argues that Gascoigne was the agent behind the entertainment's publication.

[11] Richard Jones published the following works by Gascoigne later that year: *A Delicate Diet, for Daintimouthde Droonkardes* (London, 1576; *STC* 11640), dated August 22; and *The Spoyle of Antwerpe*, which reports a November event (London, 1576; *STC* 11644).

[12] Gascoigne states in his preface that he did not write the tale, which Gabriel Heaton argues was actually written by Robert Garrett. See *Writing and Reading Royal Entertainments: From George Gascoigne to Ben Jonson* (Oxford University Press, 2010), 31. The evidence for Elizabeth's request comes from *The Queenes Maiesties Entertainement at VVoodstock*, sig. c3r.

his language skills by presenting the tale in English, Latin, Italian, and French, and he prefaced it with his own material: a dedicatory poem and a letter to Elizabeth that he accurately labeled a "tedyous preamble."[13] The frontispiece featured a pen and ink drawing of Gascoigne dressed partly as a soldier and partly as a scholar, armed with sword and pen and kneeling before the Queen. This drawing and the poem that follows make clear that Gascoigne is poised to serve Elizabeth in whatever capacity she chooses. The poem states directly that Gascoigne is ready "to serve yow so as maye become me beste / In feilde, in Towne, in Cowrte, or any where. / Then peerless prince, employe this willinge man."[14] The manuscript indicates Gascoigne's readiness to profit from Elizabeth's interest in pageantry, and it follows that he would try to make the most of his participation at Kenilworth. Although *Princelye Pleasures* does not explicitly praise Gascoigne's contributions, it presents him as a successful courtly writer simply by placing him in the company of more experienced courtiers and underscoring that he had the ear of the Queen.

However, this promotion of Gascoigne is only a small part of the book's functions. It presents a collection of literary devices penned by a team of male courtiers and would-be courtiers, and Gascoigne is one of seven authors it identifies. It also attributes authorship to well-established courtly poets George Ferris and William Hunnis (the latter of whom served as Master of the Children of the Chapel Royal); London headmaster Richard Mulcaster; and three writers who were better known as an educator (John Badger), a historian (William Patten), and an actor (Harry Goldingham). The book does not clearly indicate that Gascoigne was the entertainment's lead writer, and he was not the book's primary agent. His name appeared in none of the preliminary matter; instead, the printer's note reveals Richard Jones as the principal agent behind its publication. Jones explains, "I haue with much trauayle and paine obtained the very true and perfect Copies, of all that were there presented and executed."[15] Because he describes his actions using the words "recover" and "obtain," it is unclear whether he gathered individual pageants from various sources, or whether he received the entire text from one source.[16] It is possible that Gascoigne or another writer amassed the devices and presented them to Jones as a package ready for printing, but Jones insists that he was the driving force behind its publication. He chose not to reference Gascoigne on the title page or in his long note, so he must not have published the book because he found

---

¹³ BL, MS Royal 18 A.xlviii, f. 3.   ¹⁴ Ibid., f. 2.
¹⁵ *Kenilworth Illustrated*, 52.   ¹⁶ Ibid., 52.

Gascoigne marketable.[17] He published it because he saw potential in its content to appeal to his readership.

In his printer's note, Jones makes clear that he published the book primarily for financial gain. He explains that he sought and compiled the devices presented at Kenilworth because they

> haue been sundrie tymes demaunded for, aswell at my handes, as also of other Printers, for that in deede, all studious and well disposed yong Gentlemen and others, were desyrous to be partakers of those pleasures by a profitable publication; I thought meete to trye by all meanes possible if I might recouer the true Copies of the same, to gratifye all suche as had requyred them at my handes, or might hereafter bee styrred with the lyke desire.[18]

Jones finds potential in this book to entertain and to instruct, and he implies both moral lessons for his readers and monetary reward for himself when he calls the book "profitable." Pleasurable reading, moral profit, and financial gain motivate the rest of Jones' catalog as well. His many short prefaces are self-aware marketing tools that explain to readers why they should buy his books. The words "profit" and "pleasure" appear in many of these prefaces, which tend to emphasize a book's instructional value or its delightful aspects, and his titles likewise advertise books as "profitable" and "pleasant." As several of his prefaces reveal, money was always Jones' central motivation, and he frequently appealed to readers' pocketbooks. At the beginning of *The Copy of a Letter* by Isabella Whitney (1567), he urges readers to "bye this same Booke... And you (I know) wyll say you haue / bestowed your mony well."[19] The low cost of *A Handefull of Pleasant Delites* (1584) makes it a great value: "Doubt not to buy this pretie Booke, / the price is not so deare."[20] Jones is particularly forthright about his aims in a preface to *Brittons Bovvre of Delights* (1591): "I am (onely) the Printer of them, chiefly to pleasure you, and partly to profit my selfe, if they prooue to your good liking: if otherwise, my hope is frustrate, my labour lost,

---

17 Sandra Logan also recognizes Jones' agency in publishing *Princelye Pleasures*, but she speculates that he published it because Gascoigne was so marketable (*Text/Events*, 106–10). Although Logan argues that we should understand the text's meaning "as emanating more from the printer, Richard Jhones, than the poet," she mainly analyzes how it represents Gascoigne's authorship, concluding that it "becomes less an account of the event and more an account of the poetic project of Gascoigne" (106, 133).

18 *Kenilworth Illustrated*, 52. Similar claims appear in later printed entertainment as well; cf. the preface to *A Relation of the Late Royall Entertainment Given by the Right Honorable the Lord Knovvles, at Cawsome-House neere Redding* (London, 1613; *STC* 4545): "as much as this late Entertainment hath beene much desired in writing, both of such as were present at the performance thereof, as also of many which are yet strangers both to the busines and place" (sig. A2r).

19 Isabella Whitney, *The Copy of a Letter* (London, 1567; *STC* 25439), sig. A1v.

20 *A Handefull of Pleasant Delites* (London, 1584; *STC* 21105), sig. A1v.

and all my cost is cast away."²¹ Jones did not write as directly of money in the Kenilworth book, but his focus on profit clearly guided his choice to publish it. The entertainment must have been marketable, popular, and profitable, as it appeared in various editions of at least four formats that emphasize its timeliness or lasting value.

In deciding to publish *Princelye Pleasures*, Jones drew from a few precedents but offered something new: an entertainment pamphlet that focused on pageantry scripts. *The Pastime of the Progresse*, which appeared before it, would have demonstated readerly interest in Elizabeth's travel. Jones provides our only evidence of this book. His preface mentions "a Report thereof lately imprinted by the name of the Pastime of the Progresse: which (in deede) doth nothing touche the particularitie of euerye commendable action, but generally reherseth hir Maiesties cheereful entertainement in all places where shee passed: togither with the exceeding ioye that her subiects had to see hir."²² According to Jones, this book provided an overview of Elizabeth's progress but lacked specific details or scripts of the Kenilworth pageantry. Earlier books had described accounts of royal processions. *The Noble Tryumphaunt Coronacyon of Quene Anne Wyfe vnto the Moost Noble Kynge Henry the viij* (1533) is a nine-page prose description of Anne's coronation. Its format differs substantially from the compilation of songs and pageantry verse in *Princelye Pleasures*. Richard Mulcaster's book of Elizabeth's coronation festivities, entitled *The Passage of Our Most Drad Soueraigne Lady Quene Elyzabeth through the Citie of London to Westminster the Daye Before Her Coronacion* (1558), appears in format more like later country house pamphlets because it provides lengthy narratives of the event combined with verses from the pageantry.²³ But as a commissioned piece of royal propaganda, Mulcaster's text focuses almost exclusively on Elizabeth.²⁴ In *Princelye Pleasures*, Jones deviated from these precedents when he fashioned the book not as narrative news or as royal propaganda, but as an elite literary text in the style of a poetry collection and in line with his own specializations.

Jones identifies the literary devices as the entertainment's primary appeal to his readers. He explains that *The Pastime of the Progresse* "made verye

---

²¹ Nicholas Breton, *Brittons Bovvre of Delights Contayning Many, Most Delectable and Fine Deuices, of Rare Epitaphes, Pleasant Poems, Pastorals and Sonets* (London, 1591; *STC* 3633).

²² *Kenilworth Illustrated*, 52.

²³ Mulcaster's book was printed in two editions in 1558, and it is unclear which came first. I give the title of *STC* 7590; the other edition is *STC* 7591.

²⁴ William Leahy briefly outlines the evidence that Mulcaster was paid by the Crown to produce this pamphlet, which appeared just nine days after the procession. See *Elizabethan Triumphal Processions* (Aldershot: Ashgate, 2005), 60–1.

many the more desirous to haue this perfect Copy: for that it plainlye doth
set downe euery thing as it was in deede presented."[25] He suggests that early
news of the event was so popular that he already had a wide readership
hungry for more. He expects that his readers will value accuracy and breadth
and therefore imagines this book functioning somewhat as news. It offers
more and better information than the earlier publication, including "the
very true and perfect Copies" of performed pageantry and "one Moral and
gallant Deuyce, which neuer came to execution, although it were often in a
readinesse."[26] At the same time, the preface repeatedly underscores that the
text is a literary one. It is a "true" copy not because it captures all the sights
and sounds of a current event, but because it provides the most complete
script of the literary devices, including those that were not performed.
It is these devices, the "sundry pleasaunt and Poeticall inuentions," that
Jones claims his readers sought.[27] The book's title page likewise indicates
that while Jones valued the text's timeliness as a recent event, he marketed
it primarily as literature. The full title reads: *The Princelye Pleasures, at
the Courte at Kenelwoorth. That is to Saye. The Copies of All Such Verses,
Proses, or Poeticall Inuentions, and Other Deuices of Pleasure, as Were There
Deuised, and Presented, by Sundry Gentlemen, before the Qvenes Maiestie: in
the Yeare 1575.*[28] The title advertises the performance's location and royal
audience, but it does not lead with the name of any one writer or the
authority of its host, Robert Dudley, the Earl of Leicester. Instead, the title
presents the text as a collection of verse and prose, highlights its function
as pleasurable reading, and identifies it as courtly literature composed by
gentlemen.

Jones is often remembered for his prolific publishing of ballads and other
popular matter. R. B. McKerrow identifies his publications as mostly "of a
popular character," and Alexandra Halasz estimates that at least 75 percent
of his catalog consists of ballads, pamphlets, and small books.[29] But, as
Kirk Melnikoff's revisionist examination reveals, Jones began to specialize
in more elite literature as his career progressed. While ballads were a staple
of his early business, he became significantly involved with the more elite
markets for poetry collections, chivalric literature, and courtesy manuals

---

[25] *Kenilworth Illustrated*, 52.   [26] Ibid., 52.   [27] Ibid., 52.   [28] Ibid., 52.

[29] R. B. McKerrow, ed., *A Dictionary of Printers and Booksellers in England, Scotland and Ireland,
and of Foreign Printers of English Books 1557–1640* (London: Bibliographical Society, 1910), 159;
Alexandra Halasz, *The Marketplace of Print: Pamphlets and the Public Sphere in Early Modern
England* (Cambridge University Press, 1997), 26. Jones' extensive catalog also included a good deal
of standard fare, such as translations of the Bible, prayers and sermons, sensational news reports,
books of religious instruction, and domestic manuals.

starting in the middle of the 1570s.[30] During and after this time period, several of Jones' prefaces to conduct books and literary texts identify him as a gentlemen's publisher. The title pages and prefaces to *Cyuile and Vncyuile Life* (1579), *Brittons Bovvre of Delights* (1591), *Pierce Penilesse His Supplication to the Diuell* (1592), *The Arbor of Amorous Deuices* (1597), and *Phillis and Flora* (1598) address "the Gentlemen Readers"; declare the contents "fit to bee read" by and "acceptable" to gentlemen; and depict Jones as a publisher who strives to please this particular demographic.[31]

Jones' preface to the Kenilworth book, published right at his turn in focus from more popular materials to more elite markets, targets both this gendered, genteel readership and a wider audience. He chose to publish *Princelye Pleasures* in octavo. Because octavos were more likely than quartos to be bound for preservation in personal libraries, Arthur F. Marotti suggests that octavo books may have carried more prestige than their quarto counterparts.[32] Jones' preface fashions him primarily as a publisher for "studious and well disposed yong Gentlemen," but he adds that the book also serves "others" who hoped to experience its delights vicariously.[33] This approach is a hallmark of Jones' publications in the 1570s and 1580s. His printer's note to a conduct book published the same year, Thomas Twyne's *The Schoolemaster, or Teacher of Table Philosophie*, says it will instruct and please people of "al estates," both "hie" and "low": "What so you be, or where you do soiourne / This pleasant pithy booke wyll surely serue your turne."[34] Jones advertises a book printed the following year to "younge Gentlemen and others," and he insists that *The Treasurie of Commodious Conceites* (1584) has something to teach housewives of all ranks, "As well the Gentles of degree, as eke the meaner sort."[35] Similarly, when placed

---

[30] Kirk Melnikoff, "Jones's Pen and Marlowe's Socks: Richard Jones, Print Culture, and the Beginnings of English Dramatic Literature" in *Studies in Philology* 102.2 (2005): 184–209. About one-third of Jones' publications were literary, and many of these books appear later in his career. See also Melnikoff, "Richard Jones (fl. 1564–1613): Elizabethan Printer, Bookseller and Publisher" in *Analytical and Enumerative Bibliography* 12 (2001): 156–7.

[31] *Cyuile and Vncyuile Life a Discourse Very Profitable, Pleasant, and Fit to Bee Read of All Nobilitie and Gentlemen* (London, 1579; *STC* 15589.5); Nicholas Breton, *Brittons Bovvre of Delights* (London, 1591; *STC* 3633); Thomas Nash, *Pierce Penilesse His Supplication to the Diuell* (London, 1592; *STC* 18371); *The Arbor of Amorous Deuices VVherin, Young Gentlemen May Reade Many Plesant Fancies, and Fine Deuises* (London, 1597; *STC* 3631); *Phillis and Flora* (London, 1598; *STC* 19880).

[32] Arthur F. Marotti, *Manuscript, Print, and the English Renaissance Lyric* (Ithaca: Cornell University Press, 1995), 288.

[33] *Kenilworth Illustrated*, 52.

[34] Thomas Twyne, *The Schoolemaster, or Teacher of Table Philosophie* (London, 1576; *STC* 24411), sig. A2r–A2v.

[35] *The Covrte of Ciuill Courtesie* (London, 1577; *STC* 21134.5); *The Treasurie of Commodious Conceites* (London, 1584; *STC* 19426), sig. A1v.

in context with Jones' other publications, *Princelye Pleasures* offers diverse potential reading experiences to multiple types of readers. It could serve as a literary keepsake for those who attended the progress or access to court pageantry for a literate public of lower ranks.

It especially taps into an emerging area of expertise for Jones: the poetry collection. The language on the title page of *Princelye Pleasures* mimics that of poetry anthologies published by Jones and others. Examples include *The Paradyse of Daynty Deuises Aptly Furnished, with Sundry Pithie and Learned Inuentions: Deuised and Written for the Most Part, by M. Edwards, Sometimes of her Maiesties Chappel: the Rest, by Sundry Learned Gentlemen, Both of Honour, and Woorshippe* (1576), which Jones printed for another publisher; collections of Nicholas Breton's verse published by Jones; Gascoigne's *A Hundreth Sundrie Flowres Bounde Vp in One Small Poesie* (1573), which includes the "diuers excellent deuises of sundry Gentlemen"; and many later books.[36] Like a poetic miscellany, the Kenilworth book identifies the author of each device following that text. The book's portable octavo format is also consistent with collections of lyric poetry and other devices.[37] In 1576, Jones was just beginning to establish himself as a publisher of collected vernacular poetry; from 1573 to 1597, he would print at least eleven collections and enter three more in the Stationers' Register.[38] *Princelye Pleasures* helped him carve out that specialty.

Jones' emphasis on the literary aspects of the Kenilworth performance becomes especially apparent when compared to Langham's *Letter*. The two books reveal radically different choices about which parts of the performance were engaging and noteworthy. Whereas *Princely Pleasures* provides scripts of the pageants penned by court poets and hopeful courtiers, *A Letter* gives prominence to the country shows and non-pageantry festivities: bear-baiting, fireworks, hunting, banquets, gifts, music, and dancing. Langham describes individual pageants only in vague terms, such as "a proper poezi in English ryme and meter."[39] He copies two poems, a Latin verse hanging over the castle entrance at Elizabeth's arrival, and lyrics to one song he managed to obtain. His lack of transcriptions of other verse appears to derive from a combination of lack of access and interest in other elements of the performance. Langham addressed the letter to mercer Humphrey Martin, who did not attend the event. Because he aims to

---

[36] *The Paradyse of Daynty Deuises* (London, 1576; *STC* 7516); Nicholas Breton, *A Floorish Vpon Fancie* (London, 1577; *STC* 3654); George Gascoigne, *A Hundreth Sundrie Flowres* (London, 1573; *STC* 11635).
[37] Marotti, *Manuscript*, 287–8.   [38] Melnikoff, "Jones's Pen," 195–6.
[39] Robert Langham, *A Letter*, sig. B3v.

recreate the performance for Martin, he takes care to explain the audience's and his own reactions to individual moments. For example, as he describes the Savage Man played by Gascoigne, he notes,

> this Sauage for the more submission brake his tree a sunder, kest the top from him, it had allmost light vpon her highnes horshed: whereat he startld and the gentlman mooch dismayd. See the benignitee of the Prins, az the foot men lookt well too the hors, and he of generozitee soon callmd of himself, no hurt no hurt quod her highnes. Which woords I promis yoo we wear all glad too heeer, and took them too be the best part of the play.[40]

As the account of one spectator, *A Letter* reveals Langham's prejudices, preferences, and agendas – especially his desire to represent the performance as a grand success for Leicester, from whom he sought continued patronage.[41] *A Letter* never identifies its publisher, but whoever served that role valued Langham's text for the news it provided about a popular current event. By contrast, Jones' publication offers only short narrative explanations and focuses mainly on pageantry verse. Instead of an eyewitness account, it provides a behind-the-scenes look at the invention of literary devices, as it adopts the perspective of the courtiers and aspiring poets who devised the pageantry.

Princelye Pleasures privileges intention over actual performance. As a comparison to Langham's *Letter* highlights, more of Jones' book is about pageants that were not performed than about what really happened during Elizabeth's visit. The narrator spends a good deal of time describing a planned but unperformed water skirmish between Sir Bruce and Captain Cox. He explains,

> surely if it had bene executed according to the first inuention, it had bene a gallant shewe... This had not onely bene a more apt introduction to [the Lady of the Lake's] deliuerie, but also the skirmish by night woulde haue bene both very strange and gallant: and thereupon her Maiestie might haue taken good occasion to haue gone in her barge vpon the water, for the better executing of her deliuerie.[42]

The narrator's inclusion of this device does not promote Gascoigne or any other individual writer, but instead gives the reader insight into an alternative performance that he claims would have been more pleasing and unified than the actual event. After a relatively long description of the skirmish that did not happen, the narrator provides this sentence:

---

[40] Ibid., sig. C3v–C4r.   [41] See Goldring, "A Mercer," 262.

[42] *Kenilworth Illustrated*, 62–3. For the same passage in "A Briefe Rehearsall" in *The VVhole Woorkes*, see sig. BIV–B2r.

"And nowe you haue asmuch as I could recouer hitherto of the deuises executed there: the countrie shewe excepted, and the merry marriage: the which were so plaine as needeth no further explication."[43] Langham's *Letter*, by contrast, devotes several pages to detailed descriptions of these fascinating shows, which Jones evidently found irrelevant to his project and unappealing to his intended readers: those who considered themselves elite or, more likely, those with elite ambitions who desired an insider experience.

By including the unperformed Zabeta pageant, Jones especially crafted *Princelye Pleasures* as court gossip for those with elite ambition. Half of the book is dedicated to the Zabeta script, the inclusion of which changes the tenor and implications of the devices that came before. The narrator claims that the pageant was not performed because of "seasonable weather," which might genuinely have been the case; rainy weather interfered with many plans on progress.[44] Because the pageant is a fairly bold argument for royal marriage, some scholars have speculated that Elizabeth censored it in performance.[45] Its subsequent publication could have appeared defiant and been a counterproductive move for Gascoigne, who sought her favor, but the unperformed pageant does what all country house entertainments do: advise the Queen. After Diana and Mercury endorse celibacy, Iris brings a message from Juno that argues more forcefully for marriage than any earlier character has for virginity. She explains "How necessarie were / for worthy Queenes to wed"; urges Elizabeth that her "Countrey craues consent"; proposes that Elizabeth's virginity has caused only hardships; and concludes that "A world of wealth at wil, / you hencefoorth shall enioy: / In wedded state."[46] The argument at the beginning of the pageant clarifies that this is no unresolved debate; it imagines the final speech by Iris "Perswading the Queenes Maiestie that she be not caryed away with *Mercuries* filed speach, nor *Dyanaes* faire words, but that she consider all things by the proofe, and then shee shall finde much greater cause to followe *Iuno* than *Dyana*."[47] The presence of this pageant in *Princelye Pleasures* accentuates more subtle references to women's weakness and challenges to female authority in earlier episodes. By including multiple unperformed devices, Jones constructs not an accurate narrative of a current event, but a literary text with a life and meaning of its own. Although Jones claims that the Zabeta pageant was

---

43 *Kenilworth Illustrated*, 63; "A Briefe Rehearsall," sig. B2r.
44 *Kenilworth Illustrated*, 73; "A Briefe Rehearsall," sig. C2v.
45 See, e.g., Wall, *Imprint of Gender*, 134. Alternately, Heaton suggests in *Writing and Reading* that Leicester canceled it for fear of its offending Elizabeth (28).
46 *Kenilworth Illustrated*, 73; "A Briefe Rehearsall," sig. C2r–C2v.
47 *Kenilworth Illustrated*, 64; "A Briefe Rehearsall," sig. B2v.

"prepared and redy" for performance, it functions in print similarly to closet drama.[48] Jones presents unperformed pageants as intellectually and aesthetically superior to some festivities actually performed, and he offers his readers a glimpse into a seemingly private, elite literary culture that would normally be closed to them.[49]

Like Jones, bookseller Thomas Cadman regarded printed country house entertainment as literature with lasting value. He chose to publish *The Queenes Maiesties Entertainement at VVoodstock* (1585) ten years after the performance. An account of a decade-old event might seem outdated, but Cadman identified its potential to speak to the political moment of the mid-1580s. In 1575, the Woodstock performance would have advanced Sir Henry Lee's ambitions, with its portraits of love-struck men serving as metaphors for Lee's relationship with Elizabeth, and scholars have connected its emphasis on romantic love to the question of Elizabeth's own marriage prospects in the mid-1570s.[50] But when the political context changes ten years later, so do our available interpretations of the text. The personal politics of the performance are no longer especially relevant, and although the only known copy of this book is missing its title page and first signature, the rest of the text does not mention Lee.[51] Instead, Cadman's book engages with a more precarious time of heightened religious wars on the Continent and closer to home. Irish Catholics had revolted against Elizabeth during the Second Desmond Rebellion in 1579–83; Elizabeth and her advisors had Mary, Queen of Scots executed in early February 1585; the French wars of religion had evolved into open warfare; and Anglo–Spanish tensions had come to a head.[52] When placed in this context, the Woodstock book takes on new meaning in a time of warfare and promotes an ideal behind many of Cadman's publications: the willingness to sacrifice personal desires for the good of one's country.

Cadman was a less prolific publisher than Jones. Although one 1574 book is attributed to him, he was otherwise active for only six years (1584–9), during which time he published or sold about thirty books.[53] The vast majority of his catalog focuses on war, Spain, or courtly literature. He published a handful of medical and instructional texts that

---

[48] *Kenilworth Illustrated*, 73; "A Briefe Rehearsall," sig. C2v.

[49] Marta Straznicky describes female-authored closet drama in similar terms in *Privacy, Playreading, and Women's Closet Drama, 1550–1700* (Cambridge University Press, 2004), 1–18.

[50] See Chapter 2 for analysis of the performance's use of Petrarchan rhetoric.

[51] The title *The Queenes Maiesties Entertainement at VVoodstock* comes from a running header, and the text begins in the middle of a sentence at signature B1r.

[52] See, e.g., Mark Charles Fissel, *English Warfare 1511–1642* (London: Routledge, 2001); Paul E. J. Hammer, *Elizabeth's Wars: War, Government, and Society in Tudor England, 1544–1604* (Basingstoke: Palgrave, 2003).

[53] *STC*, 3:36.

were relevant to wartime, such as *The Schoole of Horsmanship* (1585), *A Most Excellent and Compendious Method of Curing Woundes* (1588), and *A Prooued Practise for All Young Chirurgians, Concerning Burnings with Gunpowder* (1588) – the last of which explains on its title page that the author wanted it printed "for the benefyte of his country."[54] Cadman published William Warner's *Albions England* (1586), a long patriotic poem that chronicles England's history, and many of his publications describe and glorify England as a nation, especially in contrast to Spain.[55] Translations from French and Spanish aim to educate Cadman's readers about the Continental wars and Spanish imperialism at a time of heightened Anglo–Spanish tension.[56]

In fact, because many of Cadman's publications together serve as a call to arms, we might accurately describe him as a wartime propagandist. Thomas Churchyard's *A Scourge for Rebels* (1584), which responds to the recent "troubles of Ireland," asks these questions: "Is there any labour more laudable, seruice more famous, life more toilesome, or exercises more noble, then stil to be busied for the preseruation of a Prince and countrie? . . . Deserues not that man an euerlasting renowme, that refuseth no iourney, shuns no seruice, nor auoydes no action to doe his countrie good?"[57] Three years later, Cadman published an anonymous pamphlet with even stronger language. Its full title reads: *An Oration Militarie to All Naturall Englishmen, Whether Protestants, or Otherwise in Religion Affected, to Moue Resolution in These Dangerous Times Herein Is Expressed the Delight of Libertie, and the Tyrannie of the Enemie: With a Praier Both Pithie and Necessarie Written by a Zealous Affected Subiect* (1588). Addressing his "worthy Countrymen," the writer aims "to animate each of you, (if it may be) to more resolution."[58] He speaks of the wars in France and the Low Countries and asks his readers to "consider the thraldome of your neighbours subiected to the tyranie of Spanish gouernment, and the double dealing of the Popes feined holines."[59] If the English do not actively fight Spanish forces, he predicts they will see "Religion defaced, our Countrie ruinated, our Souereigne Princesse iniured, our wiues and virgins defiled, our infants tost on pikes, and our

---

[54] Christopher Clifford, *The Schoole of Horsmanship* (London, 1585; *STC* 5415); Franciscus Arcaeus, *A Most Excellent and Compendious Method of Curing Woundes* (London, 1588; *STC* 723); William Clowes, *A Prooued Practise for All Young Chirurgians, Concerning Burnings with Gunpowder* (London, 1588; *STC* 5444).

[55] William Warner, *Albions England* (London, 1586; *STC* 25079).

[56] *A Declaration Exhibited to the French King* (London, 1587; *STC* 13100); *The French Kinges Declaration* (London, 1589; *STC* 13098.5); Juan Gonzalez de Mendoz, *New Mexico. Otherwise, The Voiage of Anthony of Espeio* (London, 1586; *STC* 18487).

[57] Thomas Churchyard, *A Scourge for Rebels* (London, 1584; *STC* 5255), sig. A4v.

[58] *An Oration Militarie* (London, 1588; *STC* 18836.5), sig. A2r.   [59] Ibid., sig. A2v.

goods the greedie Spaniardes spoyle. Take courage Countreymen, and if they come, resolue on victorie or death: if they come not, determine some of you to braue the cowardes at their doores."[60] As these publications defend violent means of taming Irish rebels and endorse war against Catholic Spain, they define England as an increasingly powerful Protestant force. In 1589, Cadman published two political tracts that make this perspective even more explicit: one extols the virtues of the English Navy and the other condemns the "Romish holie League" for its wickedness.[61]

At the same time, Cadman shows substantial interest in court plays and prose romance, and this second specialty overlaps in interesting ways with his promotion of wartime pamphleteering. Cadman published several works by John Lyly and Robert Greene, including Greene's romances *Penelopes VVeb* (1587) and *Pandosto* (1588), along with his foray into war propaganda, *The Spanish Masquerado* (1589).[62] Because Greene's romances are addressed to female readers, it is possible that Cadman was cultivating a female readership as well as the male one for which we assume he published calls to arms. Of his six extant 1584 publications, three are editions of Lyly's *Campaspe* and two are Lyly's *Sapho and Phao*, all identified on their title pages as "played before the Queenes Maiestie."[63] Just as Cadman's pamphlets idealize men who surrender their personal lives for the country's good, both Lyly plays emphasize that monarchs must often sacrifice personal happiness and love in favor of fulfilling the demands of public office. This collection of texts reveals interest in gender, war, and royalty, and it imagines Elizabeth as a Virgin Queen and an international military leader rather than as a marriageable young woman. Above all, many of Cadman's publications share endorsement of personal sacrifice for the greater good.

Cadman's Woodstock text was not the first time all of these particular pageants appeared in print. Six years earlier, Henry Denham published a version of the speech delivered by Hemetes the hermit. This pageant was appended to Abraham Fleming's English translation of Synesius' *A Paradoxe, Prouing by Reason and Example, That Baldnesse Is Much Better Than Bushie Haire* (1579).[64] The title page identifies the Hemetes text as

---

[60] Ibid., sig. A3v.

[61] *An Answer to the Vntrvthes, Pvblished and Printed in Spaine, in Glorie of Their Svpposed Victorie Atchieued against Our English Navie* (London, 1589; *STC* 17132); *The Birth, Purpose, and Mortall VVound of the Romish Holie League* (London, 1589; *STC* 15106).

[62] Robert Greene, *Penelopes VVeb* (London, 1587; *STC* 12293); Greene, *Pandosto* (London, 1588: *STC* 12285); Greene, *The Spanish Masquerade* (London, 1589; *STC* 12309).

[63] *STC* 17047.5, 17048, 17048a, 17086, and 17086.5. The sixth publication is *A Scourge for Rebels*.

[64] *A Paradoxe* (London, 1579; *STC* 23603).

"pronounced before the Queenes Maiestie" and "Newly recognised both in Latine and Englishe" by Fleming. Fleming introduces *Paradoxe* at some length in a prefatory note, and then attaches the Hemetes text without further comment. These two texts, very different in content, are linked because they were translated by the same man around the same time. Fleming's Hemetes text appears to be taken from Gascoigne's presentation manuscript (or one derived from the same source). It includes English and Latin translations that vary only slightly from the original, and it makes no mention of Woodstock, Lee, or Gascoigne. Although Fleming identifies the text as performed before Elizabeth, he otherwise removes it from its original context and presents it as light, pleasurable reading. In his translating and editing, Fleming often sought to make international and scholarly texts accessible to a wider audience, and he apparently identified the Hemetes pageant as worth disseminating more widely than Gascoigne's presentation manuscript enabled.[65]

Cadman's version is more extensive. In addition to the Hemetes tale, it includes verses delivered by the Fairy Queen, a lottery for the ladies in attendance, and a romance play about Princess Caudina. It appears to derive not from Fleming's or Gascoigne's texts, but from an eyewitness letter like Langham's. The Woodstock narrator writes to a single person, "good sir," whom he addresses as a superior (sig. c2r). He assures his audience that this is no trifling text, but a deeply rewarding one for a learned reader: "you shoulde finde no lesse hidden then vttered, and no less vttered then shoulde deserue a double reading ouer, euen of those (with whom I finde you a companion) that haue disposed their houres to the study of great matters" (sig. B1r). Unsurprisingly, this book does not emphasize its topicality and mentions no dates in its text. It is styled more as a literary work than as a news pamphlet. On the page, it presents a hodgepodge of literary kinds: some parts appear with speech prefixes as drama or dialogue, other sections are divided into lines of verse, and still others are printed in blocks of text as prose narrative. *Princelye Pleasures* and Sidney's "Lady of May" share this physical appearance. Its lengthy stage directions, which describe the action and setting, are usually in italics to differentiate the eyewitness narration from the performance script. These directions are written in both past and present tense; the combination of tenses gives the reader a sense of immediacy, as if the performance is currently happening. Although the text could have served as historical record, that is not its primary function.

---

[65] For more on Fleming's career, see especially Clare Painting-Stubbs, "Abraham Fleming: Elizabethan Maker of Indexes and 'Tables'" in *The Indexer* 29.3 (2011): 109–13; Sarah C. Dodson, "Abraham Fleming, Writer and Editor" in *University of Texas Studies in English* 34 (1955): 51–66.

Instead, its present-tense descriptions and layout emphasize its literary qualities. Because Cadman published the entertainment during a period of few progresses and no surviving country house entertainments, it might have appealed to an audience who desired more courtly performances than were currently happening.

Without a title page or printer's note, we cannot be sure how Cadman marketed the Woodstock entertainment, but the surviving text presents a nationalistic perspective. Together, the several pageants offer a positive view of England in an uncertain, unstable time. The Hemetes tale calls England "a countrie of most peace" and "a place, where men were most strong, women most fayre, the countrey most fertile, the people most wealthy, the gouernment most iust, and the Princes most worthy" (sig. B2v). A later pageant calls England "this famous realme" and says that Elizabeth's name is "knowne to all mens eares" (sig. D3r–D3v). When the Fairy Queen says of Elizabeth, "you haue no mate," it might remind us that she is the Virgin Queen, but, more likely, it declares her superiority over pretenders to the English throne and the Catholic monarchs with whom she was at war:

> your face, your grace, your gouernment of state,
> your passing sprite whereby your same is blowen:
> doe knowe by certein skill you haue no mate:
> and that no man throughout the worlde hath seene
> a prince that may compare with th' English Queene.
>
> (sig. C1r)

The Woodstock text also presents Elizabeth as a peacemaker who will end the religious wars in a satisfying way. It opens with a scene of knights fighting, and Hemetes instructs them to stop because "vyolence must giue place to vertue" (sig. B1r). Later the Fairy Queen speaks of observing Elizabeth's transformative love and "gratious speech appeasing cruell fighte" (sig. C1r). In 1585, it would have been imperative to represent Elizabeth as a monarch who would keep her country safe.

Meanwhile, several lines encourage sacrifice on behalf of one's country. Hemetes notes that "nothing notable is woon without difficulty" (sig. B4r), and the final pageant is all about this point. When Princess Caudina runs away to find her true love Contarenus, she does not overcome obstacles to marry her chosen suitor, as we might expect from a dramatic comedy; instead she begrudgingly follows her father's wishes and sacrifices that personal desire for the good of her country. Although Contarenus loves Caudina dearly, he concludes: "You must regard the common weales good plight, / and seeke the whole not onely one to saue," and Caudina responds:

"Well sith he yeelds which hath most right in me, / Ah Countries good I yeeld my selfe to thee" (sig. F3v–F4r). During war time and in context with Cadman's other publications, this play would emphasize sacrifice for England's good. The book is not explicitly about religion and never mentions Spain, but in 1585 its praise of England's peaceful government and Elizabeth's superiority compared to other monarchs would have hinted at Anglo–Spanish relations and the religious wars. The text ends with a prayer for the land "where vertuous Queene doth stately scepter sway" and a character who vows to spread the news of Elizabeth's glory: "As for my selfe I wil spread farre and neere, / for princely prayse that she deserueth best" (sig. G3r). This text was not necessarily designed as war propaganda, but in Cadman's bookshop it could become a call to broaden Elizabeth's fame and to defend against Spanish attack.

As early examples, the printed Kenilworth and Woodstock books teach us a great deal about printed country house entertainment texts. Jones' preface and career underscore that monetary profit was a central motivation behind entertainment publication and that publishers expected these books to appeal to elite and popular markets. As Jones targeted this wide readership, he presented his book somewhat as sought-after news but chiefly as literature that would generate pleasure and moral benefit. Cadman followed his lead and published devices ten years removed from their original performance because they spoke to the current political situation. Both examples reveal that these publishers chose to finance and print Elizabethan country house entertainment because they identified its appeal to audiences of political pamphlets and lyric verse. Wendy Wall has proposed that Gascoigne's 1587 *VVhole Woorkes* and Sidney's 1598 *Arcadia* elevated pageantry to literature when they printed country house entertainments as part of an author's complete works, but Jones and Cadman saw its potential function as literature earlier than that.[66] *Princelye Pleasures* and the Woodstock pamphlet reveal that stationers valued the scripts and descriptions of country house pageantry not only for their function as timely gossip, but also for their lasting value as literature.

Regional Publishing: Joseph Barnes and *Speeches Delivered*

Princelye Pleasures, *The Queenes Maiesties Entertainment at VVoodstocke*, and most other printed books of Elizabethan pageantry were published and sold in London. These books support Jean Wilson's argument that

---

[66] Wall, *Imprint of Gender*, 115.

printed entertainments allowed "the country as a whole" to learn about pageantry performed "where they could not view it," but a book of three 1592 entertainment texts entitled *Speeches Delivered to Her Maiestie This Last Progresse* provides an alternate view of their use value.[67] *Speeches Delivered* is unique among Elizabethan entertainment books for two reasons: it is the only example published outside London, and it is the only known printed collection of multiple Elizabethan great house pageants. It was published in 1592 by Oxford University printer Joseph Barnes, and it provides texts of three entertainments performed during that year's progress at Bisham Abbey in Berkshire, Sudeley Castle in Gloucestershire, and Rycote Park in Oxfordshire. When we examine these three entertainments alongside other country house shows, as Chapter 2 has demonstrated, we see that they engage in a debate with the rest of the genre about appropriate, gendered relationships between the Queen and her courtiers. However, the printed book downplays this aspect of the performances. As printed texts, they become less about gender roles and the personal politics of young people vying for employment and more about another issue with which the genre grapples: the relationship between geography and identity. Barnes' grouping of these specific entertainment texts, which were not the only progress performances in 1592, accentuates shared themes in their content, especially their endorsement of militant Protestantism and negotiation of conflicting ideologies about emerging nationalism.

The publisher's interpretation of these entertainments and their market value shapes our own. In a preface, Barnes announces that he "gathered" them of his own accord (sig. A1v). Because the word "gather" connotes the bringing together or compiling of disparate pieces into one collection, this language underscores Barnes' agency.[68] Although Barnes served as

---

[67] Wilson, *Entertainments for Elizabeth I*, 10. Three known copies of *Speeches Delivered* survive. Humphrey Dyson owned one in the seventeenth century that is currently held at the BL (shelf mark c.33.e7). I have been able to trace the ownership of the other two only to the late eighteenth and early nineteenth centuries. The copy at HEH (shelf mark 59209) was owned by Mark Masterman Sykes (1771–1823) and Richard Herber (1773–1833), and the Folger Shakespeare Library copy (shelf mark HH27) was owned by Robert Leicester Harmsworth (1870–1937).

[68] *OED*, "gather" *v.*, def. 3, 5. The word is used in the same manner as an entry in the Stationers' Register on September 20, 1578: "the enterteignement of the Quenes Maiestie in Suffolk and Norffolk; gathered by Thomas Churchyard" is licensed to Henry Bynneman (Edward Arber, ed., *Stationers' Register: A Transcript of the Registers of the Company of Stationers of London, 1554–1640, A.D* [1875; reprint, New York: Smith, 1950], 2.338). The entry identifies the entertainment's lead writer, Churchyard, as the agent who prepared the text. It is worth noting that, unlike country house entertainments, at least some civic entries were funded by the company that financed the pageantry rather than by a stationer. Tracey Hill makes this point about Lord Mayor's Shows in *Pageantry and Power: A Cultural History of the Early Modern Lord Mayor's Show, 1585–1639* (Manchester University Press, 2010), 214–69.

university printer, he made his own decisions about what to publish and, as was true of the Elizabethan printers at Cambridge, his publications were not strictly university texts.[69] As Harry Carter says of Barnes in *A History of the Oxford University Press*, "The business was his own and the profit or loss was his."[70] Barnes mainly chose publications by and for an educated male readership tied to the university or region. Like Jones and Cadman, Barnes was a businessman who sought to publish books that would sell. In a printer's note in 1585, Barnes asks Sir Walter Ralegh to be a patron of a "smal" and "pleasant" work; he explains, "It is commended to me by men of good iudgement and learning, and it will be the better commended hereafter if it may go out vnder your worships protection."[71] Barnes does not talk of money, but he implies financial motivation when he expresses his desire for the book to circulate widely with Ralegh's recommendation. He advertises support and interest in this book from learned men, whom he saw as his primary audience.

A survey of Barnes' career reveals his specializations in theological debate and local publication. During his tenure as printer to Oxford University from 1584 to 1617, his press produced more than 300 books, most of which have scholarly value or regional appeal, such as sermons and treatises composed by area preachers and Oxford-educated theologians, political and philosophical tracts, theses, academic drama, and lectures delivered at Oxford.[72] Barnes published numerous Latin texts and some Greek ones, and many of his books intervened in political and religious controversy. In the first two decades of his career, he published mostly religious tracts and sermons. Although his publications include several works by Continental Protestant scholars Zacharias Ursinus and Théodore de Bèze, the majority of his authors were Oxford men who advertise connections to the university and Oxfordshire, such as John Case, John Prime, John Chardon, Thomas Holland, and John Howson. Barnes' catalog is dominated by the work of these and a select few other local theologians known for their Protestant, often Calvinist, perspective. His authors typically sign their prefaces from university locations, such as "At Corpus Christi College in Oxford" or "From Exeter College in Oxford," and several write dedications to Oxford

---

[69] David McKitterick's survey of the careers of Thomas Thomas and John Legate reveals that both men needed to publish a wider range of books to survive financially. Although they had distinct priorities and preferences in the works they chose to publish, both produced several works by local authors or with local interest in the late Elizabethan period. See *A History of Cambridge University Press*. Vol. 1: *Printing and the Book Trade in Cambridge 1534–1698* (Cambridge University Press, 1992), 73–135; *STC*, 3:105, 3:168.

[70] Harry Carter, *A History of the Oxford University Press* (Oxford: Clarendon Press, 1975), 1:23.

[71] John Case, *The Praise of Mvsicke* (Oxford, 1586; *STC* 20184). Unlike Jones, Barnes rarely wrote printer's notes. In fact, this is the only example I have found besides *Speeches Delivered*.

[72] For a list of his publications, see *STC*, 3:14.

men or university patrons.[73] John King thanks Thomas Egerton for "your loue to our Vniversity," and Laurence Humphrey praises Leicester for being "a speciall Patrone of our Vniuersity."[74] Barnes also issued volumes of poetry with contributions from members of the university that memorialized or honored prominent figures, including a posthumous tribute to Philip Sidney in 1587, verses and addresses on the occasion of Queen Elizabeth's death in 1603, and a poetic celebration of the newly crowned King James in 1603.[75] He published sermons delivered at the university, the town of Oxford, or the surrounding area. David McKitterick suggests that some area authors sought Cambridge University printer Thomas Thomas out of convenience and perhaps as an alternative to the London trade, and the same may have been true of Barnes, who operated England's westernmost press.[76]

Several of his books' preliminaries and content suggest the existence of a somewhat fixed readership united through shared experiences and locality. The word "our" appears in many notes by Barnes' authors. John Prime writes to Thomas Cooper, the Bishop of Winchester, that his book is designed for "your Lordships countrimen and mine, the Cittizens of *Oxforde*."[77] When Prime identifies himself as writing "[h]ere before the towne" and labels "us" as "both Vniuersity and Towne," he envisions a group of readers and writers who share location.[78] Some preliminaries refer to other books published by Barnes and imply a relatively consistent readership. For example, Prime's preface to his 1585 sermons preached in Oxford references Thomas Bilson's *The True Difference betweene Christian Subiection and Vnchristian Rebellion*, which was published that same year by Barnes and which supports political resistance on the Continent.[79] Barnes also published Thomas Spark's *Ansvvere to Master*

---

73 There are too many examples to list in full. The two quoted here are John Rainolds, *A Sermon vpon Part of the Eighteenth Psalm* (Oxford, 1586; *STC* 20621), sig. A4r; and John Chardon, *A Sermon vpon Part of the Ninth Chapter of the Holy Gospel of Iesvs Christ According to S. Iohn* (Oxford, 1586; *STC* 5002).

74 John King, *Lectvres vpon Ionas* (Oxford, 1597; *STC* 14976), sig. *4v; Laurence Humphrey, *A View of the Romish Hydra and Monster* (Oxford, 1588; *STC* 13966), sig. *9r.

75 *Peplvs. Illvstrissimi Viri D. Philippi Sidnaei Svpremis Honoribvs Dicatvs* (Oxford, 1587; *STC* 22552); *Oxoniensis Academiae Funebre Officium in Memoriam Elisabethae Reginae* (Oxford, 1603; *STC* 19918); *Academaie Oxoniensis Pietas erga Serenissimvm et Potentissimvm Iacobvm Angliae Scotiae Franciae and Hiberniae Regem* (Oxford, 1603; *STC* 19019).

76 McKitterick, *A History of Cambridge University Press*, 1:86–7.

77 John Prime, *The Consolations of David, Breefly Applied to Queene Elizabeth in a Sermon Preached in Oxford the 17. of Nouember* (Oxford, 1588; *STC* 20368), sig. A2r.

78 Ibid., sig. A3v.

79 John Prime, *A Sermon Briefly Comparing the Estate of King Salomon and His Subiects Togither with the Condition of Queene Elizabeth and Her People* (Oxford, 1585; *STC* 20371); Thomas Bilson, *The True Difference betweene Christian Subiection and Vnchristian Rebellion* (Oxford, 1585; *STC* 3071).

Iohn de Albines (1591), which offers a line-by-line critique of de Albines' Catholic treatise.[80] These publications indicate that Barnes' audience consisted primarily of learned readers interested in political and theological debate. Late in Elizabeth's reign, Barnes published a group of texts that consider the morality of theatrical festivities. While Huw Roberts condemns "mischievious May-games" for promoting "fleshly lusts," printed sermons by Thomas Holland and John Howson defend royal festivals in response to recent attacks.[81] These books, which originated as sermons preached in Oxford, exemplify Barnes' interests in learned debates and local events.

Not all of Barnes' publications envision such a narrow readership consisting of local, educated men; some speak to a wider public. John Rider's Latin–English dictionary, for example, has the following full title: *Bibliotheca Scholastica. A Double Dictionarie, Penned for All Those That Would Haue within Short Space the Vse of the Latin Tongue, Either to Speake, or Write. Verie Profitable and Necessarie for Scholars, Courtiers, Lawyers and Their Clarkes, Apprentices of London, Travellers, Factors for Marchants, and Briefly for All Discontinuers within Her Majesties Realmes of England and Ireland.*[82] The book still has an Oxford connection; the title page identifies Rider as possessing a master of arts degree from Oxford University. As with this book, several examples from Barnes' catalog advertise regional connections but look beyond Oxford to national and international concerns.

In deciding to publish *Speeches Delivered*, Barnes must have recognized something in its content that would appeal to his readers' interests in international Protestantism, political debate, and books about the university and surrounding area. Additionally, country house entertainment texts had sold well in London the previous year. After the Queen visited Oxfordshire in 1592, Barnes may have hoped to capitalize on existing demand for the performance texts, as Jones claimed of the Kenilworth entertainment.[83] Besides *Speeches Delivered*, Barnes published only two other "speculative" books in the vernacular in 1592: Nicolas Breton's *The Pilgrimage to Paradise*

[80] Thomas Spark, *An Ansvvere to Master Iohn De Albines, Notable Discourse against Heresies (as His Frendes Call His Booke) Compiled by Thomas Spark Pastor of Blechley in the County of Buck.* (Oxford, 1591; *STC* 23019).

[81] Huw Roberts, *The Day of Hearing* (Oxford, 1600; *STC* 21089); Thomas Holland, *D. Elizabethae Dei Gratia Angliae Reginae a Sermon Preached in Pavls Chvrch in London the 17. of November* (Oxford, 1599; *STC* 13596.5); John Howson, *A Sermon Preached at St. Maries in Oxford, in Defence of the Festivities of the Church of England, and Namely That of Her Maiesties Coronation* (Oxford, 1602; *STC* 13884).

[82] *Bibliotheca Scholastica* (Oxford, 1588; *STC* 21031.5).

[83] The Cowdray and Elvetham books of 1591 were both popular enough to be reprinted the same year; see Chapter 5 for more. *Speeches Delivered* was apparently not reprinted after its initial run.

and Thomas Churchyard's *A Handefvl of Gladsome Verses, Giuen to the Queenes Maiesty at Woodstocke this Prograce*.[84] These books and their preliminaries again underscore Barnes' role as a publisher of elite, regional material. *The Pilgrimage to Paradise* is a religious allegory about salvation. Its author was an amateur courtly poet, and unlike almost of all Barnes' other authors, Breton had no clear ties to Oxford.[85] Through this publication, he tried to establish himself as a learned writer who would appeal to Barnes' readership. Breton's prefatory note, "To the Gentlemen studients and Scholers of Oxforde," humbly introduces his "simple fruites" and hopes for their "vndeserued fauours."[86] The other preliminaries, an English note by John Case and Latin verses by William Gager, demonstrate the endorsement of established Oxfordians also published by Barnes. As they vouch for the newcomer, they legitimize the book's relevance to Barnes' readers. Churchyard's book presents a collection of commendatory verses handed to Elizabeth during her progress visit to Woodstock in Oxfordshire, and Churchyard's apology represents it as a haphazard collection by a self-effacing writer who cannot compete with "learned" poets: "so happing on a few voluntary rimes I haue as it were by good fortune, peeced or compounded vp a booke."[87] These prefaces by Churchyard and Breton indicate that Barnes had a reputation as a publisher of learned material, which we would expect from a university printer.

Several of Barnes' Latin and Greek publications that year also commemorate the progress as an important local event. In one book, John Sanford describes in Latin verse the banquet during Elizabeth's visit on September 22, 1592 to Magdalen College, Oxford.[88] Barnes also published two academic plays by Gager, who helped oversee performances for the visit. Gager's tragicomedy *Ulysses Redux* includes an epilogue by Momus that defends academic drama. It satirizes John Rainolds, a Puritan leader in Oxford and an author published by Barnes on multiple occasions, who had

---

[84] Nicolas Breton, *The Pilgrimage to Paradise* (Oxford, 1592; *STC* 3683); Thomas Churchyard, *A Handefvl of Gladsome Verses* (Oxford, 1592; *STC* 5237). I use "speculative" as Alan B. Farmer and Zachary Lesser do, to designate publications printed for profit by stationers who saw them as worthwhile investments. See "The Popularity of Playbooks Revisited" in *Shakespeare Quarterly* 56.1 (2005): 1–32. In 1592, Barnes also printed Hereford church visitation articles (*STC* 10215.5), a non-speculative publication that he would have printed on demand.

[85] Breton's prefatory note to the students and scholars at the university reveals that he considered himself an outsider without academic credentials. At this time, Breton was trying to build his reputation as a courtly poet; the "Phillidon and Coridon" song in the Elvetham entertainment (1591) is attributed to him. Even though *The Pilgrimage to Paradise* was also sold in London and therefore sought a wider audience, the prefatory material advertises it primarily to an educated Oxford readership.

[86] *The Pilgrimage to Paradise*, sig. *3r.   [87] *A Handefvl of Gladsome Verses*, sig. A2v.

[88] John Sanford, *Appolinis et Musarum* (Oxford, 1592; *STC* 21733).

denounced university plays as immoral.[89] Barnes pieced together regional records of the 1592 progress that showcase timely debates about religion and politics as they celebrate the royal visit. Like Barnes' other publications, *Speeches Delivered* targeted an audience largely consisting of well-educated men, and its inclusion in Barnes' catalog highlights its debates about international politics and definitions of English cultural identity.

In his printer's note to *Speeches Delivered*, Barnes interprets its significance narrowly as a valuable piece of news about the recent progress, and he legitimizes it as masculine and elite. His short preface resembles Churchyard's apology in its guise of humility and emphasis on random creation: "I Gathered these copies in loose papers I know not how imperfect, therefore must I craue a double pardon; of him that penned them, and those that reade them. The matter of small moment, and therefore the offence of no great danger" (sig. A1v). As opposed to the "true" and "perfect" copies often advertised on title pages, Barnes has collected "loose" and "imperfect" texts. To emphasize their origins in aristocratic manuscript culture and to excuse any errors, Barnes downplays the significance of their "matter" using a similar strategy to Philip Sidney's famous apology for his "triflinglie handled" *Arcadia*, a work also compiled from "loose sheetes of paper."[90] Barnes values these texts not for their accuracy in recording historic events for all time, but for their timeliness. In performance, these entertainments showcased the collaborative efforts of many devisers, including the authorship of Elizabeth Russell, the acting of the Russell daughters and Elizabeth Brydges, and the contributions of household mistresses Frances Brydges and Margery Norreys. Barnes' preface obscures these collaborative origins and female devisers by presenting the book as the work of a single male author: "him that penned them." By emphasizing his role as collector, Barnes enables the entertainment devisers to perform the part of humble courtier-poets unaware of their advertisement in print. Because Gager's recent dispute with Rainolds reveals that the Puritan anti-theatrical movement was alive in Oxford and affected play-devising beyond the commercial stage, Barnes' preface might have protected them from personal attacks. He also implies that a single masculine writer is necessary for print publication, at least within his particular community. None of his publications indicate

---

[89] William Gager, *Meleager* (Oxford, 1592; *STC* 11515); Gager, *Vlysses Redux* (Oxford, 1592; *STC* 11516). For more on the dispute between Gager and Rainolds, see J. W. Binns, "Women or Transvestites on the Elizabethan Stage?: An Oxford Controversy" in *Sixteenth Century Journal* 5.2 (1974): 95–120; K. Young, "William Gager's Defence of the Academic Stage" in *Transactions of the Wisconsin Academy of Sciences, Arts, and Letters* 18 (1916): 593–638.

[90] I quote from the first printed edition of *The Covntesse of Pembrokes Arcadia* (London, 1590; *STC* 22539), sig. A3r–A3v.

a female author, and most boast a single male one. Churchyard might have cobbled together disparate pieces in *A Handefvl of Gladsome Verses*, but his collection is united through his authorship. Perhaps Barnes assumed his readers would expect the same from *Speeches Delivered.* Because he was affiliated with the university and targeted those who wished to read learned materials, most of his intended readers were male as well. In a short preface, Barnes transforms three loosely connected, collectively devised theatrical pieces into one single-authored printed work.

The book's title page also markets it as a recent event produced by the local elite. Its full title reads: *Speeches Delivered to Her Maiestie This Last Progresse, at the Right Honorable the Lady Rvssels, at Bissam, the Right Honorable the Lorde Chandos at Sudley, at the Right Honorable the Lord Norris, at Ricorte* (see Figure 4.1). The most important marker of the book's status, legitimacy, and appeal is its association with "Her Maiestie," and the title emphasizes her hosts' elite status by repeating the words "right honorable" three times. The local family and place names advertise the book's appeal to the Berkshire-Gloucestershire-Oxfordshire region. Yet the book was not designed for all literate locals, but for an educated elite. Although the printed Elvetham entertainment (1591) translates Latin speeches into English because "all our Countrey-men are not Latinists," Barnes offered no English translations of Latin and French phrases.[91] There are only a handful of such phrases, so readers who did not know Latin or French could still follow, but the lack of translation reveals that Barnes was not concerned with widespread popular appeal.

He was also not especially concerned with providing a comprehensive record of the event. His printer's note and title page emphasize timeliness ("This Last Progresse"), and the book's language occasionally resembles a newsletter or diary ("The 28. of September, her Maiesty went from Oxforde to Ricort" [sig. C1V]). However, *Speeches Delivered* lacks a running narrative of the event and has fewer descriptive details of the estates, the hosts' preparation, and the performances' sights and sounds than the news-like pamphlets of the previous year's entertainments at Elvetham and Cowdray. The book's design also highlights its literary qualities. Its three texts are presented on the page as dramatic literature. They appear as the text of one continuous play with three acts and multiple scenes, including speech prefixes and stage directions in italics. The word "speeches," which is infrequently used on Elizabethan title pages, suggests language and literariness

---

[91] *The Honorable Entertainement Gieuen to the Queenes Maiestie in Progresse, at Eluetham in Hampshire,* sig. B2v.

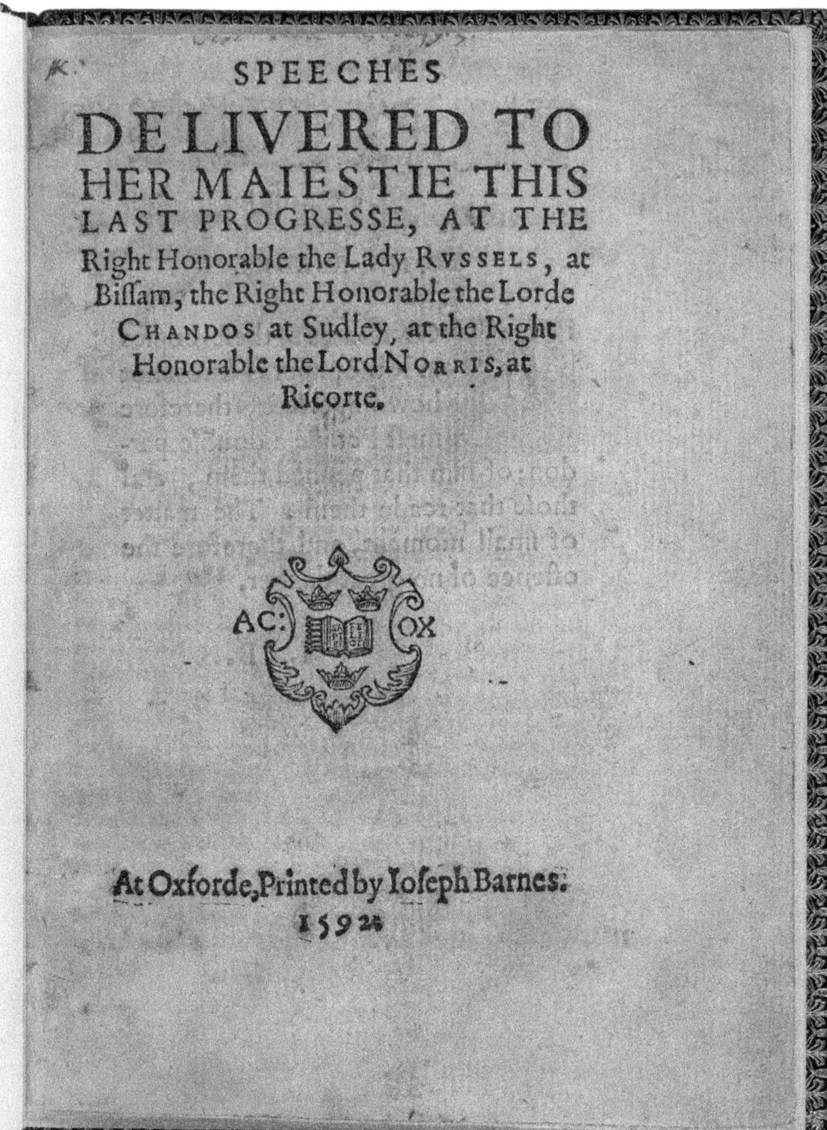

4.1 Title page of *Speeches Delivered* (1592). Folger Shakespeare Library, shelf mark STC 7600.

rather than music, visual spectacles, or any other component of entertainments on progress.[92] According to the *OED*, the word "speech" can indicate a conference between two people, so it underscores an intimate and mutual exchange between the Queen and her hosts in a way that "entertainment" or "device" might not.[93] It also ties the book to the many political and theological speeches in Barnes' catalog. The title therefore represents its texts as political conferences between the local elite and the monarch – an appropriate introduction to a book that both establishes and undermines a definition of England centered on the Queen.

Certain aspects of the Bisham, Sudeley, and Rycote entertainments support the notion that the Tudor period saw the rise of a state increasingly centered on the monarch.[94] They define England as Elizabeth's kingdom as they collectively celebrate the fourth anniversary of the defeat of the Spanish Armada and declare England's position as a Protestant world power. In the Bisham text, when Sybil celebrates the Queen's central role in England's economy and in international politics, she calls Elizabeth "the Queen of this Islande, the wonder of the world" (sig. A3v). The unperformed pageant at the end of the Sudeley text echoes Sybil by calling Elizabeth one who brings "the whole world astonishment" and "the worldes wonder that leades England into euery land, and brings all lands into England" (sig. B3r–C1r). The Norreys sons' letters in the Rycote text come from Ireland, France, and Flanders – areas where England most exerts military power – and as they boast of the Protestant allies' success against Spain, they position England internationally as a powerful Protestant nation. These moments show royal patriotism, as well as a kind of national pride.

Yet the three texts together reveal an unstable definition of the word "country." The Bisham text employs it to refer to a nation when comparing England to "other countries" and celebrating the following:

> that our horses are ledde vvith a whipp: theirs vvith a Launce, that our Riuers flow with fish, theirs with bloode: our cattel feede on pastures, they feede on pastures like cattel: One hande she [Elizabeth] stretcheth to *Fraunce*, to weaken Rebels; the other to *Flaunders*, to strengthen Religion; her heart to both Countries, her vertues to all. (sig. A3v)

---

[92] According to the examples available in *Early English Books Online* (*EEBO*), the word "speech" appears mostly on title pages of grammar guides or news pamphlets about political and theological speeches. It also appears on the title pages of a few other royal entertainment texts.

[93] *OED*, "speech," *n.*, def. 1.

[94] See, e.g., G. R. Elton, *The Tudor Revolution in Government: Administrative Changes in the Reign of Henry VIII* (Cambridge University Press, 1953), 1–9.

With the striking juxtaposition of bloody war and bountiful harvest, this passage creates the image of a peaceful, prosperous England in contrast to countries plagued by civil war. It praises Elizabeth for intervening on behalf of Continental Protestants in their religious wars, and when it uses this intervention to exemplify her magnanimous leadership, it urges her to continue aiding Protestant allies in France and Flanders despite recent setbacks.[95] The Rycote text also advocates continued involvement in Continental wars as it describes England as a "country" with international prestige. One of the soldiers' letters proudly proclaims he has "an English hearte," though his long absence has made him "a stranger in mine owne countrye" (sig. C2r). The host families at Rycote and Bisham define themselves as part of an English nation united by Protestantism and headed by a single superior sovereign, and they encourage Elizabeth not to back down from a militant Protestant foreign policy.

The Sudeley entertainment, however, uses the word "country" to label the Cotswolds as a distinct region. At the castle's entrance a shepherd humbly welcomes Elizabeth to the Cotswolds, "an vneuen country, but a people, that carry their thoughtes leuell with their fortunes, lowe spirites, but true harts, vsing plaine dealinge, once counted a Iewell nowe beggery, these hills afoorde nothing but cottages, and nothing can we present to your highnes, but shephards" (sig. B1r). On the surface, these lines emphasize the unwavering loyalty and candor of the local people with a conventional display of artificial humility, and they promise Elizabeth a safe pastoral haven for her visit. One of the many reasons she went on progress was to escape the plague, and unlike plague-ridden London or the disingenuous court environment, pastoral Gloucestershire is "healthy, and harmeles, a fresh aier, where there are noe dampes, and where a black sheepe is a perilous beast" (sig. B1r). As the Sudeley entertainment idealizes the pastoral region, it assures Elizabeth that she has entered a peaceful territory where her health and person will remain safe. Yet ambiguous syntax makes it possible that the phrase "one counted a Iewell nowe beggery" describes not the people's forthright dealing, but the Cotswolds region. Whether or not the

---

[95] In 1592, England had allied with Protestants in France against the Catholic League and with the Low Countries in their rebellion against Spanish rule. Flanders became particularly important territory because it could be used as a starting point for Spanish invasions of England. However, the devastating economic and human cost of war had caused the Queen to question England's military involvement in these areas. In May 1592, two days of fighting Catholic League and Spanish forces killed about 500 English soldiers; in response, England signed a June agreement with France that moved from offensive measures to a defensive position. See Fissel, *English Warfare*, esp. 164; Hammer, *Elizabeth's Wars*, 178–80; R. B. Wernham, *After the Armada: Elizabethan England and the Struggle for Western Europe 1588–1595* (Oxford: Clarendon, 1984).

hosts intended the performance to do so, the entertainment text alluded to area poverty and criticized royal policy, as Elizabeth's ban on tobacco growth and attempts to regulate the wool industry left the area in financial disarray.[96] This context can inform our interpretation of Elizabeth's visit in September, and because circumstances did not change for the rest of the year, it would have been relevant to the book's early readers as well. The text draws attention to the wool industry when the shepherd presents Elizabeth with a "lock of wooll Cotsholdes best fruite, and my poore gift" (sig. B1r). The gift simultaneously touts a source of local pride and exposes the region's need for royal favor. The opening speech's emphasis on the language of poverty alludes to the actual troubles of Winchcombe, the town closest to Sudeley, in a plea for royal assistance, yet its proud tone represents the area as self-sufficient. It also presents "the honorable Lord and Lady of the Castle," for whom this welcoming address speaks, as powerful local authority figures invested in securing their region's welfare (sig. B1r).

This text's representation of the Cotswold region as superior to the court and city is a familiar move in pastoral literature, but when the Sudeley shepherd spends more lines defining and celebrating the Cotswold region as an independent "country" than praising the Queen, his speech begins to appear ambivalent about the Queen's arrival and authority. In the final scene of the Sudeley entertainment, which the text explains "shoulde haue beene presented to her Maiestie . . . but the weather so vnfit, that it was not," a character called "the great Constable and commandadore of Cotsholde" delivers a speech to Elizabeth (sig. B3r). He speaks only the "Rammish tongue" and needs an interpreter to converse with her (sig. B3r), which playfully emphasizes difference between this area and other parts of England and represents Gloucestershire almost as a foreign place. An earlier line in the invocation implies the same. When the shepherd celebrates the novelty of Elizabeth's visit, which fills "eies with wonder," he underscores that she is not normally at the center of Gloucestershire life (sig. B1r). The Bisham text also highlights the novelty of Elizabeth's visit – its wild man notes that the event is "vnusuall to these Woods" – but it stresses the host family's complete submission to her in such lines as: "vve doe all Homage, accounting nothing ours but what comes from you" (sig. A4v). It celebrates the positive transformative potential of Elizabeth's visit in a way

---

[96] Especially devastating levels of unemployment, poverty, and famine hit Gloucestershire in the 1570s and 1590s, and the wool industry suffered during these periods. See David Rollison, *The Local Origins of Modern Society: Gloucestershire, 1500–1800* (London: Routledge, 1992), 21–44, 77; R. Perry, "The Gloucestershire Woollen Industry, 1100–1690" in *Transactions of the Bristol and Gloucestershire Archaeological Society* 66 (1945): 49–137.

that the Sudeley entertainment does not. Characters at Bisham are amazed that she condescends "to visite the bare Farmes of her subiects," which are then "blessed with her presence" (sig. A3v). By contrast, the Sudeley text appears more ambivalent about the Queen's relationship to the area. Its emphasis on regional culture supports the claims of such scholars as John M. Adrian, Robert W. Barrett, Jr., and David Rollison that regionalism was often a more crucial aspect of individual experience than was nationalism in the early modern period and that local identity played a central role in early definitions of Englishness.[97] The Sudeley text tries to balance an ideology of regional independence with a concept of Englishness rooted in royal loyalty, but it exhibits uncertainty about how to do so. When it never claims that Elizabeth's authority supersedes that of her host or even its Constable, it exposes subtle friction between local patriotrism and royal authority in a similar way to the Kenilworth performance.

This friction also affects our interpretation of *Speeches Delivered* as a whole, as the Sudeley text articulates most clearly an issue lurking in the others with which it was published. As discussed in Chapter 2, the Bisham text offers several characters who are originally ignorant or skeptical of Elizabeth's authority, including a wild man, the rude god Pan, and the boastful goddess Ceres. Even though each challenge is dismissed or overcome, its printed context might encourage us to dwell on the text's repeated insistence that Elizabeth needs protection. The wild man carries a club to "beate down" those that threaten to harm her, and Pan vows to protect her from "theft," "noise," and "spies" (sig. A2r–A4r). We might linger on a strange moment in the Rycote text when the host's only daughter "hath so much forgotten" to send her regards and gives the excuse that "shee is a woman" (sig. C4r). Even though the messenger delivers her note the following day, her absence and emphasis on the limitations of her gender might cast a shadow on the entertainment's devout celebration of a female ruler's ability to unify her nation. Although these entertainments would have engaged their audience to think about the relationship between local and national interests in performance, these particular moments might not have created tension when performed and might carry hints of resistance only or primarily in their printed context. When read together, as Barnes' audience would have read them, the three entertainment texts in *Speeches Delivered* celebrate Elizabeth and England, but they sometimes privilege

---

[97] John M. Adrian, *Local Negotiations of English Nationhood, 1570–1680* (Basingstoke: Palgrave, 2011); Robert W. Barrett, *Against All England: Regional Identity and Cheshire Writing, 1195–1656* (Notre Dame: University of Notre Dame Press, 2009), esp. 11–22; Rollison, *The Local Origins of Modern Society*, 69.

the local over the national, a feature accentuated by the book's publication at Oxford. The uneasy coexistence of localism and royal patriotism in this book calls for a new definition of England not so focused on the Crown.

Books of the entertainments at Kenilworth, Woodstock, Bisham, Sudeley, and Rycote demonstrate that printed pageantry could carry meanings beyond those of the performed events, and they indicate that their publishers took the lead in shaping this meaning. When these books are read within the context of their publishers' full careers, a didactic quality emerges in all of them. Publishers read these books not as mere records or frivolity, but as literature with instructive value. The performances they interpret served to advise the Queen; in print, the entertainments advocated certain policies to audiences of courtiers, scholars, and those of lower ranks but high ambition. Despite what Barnes has told us about *Speeches Delivered*, we see that printed pageantry is not genuinely "of small moment."

"Set this downe in English"
Cowdray, Elvetham, and Printed Pageantry as National News

This chapter turns to two popular pamphlets that chronicle the 1591 performances at Cowdray and Elvetham, both of which were printed quickly after the event and then reprinted with some revision. Both performances held special potential for contentious or at least delicate interactions, the kind of wrangling over authority highlighted in Chapter 1, because both needed to deal with their hosts' complicated relationships with Elizabeth. Anthony Browne, Viscount Montague, was one of the wealthiest peers in Sussex and the most public of Elizabeth's Catholic supporters, and his estate at Cowdray was something of a haven for Catholics in Sussex, a county in which the old religion was certainly not dead.[1] The entertainment he hosted with his wife Magdalen proclaimed the couple as committed to Elizabeth and sought greater liberties for English Catholics. When Elizabeth arrived at Elvetham the following month, she entered a situation that potentially evoked even more tension. As we have seen, the entertainment gave Edward Seymour, Lord Hertford, the opportunity to stage a public apology and rewrite his reputation as a loyal political insider. When put in context with other performances that year at Cowdray and Theobalds, the Elvetham entertainment's celebration of England's international position offered an aggressively Protestant perspective that could challenge the kind of leniency the Cowdray pageants requested.

Most of the audience in attendance at Cowdray and Elvetham would have been at least partially alert to the hosts' challenging positions. But the printed records betray little of this background. Their publishers specialized in political news, especially that which placed England in an international context, and the Cowdray and Elvetham books likewise served as news

---

[1] Michael C. Questier, *Catholicism and Community in Early Modern England: Politics, Aristocratic Patronage and Religion, c. 1550–1640* (Cambridge University Press, 2006), 18–59; Elizabeth Heale, "Contesting Terms: Loyal Catholicism and Lord Montague's Entertainment at Cowdray, 1591" in Jayne Elisabeth Archer, Elizabeth Goldring, and Sarah Knight, eds., *The Progresses, Pageants, and Entertainments of Queen Elizabeth I* (Oxford University Press, 2007), 198.

while cultivating a national readership comprising both "popular" and "elite" audiences. Each publisher printed an early version with as much information as he could gather, followed by a revised edition that added more narrative detail. The later edition of each book became more queen-centered, communal, and conservative as it transitioned from a quick news pamphlet to historical record. As all of these books present cases for royal favor, they offer differing definitions of political loyalty and Englishness. They also reveal a group of stationers whose careers point to the early 1590s as a crucial moment in printed conceptions of England as a nation with some power on an international stage.

Defending Catholic Sussex at Cowdray

When Elizabeth arrived at Cowdray on a Saturday evening in August, a Porter greeted her at the estate's bridge and delivered a speech emphasizing her transformative power and her hosts' devotion to her. Elizabeth stayed for nearly a week. She was entertained with abundant music, feasting, hunting, and pageantry that included speeches by a Porter, Pilgrim, Wild Man, and Angler. We know of this entertainment from two editions of a printed quarto, both of which were produced in 1591 by the partnership of bookseller William Wright and printer Thomas Scarlet.[2] Neither title page claims to be a revised version, and both include printer's errors and possible corrections. Yet their final paragraphs betray which version appeared first. The one entitled *The Speeches and Honorable Entertainment giuen to the Queenes Maiestie in Progresse, at Cowdrey in Sussex, by the right Honorable the Lord Montacute. 1591* reveals itself as the earlier one (see Figure 5.1).[3]

---

[2] Copies of both versions are now held at the British Library: *The Speeches and Honorable Entertainment Giuen to the Queenes Maiestie in Progresse, at Cowdrey in Sussex, by the Right Honorable the Lord Montacute. 1591* (shelf mark c.33.d.11; *STC* 3907.7) and *The Honorable Entertainment Giuen to the Queenes Maiestie in Progresse, at Cowdrey in Sussex, by the Right Honorable the Lord Montecute. 1591* (shelf mark c.142.dd.23; *STC* 3907.5). Besides these printed editions, there is a manuscript copy: Woking, Surrey History Centre, LM/1329/257. It presents pageantry speeches with no narrative, song lyrics, or descriptions of any other part of the event, and it follows the earliest printed text. Folded into a small pamphlet, it shows no signs that it was enclosed in a letter. I assume that it was copied from the first printing rather than a separate eyewitness account.

[3] For an alternative theory, see Gabriel Heaton's introduction to the Cowdray entertainment in Elizabeth Goldring, et al., eds., *John Nichols's The Progresses and Public Processions of Queen Elizabeth I: A New Edition of the Early Modern Sources* (Oxford University Press, 2014), 3:548–9. Jean Wilson and A. W. Pollard both reach the same conclusion as I do. However, I disagree with Wilson's argument that the first quarto was an advance copy. Its language does not support this theory: its descriptions are too precise and sometimes weather-dependent to be plans or predictions, and its concluding claim that the entertainment pleased Elizabeth would be a bit reckless if printed in advance. Jean Wilson, *Entertainments for Elizabeth I* (Woodbridge: D. S. Brewer, 1980), 87–8; *STC*, 1:173.

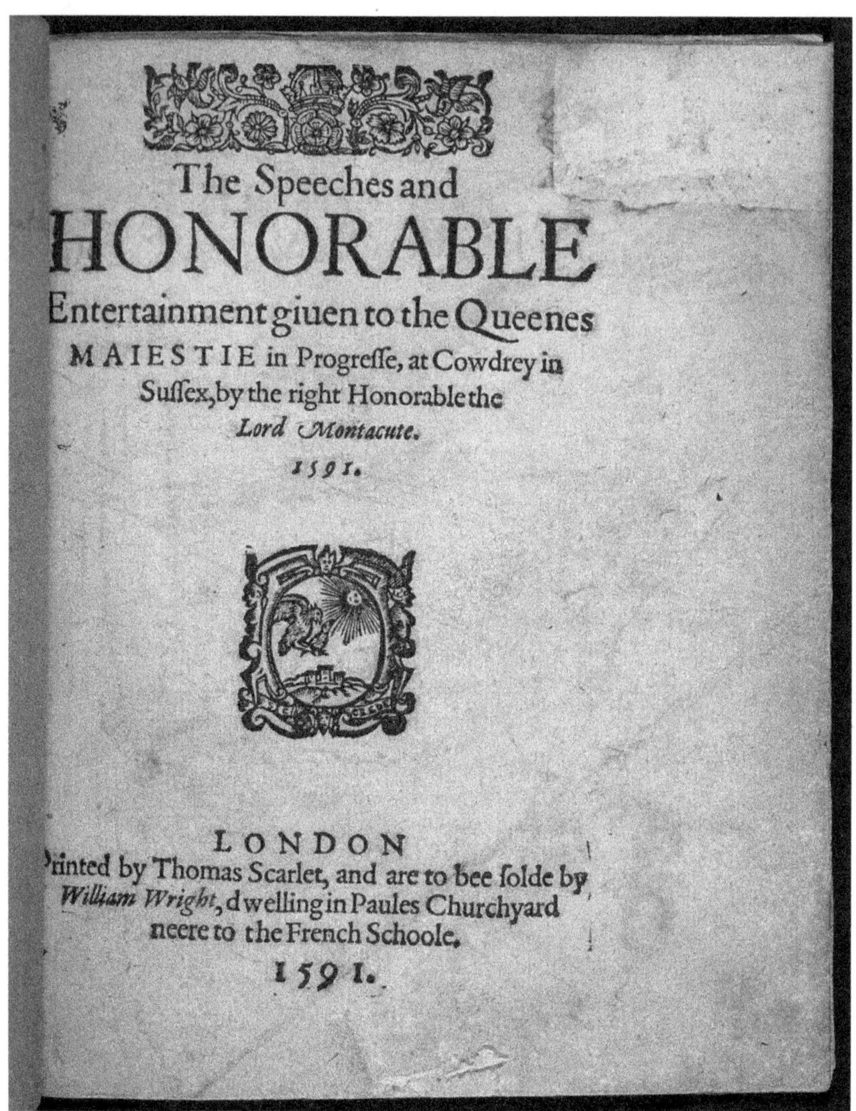

5.1 Title page of *The Speeches and Honorable Entertainment* (1591), probably the first quarto of the Cowdray entertainment. British Library, shelf mark C.33.d.11.

After it describes festivities on Saturday to Wednesday, it ends abruptly: "For the rest of the Entertainment, honorable feasting, and abundance of all things that might manifest a liberall and loyall heart, because I was not there, I cannot set downe, thus much by report I heare, and by the words of those that deserue credite, that it was such as much contented her Maiestie and made many others to wonder."[4] The other version, which excludes "Speeches" from its title, provides accounts of Thursday and Friday and ends with a description of Elizabeth's departure from Cowdray (see Figure 5.2). The two texts' many spelling and spacing variants reveal that the later version was not simply a corrected issue, but a new edition. The book was apparently popular enough to warrant this revised edition; the initial run might have sold out, and the publisher acquired further accounts of the event.

The two editions share a great deal of content, but their variants reveal somewhat different interpretations of the event and its politics. The first includes the lyrics to three songs, and the second substitutes additional details about non-pageantry elements such as hunting and dancing. Likewise, the first title ("The Speeches and Honorable Entertainment") emphasizes the pageantry orations and the second (simply "The Honorable Entertainment") does not. As is true in its genre more broadly, the Cowdray pageantry uses equivocal language that allows us to interpret its politics as conservative or defiant.[5] Although both editions of the Cowdray book include earnest statements of loyalty and rhetoric implying dissension, the first quarto encourages readers to focus more on the subversive elements and the second supports a more conservative view.

Although the political stakes of a Catholic-hosted entertainment were especially high, the Cowdray book demonstrates that the performance facilitated the same risks and rewards as others in its genre. Its hosting couple sought the same two goals of self-promotion and royal favor: they wanted to display on a grand scale their loyalty, Elizabeth's long-standing alliance with Montague, and his enduring role in local and courtly politics. In the House of Lords early in the reign, Montague argued vehemently for Catholicism as the best path for England and spoke out against anti-Catholic legislation, and he served as Lord Lieutenant of Sussex for

---

[4] *The Speeches and Honorable Entertainment Giuen to the Queenes Maiestie in Progresse, at Cowdrey in Sussex*, sig. B4v. This is the first quarto, the version I cite hereafter in this chapter unless quotations are explicitly identified as from the second edition.

[5] Previous scholarship has shifted between these perspectives. See especially Curtis Breight, "Caressing the Great: Viscount Montague's Entertainment of Elizabeth at Cowdray, 1591" in *Sussex Archaeological Collections* 127 (1989): 147–66; Questier, *Catholicism and Community*, 169; and Heale, "Contesting Terms," 189–206.

5.2 Title page of *The Honorable Entertainment* (1591), probably the second quarto of the Cowdray entertainment. British Library, shelf mark c.142.dd.23.

several years in the middle of the reign.[6] Although his biographers disagree about whether he was genuinely as obedient as he seemed, he maintained a position of power despite his religion because he was outwardly conformist.[7] Arguably the most influential Catholic in Elizabethan England, he had long constructed himself as moderate, and he actively aided England's defense against the Spanish Armada just a few years earlier. Yet Montague had radical acquaintances and family members – his wife and co-host Magdalen tended to be much less moderate, for example – and his household had been accused of harboring priests and recruiting converts in the 1580s.[8] In a speech he delivered in the January following his entertainment, Montague revealed that Elizabeth had been advised it was too "daungerous" to visit his house. Rumors held that he was "a daungerous man to the state" who housed "sixe score Recusantes that neuer cam to churche" – accusations he calls "a wonderfull vntruthe."[9] In the same speech, Montague emphasized his willingness to fight for England: "yf the Pope or the Kinge of Spayne or anye other forreyne Potentate shoulde offer to invade this Realme, for anye cause whatsoeuer; I woulde be one of the fyrst that shoulde beare armes agenst him or them for my prynce and cowntrye."[10] Finally, he identified his relationship with Elizabeth as a close one, built on mutual benefit and trust. He repeatedly emphasized that he had nothing to hide; of Elizabeth, he said, "she knoweth the worst

---

[6] Montague spoke out against the ecclesiastical supremacy bill in 1559 and the 1563 bill to incite the death penalty for refusal to take the Oath of Supremacy, and, along with the Protestant Lord Buckhurst, he served as Lord Lieutenant of Sussex from 1569 to 1585. See Montague's 1559 speech to Parliament, Oxford, Bodleian Library, MS Eng.th.b.2, 840–3; Timothy J. McCann, "The Parliamentary Speech of Viscount Montague against the Act of Supremacy, 1559" in *Sussex Archaeological Collections* 108 (1970): 50–7; Roger B. Manning, "Anthony Browne, 1st Viscount Montague: The Influence in County Politics of an Elizabethan Catholic Nobleman" in *Sussex Archaeological Collections* 106 (1968): 103–12.

[7] Questier in *Catholicism and Community* (117–49) questions Montague's actual loyalty; Roger B. Manning maintains that his success derived from "unquestioned loyalty to the queen" and "scrupulous moderation." See *Religion and Society in Elizabethan Sussex: A Study of the Enforcement of the Religious Settlement 1558–1603* (New York: Leicester University Press, 1969), 160. For an example of Montague's outward conformity, see his 1559 speech, in which he insists that "ther lyveth no subiect in this Realme" who will better "put his life in adventure to serve my Soveraigne Ladye then I woulde, nor woulde be more loath to offend her, nor more glad to please her highnes." Oxford, Bodleian Library, MS Eng.th.b.2, 842.

[8] Questier, *Catholicism and Community*, 159–65; Manning, "Anthony Browne," 109–10; Richard Smith, *The Life of the Most Honovrable and Vertvovs Lady the La. Magdalen Viscovntesse Montagve* (*STC* 22811; London, 1627). See also Montague's 1592 speech at West Morsley: Woking, Surrey History Centre, LM/1856, fol. 1v. Smith's *Life* is a posthumous biography of Magdalen that represents her as an embattled saint. Written by her priest, it uses an idealized version of Magdalen to argue for the superiority of the Catholic faith. Although we should approach this book with skepticism, some of its descriptions are supported by other accounts.

[9] Woking, Surrey History Centre, LM/1856, fol. 1v.   [10] Ibid., fol. 2r.

of me, and so I woulde haue her she knoweth also my faythfull and Loyall harte towards her."[11] This speech demonstrates how burdensome Montague found the ubiquitous anti-Catholic prejudice of late Elizabethan England and how he fought against it. The performance and subsequent printed texts reveal the same agenda.

Those who analyze the Cowdray performance generally agree that Montague used it to put forth definitions of honor and loyalty that were not tied to religious affiliation.[12] The printed book extends this aim and shows off Montague's well-crafted public persona to an even wider audience. Because that particular progress took Elizabeth to more Catholic homes than did any other, Mary Hill Cole speculates that one of its central goals was to strengthen loyalties and ascertain viewpoints of southern Catholics.[13] Likewise, the hosting family wanted to test Elizabeth's attitude toward them and their region, and their performance lobbied for more lenient government policy toward Catholics.[14] In short, it benefited the family, Elizabeth, and English Catholics to claim that the event staged a positive alliance. The Cowdray book does exactly that. Both versions emphasize that Elizabeth enjoyed and approved of the entertainment. The first describes her as "well pleased" and Montague as "throughly comforted with her Highnesse gracious acceptance" (sig. B4v), and the second says that she spoke up during the first pageant to agree that "there was none more faithfull" than Montague (sig. A3v). Because the narrator advocates on Montague's behalf, it is possible that Montague helped get it published, or perhaps the narrator hoped to earn his patronage by representing him positively in print. Just as hosts entertained Elizabeth in the hopes of receiving reciprocation, publishers and writers often dedicated books to influential patrons for the same reason.[15]

Whether or not Montague was directly involved in the publication of the Cowdray entertainment, the primary agent behind its production was its publisher. The title page of both editions provides publication information as follows: "Printed by Thomas Scarlet, and are too bee solde by

---

[11] Ibid., fol. 1v.

[12] Breight, "Caressing the Great," 147–66; Questier, *Catholicism and Community*, 169; Heale, "Contesting Terms," 189–206.

[13] Mary Hill Cole, "Religious Conformity and the Progresses of Elizabeth I" in Carole Levin, Jo Eldridge Carney, and Debra Barrett-Graves, eds., *Elizabeth I: Always Her Own Free Woman* (Aldershot: Ashgate, 2003), 72–3.

[14] Heale, "Contesting Terms," 189–206.

[15] David M. Bergeron, *Textual Patronage in English Drama 1570–1640* (Aldershot: Ashgate, 2006); Arthur F. Marotti, *Manuscript, Print, and the English Renaissance Lyric* (Ithaca: Cornell University Press, 1995), 321–4.

William Wright." The pair worked together often and shared certain agendas, so either could have financed the book and supervised its content.[16] But Wright most often published the books they produced together.[17] The Cowdray title page highlights the names of Wright and Montague (Montecute) by placing them in italics, while Scarlet's name is in roman type. This typography implies that Wright served as publisher; the italicized names appear to identify Wright and Montague as the contributors whose effort and perspectives most clearly shaped the Cowdray performance and text.[18]

Wright's main specialty was news. In the early part of his career, he published mostly sensational pamphlets: a prophecy by a Dutch girl who woke after she was presumed dead, accounts of public executions, and collections of "rare" events.[19] The title of one of his earliest publications illustrates this kind of news:

> *A Vievv of Sundry Examples. Reporting Many Straunge Murthers, Sundry Persons Periured, Signes and Tokens of Gods Anger towards Vs. What Straunge and Monstrous Children Haue of Late Beene Borne: And All Memorable Murthers since the Murther of Maister Sanders by George Brovvne, to This Present and Bloody Murther of Abell Bourne Hosyer, who Dwelled in Newgate Market. 1580. Also a Short Discourse of the Late Earthquake the Sixt of Aprill.*[20]

The repetition of "murther" and adjectives such as "straunge," "monstrous," and "bloody" draw in readers who delight in oddities and violence. Like this title, which offers an account of a "present" murder, many of Wright's title pages give specific recent dates or otherwise emphasize timeliness. He titled one publication *The Araignment, Examination, Confession and Iudgement of Arnold Cosbye: VVho Wilfvlly Murdered the Lord Burke, neere the Towne of Wanswoorth, on the 14. Day of this Present Month of Ianuary and Was Executed the 27. of the Same Moneth. 1591.*[21] The reference to "this Present Month" indicates that this publication must have appeared soon after the

---

16 The majority of the texts we can identify as published by Scarlet are political or sensational news pamphlets. See, e.g., a sensational pamphlet entitled *Sundrye Strange and Inhumaine Murthers* (London, 1591; *STC* 18286.5).

17 See, e.g., the title page to *The Pride of King Nabuchadnezzer* (London, 1591; *STC* 22689), which uses the same language as the Cowdray book: "Printed by Thomas Scarlet, and are to be sold by William Wright." The note to the reader, signed by Wright (as W.W.), identifies that the agency rested primarily with him: "Nowe as I haue caused them to bee examined by the best Copies, and to bee corrected accordingly, so I thought good to certifie thee of the same" (sig. A2r–A2v).

18 Italics are used purposefully in the rest of the book to mark important names, dates, and days of the week; they also differentiate pageants from narrative descriptions.

19 See, e.g., Eyriak Schlichtenberger, *A Prophesie Vttered by the Daughter of an Honest Countrey Man, Called Adam Krause* (London, 1580; *STC* 21818); Phillip Stubbes, *Two Wunderfull and Rare Examples* (London, 1581; 23399.7).

20 Anthony Munday, *A Vievv of Sundry Examples* (London, 1580; *STC* 18281).

21 *The Araignment* (London, n.d. [1591]; *STC* 5813).

execution. Wright later published a description of the execution itself; this book repeats no material from the earlier one and begins, "Imediatly after that Arnold Cosbie had receaued iudgement, as you haue before heard."[22] Wright designed this book as a sequel for an established readership. His publication of two separate accounts rather than one longer book underscores that he valued (and expected his readers would value) timeliness more than comprehensiveness.

In the late 1580s, Wright's career took an interesting turn. Although he still published accounts of "strange and wonderfull things," his books became less about odd individual occurrences and more about international politics and England's place in them.[23] This shift in focus began with his 1589 publication of George Peele's patriotic poem to English generals John Norreys (Norris) and Francis Drake. Its title page, which honors "the famous and fortunate Generalls of our English forces," imagines a readership united by a shared English identity.[24] Wright was especially active in the early 1590s, when he contracted Scarlet to publish a series of news stories about France and the Netherlands. An early example begins by emphasizing that the activities recorded in this "true discourse" happened up until the fifteenth day "of this present moneth of September. 1590."[25] The following year Scarlet printed for Wright *Nevves from France*, an anonymous letter about a French victory over Spain that explains on its title page, "This happened the 18. of September. 1591."[26] The letter includes this line: "It is woonderfull (my very good kinsman) to see the miseries of Fraunce, and as miraculous to compare our present estate in the contrary, she hauing beene called the Garden of the world for pleasure."[27] As this book makes explicit, a primary purpose of the international news books by Scarlet and Wright was to shore up pride in England's relative security and emerging eminence. Although battles raged on the Continent, England was not experiencing war on home soil. The kind of nationalistic language

[22] *The Manner of the Death and Execution of Arnold Cosbie, for Murthering the Lord Boorke, Who Was Executed at VVanswoorth Townes End on the 27. of Ianuarie 1591* (London, 1591; *STC* 5814), sig. A2r.

[23] I quote from the title page of *The Rare Trauailes of Iob Hortop, an Englishman, Who Was Not Heard of in Three and Twentie Yeeres Space . . . Wherein Also He Discouereth Many Strange and Wonderfull Things Seene in the Time of His Trauaile* (London, 1591; *STC* 13827.5). Another example of this kind of publication later in Wright's career is *The Strange and Cruell Martyrdome of an English Man in the Towne of Dunkerke This Present Moneth of Ianuarie. 1591* (London, 1591; *STC* 25735).

[24] George Peele, *A Farewell. Entituled to the Famous and Fortunate Generalls of our English Forces: Sir Iohn Norris & Syr Frauncis Drake Knights, and All Theyr Braue and Resolute Followers* (London, 1589; *STC* 19537).

[25] *A Discovrse of All Svch Fights, Skirmishes, Exploites, and Other Politike Attempts Which Haue Happened in France since the Ariuall of the Duke of Parma, and the Ioyning of His Forces with the Enemies* (London, n.d. [1590]; *STC* 11268), sig. A3r.

[26] *Nevves from France* (London, 1591; *STC* 11282.5).   [27] Ibid., sig. A2r.

we see here appears in several of Wright's other publications. In *The Second Part of Conny-Catching*, Robert Greene's note to readers mentions "this flourishing estate of England" and his desire to contribute to "the benefit of my countrie."[28] Wright's publications define Englishness as a crucial component of identity and, for many of these books, England's military prowess rather than its monarch inspired writers to imagine a national community.

Wright's publications also show special attention to authentication. Several of his title pages identify their sources, such as letters from the French king or the Turkish emperor. The pamphlet detailing the Dutch prophecy claims credibility by emphasizing how many reliable witnesses testified to the story's accuracy. It lists ten men "of good woorshippe and credite, that were then present" and explains that the town superintendent "had the examination of the trueth, before it was published in Print."[29] A preface to an account of a Scottish sorcerer similarly promises, "All which examinations (gentle Reader) I haue here truly published, as they were taken and vttered in the presence of the Kinges Maiestie, praying thee to accept it for veritie, the same being so true as cannot be reprooued."[30] Other of Wright's publications foreground the credentials of authors or translators. Anthony Munday, for example, was a trustworthy reporter of a public execution because he "was there present" and a suitable translator for a courtly text because he was "one of the Messengers of her Maiesties Chamber."[31] Still others emphasize the legitimacy of their printing with such phrases as "Seene and allowed" and "Published with authoritie."[32] Wright imagines a skeptical reader, and the more far-fetched the content, the more his books justify their accuracy. For Wright, valuable news did not need to be complete, but it did need to be produced quickly, accurately, and from a reliable informant. He aimed to build a reputation as a trustworthy news source.

Wright's interests in timely news and nation-building provide useful context for his publication of the Cowdray entertainment at an active time

---

[28] Robert Greene, *The Second Part of Conny-Catching* (London, 1591; *STC* 12281), sig. *3r.

[29] Schlichtenberger, *A Prophesie Vttered* (London, 1580; *STC* 21818), sig. A7v.

[30] *Newes from Scotland. Declaring the Damnable Life of Doctor Fian a Notable Sorcerer* (London, 1592; *STC* 10842.3), sig. A2v.

[31] Anthony Munday, *A Breefe and True Reporte, of the Execution of Certaine Traytours at Tiborne, the xxviii. and xxx. Dayes of Maye. 1582* (London, 1582; *STC* 18261); Palmerin D'Oliva, *The Mirrour of Nobilitie, Mappe of Honor, Anotamie of Rare Fortunes, Heroycall President of Loue*, trans. Anthony Munday (London, 1588; *STC* 19157).

[32] *The Politique Takinge of Zutphen Skonce, the VVinning of the Towne, and Beleagering of Deuenter... Seene and Allowed* (London, 1591; *STC* 26134.5); Job Hortop, *The Trauailes of an English Man... By I. H. Published with Authoritie* (London, 1591; *STC* 13828).

in his career. Early in 1591, he published a book called *The Blessed State of England. Declaring the Svndrie Dangers VVhich by Gods Assistance, the Qveenes Most Excellent Maiestie Hath Escaped in the Whole Course of Her Life. With Her Singular Vertues and Peaceable Gouernment. VVherein is Also Shewed How Greatly Foraine Nations Doe Admire and Wonder Thereat, Together with the Rare Titles of Commendation Which the Great Emperor of the Turkes Lately Sent in His Letters to Her Highnesse.* It begins with a note in which the author explains the book's purpose: "to make knowne to all hir maiesties well disposed subiectes, the louing kindnes of almightie God towards hir, the loue and affection which forreine princes beare hir, and how much the verie heathen do admire at hir proceedings."[33] When he addresses "well disposed" subjects, he implies that others might not be as receptive to such praise, and he positions the book as a kind of defense of Elizabeth. Although its title and dedication foreground Elizabeth's divine ordination and claim that all of England's strengths can be traced to her influence, its content is more about the preeminence of her collective people than about Elizabeth herself. It emphasizes England's position in the world and labels it the best nation of all. It explains that while "other countries round about vs," especially France and the Netherlands, are engaged in civil wars and riots, England is:

> the principallest place for anie man to liue in throughout the whole worlde. What else maketh the strangers to flocke so fast to Englande? thinke you it is only for religion? no I warrant you, there is of them as there is of our owne nation, manie godly professors, true Protestantes, some Papistes, some Atheists, some lacke a both sides, some Anabaptists and what not? So that in truth it is the ease, the welth, the peace, the safetie and security of England, both for their liues and goods that brings them hither in such aboundance.[34]

Like others in Wright's list, this text celebrates as proof of England's power the inability of the Spanish Armada to invade it. Yet it defines England not as a Protestant nation, but as one that welcomes and shelters a diverse group of people.

When we turn to the Cowdray books, we see suitability for Wright's list and evidence of his influence. Especially because the Cowdray entertainment marked Elizabeth's first progress to West Sussex, an area with a substantial Catholic population, it was significant news that would have appealed to readers of Wright's pamphlets about Continental wars between

---

[33] Thomas Nelson, *The Blessed State of England* (London, 1591; *STC* 18422.5), sig. A2v. The letter is dedicated to London's Lord Mayor.

[34] Ibid., sig. B3r.

Catholics and Protestants. The title pages of both editions identify the pageantry as performed during the latest royal progress. By highlighting the Queen's presence, Wright marks the text as legitimate and newsworthy. He assumed that readers would value the first edition not as a complete record, but for its function as immediate gossip about an exciting recent event. The narrator acknowledges without apology that this version is incomplete when he identifies himself at its end as an editor rather than an eyewitness. We might even speculate that this narrator was Wright himself, especially when he explains that his sources were "the words of those that deserue credite" (sig. B4v). Both editions of the Cowdray book were part of the turn in Wright's career from sensational reports to patriotic news that celebrates a diverse but unified England, and they reveal a post-Armada view of England as an emerging world power.[35] This version of England, which it shares with *The Blessed State of England*, renders possible such a thing as a patriotic Catholic.

The main pageants – the speeches by the Porter, Pilgrim, Wild Man, and Angler – are nearly identical in both editions. They share with many of Wright's other publications a celebration of Elizabeth's international fame – a common, safe choice for a late Elizabethan entertainment. The pageantry calls her "Natures glorie, Fortunes Empresse, the worlds wonder!" and one whose "government is wondered at vpon the earth" (sig. A3v, B1v). By labeling Elizabeth an "Empresse" of good fortune and a figure that strikes awe across the world, the entertainment implies that she has an international reputation and that her power extends even beyond her own kingdom. As the pageantry invites Elizabeth to wield this power over Sussex, it reveals subtle possibilities for resistance to her presence, but repeatedly rectifies these threats or eclipses them with excessive praise. In the opening pageant, a Porter greets Elizabeth in armor holding a club and a key. Although he might have had a more aggressive presence in performance, the text emphasizes his immediate submission to the Queen. Standing between two porters carved of wood, he explains that the wooden figures are men who are cursed to sleep forever and that a prophecy has declared that the walls around them would shake and sleeping men would not wake until the arrival of "the wisest, the fairest and most fortunate of all creatures" (sig. A3v). When Elizabeth appears, the wall stops shaking, and the Porter declares the house "immoueable" (sig. A3v). This particular

---

[35] The idea that the Armada defeat marked a defining moment in English history is far from new; R. B. Wernham tellingly titled his two-volume study of Elizabethan England *Before the Armada: The Emergence of the English Nation, 1485–1588* (New York: Harcourt, 1966) and *After the Armada: Elizabethan England and the Struggle for Western Europe, 1588–1595* (Oxford University Press, 1984).

word helps explain how Elizabeth's transformative presence has made the house stable, but it also might allude more subversively to Cowdray's function as an unshakable center for English Catholics. The fact that Elizabeth's presence cannot awaken the wooden porters could imply that her power has limits. Yet the book frames Cowdray's strength as the work of Elizabeth. She controls the estate, is its foundation, and pardons it for being a center of Catholicism. The text states outright that she governs the region: "The heauens guide you, your Maiestie gouernes vs" (sig. B2v). This sentence acknowledges her governance as divinely ordained, a significant point within an entertainment hosted by Catholics, and vows that the host family and their West Sussex neighbors will follow Elizabeth's rule.

These pageantry texts overall demonstrate a strong desire to please Elizabeth. The end of the welcome address has the Porter give Elizabeth the estate key and say the following:

> Enter, possesse all, to whom the heauens haue vouchsafed all. As for the owner of this house, mine honourable Lord, his tongue is the keie of his heart: and his heart the locke of his soule. Therefore what he speakes you may constantlie beleeue: which is, that in duetie and seruice to your Maiestie, he would be second to none: in praieing for your happinesse, equall to anie. (sig. A3v–A4r)

These lines emphasize the careful balance of jurisdictional power central to the genre. By labeling Montague the estate's "owner," they remind readers of his power: he remains lord of Cowdray and host of the entertainment. But they also invite Elizabeth to possess what is rightly hers as they work to establish a reciprocal relationship that provides mutual benefit. If Elizabeth contributes to the strength of Cowdray and shows Montague favor, he will be her best servant. Although many entertainments claim that their hosts exceed all others in terms of duty and service, this one adds that Montague will be "equall to anie" when he prays for Elizabeth's happiness. His Catholicism will not be a problem, and he seeks only to be treated equally with his Protestant peers. The entertainment insists that Montague is simply like any other wealthy subject, a message it underscores by never referring explicitly to his religion. In some ways it skirts the issue, but words like "heauens," "soule," and "praieing" alert attentive readers to the significance of Montague's faith. Later pageants include nods to religion as well, especially the speech by a Pilgrim who prays for Elizabeth's happiness as Montague has promised to do. Through religious language and images, the text insinuates that Montague is more devout to Elizabeth than to any other entity or belief system.

The idea that worship of Elizabeth is Montague's true religion becomes especially apparent in lines delivered by a Wild Man. He acknowledges that Montague has special reason to be grateful for Elizabeth's favor: "Abroad courage hath made you feared, at home honoured clemencie. Clemencie which the owner of this Groue hath tasted: in such sort, that his thoughts are become his hearts laberinth, surprized with ioie and loialtie. Ioy without measure, loyaltie without end, liuing in no other ayer, then that which breathes your Maiesties safetie" (sig. b2r). This second reference to Montague as "owner" continues to claim some degree of authority for him, but the entertainment again emphasizes mutual benefit as it fashions Elizabeth as lenient and merciful toward an indebted Montague. The Wild Man's lines allude to rhetoric in the Book of Common Prayer that would have been recited in English churches – "The Savior's Love, without measure, without end" and "world without end" – but substitutes Elizabeth for references to God or the Savior.[36] At the same time, this vow of devotion is framed by references to violence and terror. When the entertainment promises that Montague will protect Elizabeth, it reminds us that she and England may need protecting.

Allusions to the wars abroad underlie the Cowdray pageants as the Wild Man's speech and the rest of the text depict the current political climate as full of dissent, factionalism, and deception. The Wild Man says,

> such a disguised worlde it is that one can scarce know a Pilgrime from a Priest, a Tailer from a Gentleman, nor a man from a woman. Euerie one seeming to be that which they are not, onely do practise what they should not. The heauens guide you, your Maiestie gouerns vs: though our peace bee enuied, by you we hope it shall be eternall. (sig. b2r–b2v)

When he refers to "our peace," he simultaneously celebrates England's lack of war on home soil and acknowledges Elizabeth's relative amity toward Catholics. He urges her to institute policies that support continued peace, and he argues that she should not make judgments based on appearance or assumption because both are often false. Just as Protestants are not necessarily honest, Catholic beliefs do not make the Browne family traitors. It is tempting to interpret this passage as an aggressive insistence on religious freedom. The repeated emphasis on dishonesty could make Elizabeth sound threatened, and the word "practise" could even hint at recusancy and the practicing of Catholicism at Cowdray. But the text at every turn insists on Montague's loyalty to Elizabeth and England. In the final pageant,

---

[36] *The Book of Common Prayer: The Texts of 1549, 1559, and 1662*, ed. Brian Cummings (Oxford University Press, 2011), 7, 104.

the Angler complains of "this nibling world, where euerie man laies bait for another" (sig. B3r). He condemns liars and cheaters, including city merchants and landlords who "put such sweete baits on rackt rents, that as good it were to be a perch in a pikes belly, as a Tenant in theyr farmes" (sig. B3r). His rant implies that the host family is an exception to these complaints; Montague is no "rackt rent" landlord, but an honest peer who never hides his true self. The Angler wishes he could rid England of "all the hollowe heartes to your Maiestie" and mentions those "muddie minded" people who would not rest until "they haue disturbd the state with their trecheries" (sig. B4r). He puns on the names of freshwater fish in the pond: carps become "carpers," those who prattle and criticize, and perch becomes "pearchers," those who are overly ambitious (sig. B4r). As the Angler imagines that potential traitors and critics surround Elizabeth, he wishes they might get the punishment they deserve. His speech, like the Wild Man's, argues that Elizabeth needs protection and a trustworthy alternative, and the text holds up an alliance with Montague as exactly what she needs.

The emphasis on Elizabeth's need for protection is crucial to the text's representation of Sussex. It explains that the Wild Man's speech happens before a tree upon which hang the royal arms and those of local nobility and gentry. In performance, this tree could have presented a visual representation either of unity or of conflict between Sussex lords and the Crown, and the text reveals both possibilities. Although the Pilgrim introduces the speaker as a "rough-hewed Ruffian," this Wild Man seems rather docile and informed. He has already been tamed when we meet him, and he recognizes the Queen immediately (sig. B1r). He explains that the tree represents the shire and Elizabeth's strength; all the limbs of her kingdom are "wouen in one roote" (sig. B1v). He says, "The wall of this Shire is the sea, strong, but rampired with true hearts, inuincible: where euery priuate mans eie is a Beacon to discouer: euerie noble mans power a Bulwarke to defende" (sig. B1v). The tree's "root is so deeplie fastened, that treacherie, though shee vndermine to the centre, cannot finde the windings . . . Well wot they that your enemies lightnings are but flashes, and their thunder which filles the whole world with a noise of conquest, shall end with a softe shower of Retreate" (sig. B1v–B2r). The speech's reference to the sea evokes the defeat of the Armada and England's continuing need to fortify its southern counties against possible attacks, and it represents Sussex as crucial to these past and future efforts. Its central message is that Elizabeth will be able to hold off Spain with the help of Sussex.

The Wild Man repeatedly uses the word "arms" to describe the tree branches, which reminds us of the arms hanging on the tree, and his emphasis on the strength of Sussex men and their willingness to fight could imply that Sussex intends to defend its true religion. Its language of strength, defense, and honor presents Sussex as ready for war, and the crux is whether we interpret Sussex as aiding or resisting Elizabeth. The pageantry language argues that Montague and the Sussex arms are prepared to protect and defend England and its monarch. Although Montague and several of his neighbors are Catholic, they are steadfastly devoted to Elizabeth. They will fight for and with her. The Wild Man says this directly:

> For himselfe, and all these honourable Lords, and Gentlemen, whose shieldes your Maiestie doeth here beholde, I can say this, that as the veines are dispersed through all the bodie, yet when the heart feeleth any extreame passion, sende all their bloud to the heart for comfort: so they being in diuers places, when your Maiestie shall but stande in feare of any daunger, will bring their bodies, their purses, their soules, to your Highnesse, being their heart, their head, and their Soueraigne. (sig. B2r)

This metaphor argues that the region will fight on behalf of Elizabeth to protect her body and kingdom. Although the county is somewhat geographically distant from her, it is resolutely part of her body and follows her command. The Cowdray speeches together establish mutual obligation: the Sussex men will obey and defend Elizabeth if she promises to include and protect them. They advance an argument similar to the Cecils' at Theobalds that same year: Elizabeth can root out domestic and international treachery with the help of Montague and his county. The entertainments at Theobalds, Elvetham, and many other places construct a religious definition of England as a Protestant nation led by a Protestant monarch. The Cowdray text does not support this definition, nor is it invested in crafting a unified identity for England. Instead, the pageantry's descriptions of Sussex create a definition of England as multi-faceted and consisting of a network of independent counties that are loosely united through their shared loyalty to Elizabeth. It argues that England can be both Elizabeth's realm – a place defined by the monarch – and a conglomerate of diverse subjects.

My discussion so far offers close analysis of the passages that both editions share, and, although there is considerable potential for subversion, they overall represent Montague and Sussex as devout to Elizabeth as they insist that religious affiliation does not determine loyalty or treason. Both quartos depict the entertainment as a personal argument for favor as well as a larger claim about tolerance for Catholic subjects. But neither version prints the pageantry speeches in isolation; they frame them with narration and, in the case of the first quarto, the lyrics to three songs. The differences between the two versions affect our interpretation of the shared passages and the entertainment as a whole. Although both insist on Montague's loyalty, the song lyrics in the first quarto amplify the possible resistance that underlies this claim. By contrast, the added narration in the second quarto constructs a heightened sense of community that includes Elizabeth and embraces her authority.

The three songs in the first quarto, all absent from the other edition, together encourage a more subversive reading of the entertainment. Using love as a metaphor for political ambition and favor, these songs offer veiled critique and demand fair treatment from Elizabeth on behalf of the hosts and their Catholic neighbors. The first "Dittie," which the text explains was sung while Elizabeth hunted deer on Monday, fashions her as a Petrarchan mistress. Its blazon recalls the language of several pageants and songs in earlier country house entertainment: Elizabeth's hair is like gold, her eyes are like stars, and she is a chaste goddess and unavailable love interest.[37] The song echoes phrases from the Porter's speech as it praises her as a powerful woman who is in her advanced age a "miracle of time," "the worlds storie," "Fortunes Queen," and "Natures glory" (sig. A4r). Yet she wields her power violently. The song is accompanied by the gift of a bow for a "huntresse," and the lyrics draw on the language of hunting:

> Your eies are arrows though they seeme to smile
> which neuer glanst but gald the stateliest hart,
> Strike one, strike all, for none at all can flie,
> They gaze you in the face although they die.
>
> (sig. A4v).

When printed as part of the Cowdray entertainment, this fairly conventional rhetoric takes on greater significance. Just as earlier performances and texts used Petrarchan complaints to protest Elizabeth's hesitancy to offer favor, this song adopts hunting metaphors to critique her treatment of suitors, especially the Catholic subjects who love her, as it celebrates her status as a ruler with international power. It depicts Elizabeth as unyielding, determined, and more brutal than she seems – all qualities the entertainment both celebrates and protests depending on whether those she strikes

---

[37] See Chapter 2, pp. 51–61.

are Spaniards or Sussex Catholics. Because the song's emphasis on violence and the inability to escape Elizabeth is especially strong, it garners the reader's sympathy for those who love her and insinuates that her suitors experience an uphill battle. As it offers implied critique of Elizabeth's treatment of her Catholic subjects, it provides an apt metaphor for the Cowdray performance: Elizabeth's hosts were happy to welcome her and "gaze [her] in the face" even though they risked offending her.

The second "Dittie," turns to the perspective of a love-struck suitor who finds a way to regain power. When the lover is cast down multiple times, his love grows stronger in response. Through sustained focus on unrequited love as a metaphor, this song introduces the idea of martyrdom, which shapes our reading of the Wild Man's and Angler's speeches that surround it. The song begins with a description of the phoenix, a bird often associated with Elizabeth, and the way it rises triumphantly from ashes. When the speaker calls this bird "The rarest thing on earth except my loue," he argues that his devotion in its splendor exceeds all else, including a symbolic representation of the Queen's power (sig. B2v). The second stanza extends the metaphor:

> My loue that makes his neast with high desires,
> and is by beauties blaze to ashes brought,
> Out of the which do breake out greater fires,
> they quenched by disdain consume to nought,
> And out of nought my cleerest loue doth rise,
> True loue is often slaine but neuer dies.
>
> (sig. B2v)

Following the previous song, this one hints that the power of Elizabeth's devoted lover is even greater than her own. He is ambitious in reaching for his mistress – the foundation of his love is "high desires" – but like the phoenix, his love grows out of the ashes of rejection. Furthermore, the song dedicates all its lyrics to the lover and reserves no space for descriptions of the mistress.

The final stanza connects this personal love to the Queen's hosts and the political stakes of the entertainment when it compares the speaker's love to chamomile, which grows the more it is trodden, and to "the Palme that higher reares his head, / when men great burrhens [burdens] on the branches throw" (sig. B2v). The palm was a symbol of victory and triumph, especially as in martyrdom, and this lover indeed sounds like a martyr.[38] The images in this song, as in the previous one, are violent; the lover is

---

[38] *OED*, "palm," *n.*, def. 2b.

burned and trampled but gains strength from his suffering. In context, the song alludes to Montague's dual loyalties to Elizabeth and to the Catholic Church. Because the book presents these lyrics directly after the Wild Man's speech with no narrative interlude, it suggests that the song's setting is the same tree where the local and royal arms are hung. The line about "great burrhens" thrown on branches recalls that tree and refigures it as a symbol of martyrdom. Its declaration of defiant strength in the face of undeserved violence presents the arms not as a representation of the county's unity with the Crown, but as a warning of their willingness to use military prowess. At least, the song causes us to ask: when Sussex men take arms, where will their allegiance lie? Its final words offer a subtle critique of Elizabeth's treatment of the host family and Catholic subjects more generally. The song suggests that "Ingratitude" fancies "the tombe" (sig. b2v). The cruel mistress from the first song and this one certainly appears ungrateful, and if ingratitude is associated with death, the outlook is not good for the mistress unless she stops withholding favor to subjects who deserve it.

The third song, printed after the Angler's speech, calls for change. It builds on the Angler's implicit argument that the loyalty of Elizabeth's hosts is far superior to treacherous, prattling alternatives, and it advises her to turn unrequited love into a mutually beneficial alliance. It again speaks of love and describes it using a violent metaphor: a fish caught "vnawares" by a hook (sig. b4r). It suggests that "poore Fisher men" feel love deeply, although their external appearance and behavior might indicate otherwise: "rich pearles are found in hard and homely shels / Our habits base, but hearts as true as steele" (sig. b4v). Like these fishermen, Montague and his wife are more dedicated servants than their religious affiliation might make others assume. Loyal subjects are found in surprising places. According to the song, the fisherman's motto is: "Loue me and Ile loue thee" (sig. b4v), which aptly summarizes this version of the Cowdray entertainment. Through the performance and printed texts, Montague and Magdalen alternately ask, beg, and demand the Queen to love and favor them, and when this song uses the inclusive pronouns "we" and "our," it underscores that the hosts stand in for English Catholics more broadly. At its end, the song declares "our" perseverance: like a patient Angler "content to tarrie" until fish bite, "we neuer leaue" until we are satisfied (sig. b4v). It concludes with a warning, "We count them lumps that will not bite at loue," which suggests that those who do not return affection are diseases that must be wiped out (sig. b4v). This last stanza delivers a clever equivocation: it pronounces either the hosts' steadfast dedication to Elizabeth or the kind of threatening perseverance we see in the previous song. When it emphasizes that the hosts will love and protect Elizabeth if she treats them well, it offers a plea and a promise, but also a warning and a critique.

When we examine the three songs together, their critical tone and collection of violent imagery contribute to a more defiant version of the entertainment. As a cruel Petrarchan mistress, Elizabeth is more silent and unreasonable in this version. These qualities distance her from the host family, and her silence suggests simultaneously her own resistance and her vulnerability as a woman whom men desire to control. The presence of these songs encourages us to pay more attention to language that threatens to undermine the pageantry's message of devout loyalty to royal authority. It highlights tension, struggle, and resistance beneath the necessary posturing of royal entertainment. It heightens the pageantry's focus on factional politics, and it even hints at martyrdom. Taken together with the pageantry speeches, the song lyrics impart the message that Elizabeth had better value the strengths and devotion of this region, tolerate their continued Catholicism, and discontinue undeserved censure in order to retain them as her allies.

The book in its second version does not offer such an ultimatum; without the songs, it becomes more conservative and optimistic. In place of the lyrics to the first song, this edition identifies the violent blazon simply as "a sweet song" (sig. A4v). It does not permit readings of the song as veiled protest; instead, it interprets it for us as pleasant, light entertainment. Without the Petrarchan metaphors in the three songs and with added description about Elizabeth's positive interactions at Cowdray, the second quarto represents the Queen as more accessible and receptive than does the first. After the Porter's speech, in which the entertainment first declares Montague's loyalty and offers Elizabeth the key to his heart, the narrator adds: "Wherewithall her Highnes tooke the keye, and said she would sweare for him, there was none more faithfull: Then being alighted, she embraced the Ladie *Montecute*, and the Ladie *Dormir* her daughter. The Mistresse of the house (as it were weeping in her bosome) said, *O happie time, O ioyfull daie!*" (sig. A4r). The book shows the Queen taking Montague's gift and responding with a testament to his dependability. This important gesture completes the exchange Montague initiated in the welcome address. Once Elizabeth attests to the truth behind his self-representation, any hints of subversion in his claim to ownership fade away.

The added narration about Elizabeth's interaction with the household mistress and her daughter represents them as intimate friends. Elizabeth steps off her horse to greet these women, embraces them, and brings about a heightened emotional response from Magdalen. This seemingly personal

moment interprets a public performance as illustrating a successful political alliance between two powerful women. A posthumous biography of
Magdalen suggests that she was less of a conformist than was her husband,
and even if only part of this account is true, Magdalen may have had
even more reason than did her husband to perform the role of a loyal
subject.[39] She was no shrinking violet, and although only one record of
the entertainment mentions her briefly, she would have been an imposing
presence at the performance in body and spirit.[40] Her presence might have
even added tension to the event. The first quarto excludes her entirely,
and when the second quarto reveals that she co-hosted the occasion, it
describes her contribution (and the participation of her daughter, Elizabeth Dormir) as evidence of a solidified alliance with the Queen. When the
second quarto later explains that the Queen knighted Elizabeth Dormir's
husband, Robert, and brother, George, at the end of her stay at Cowdray,
it offers the implicit claim that these women and their family's interactions
with Elizabeth led to genuine reward.

Fuller descriptions of the Queen's reactions make the event seem more
reciprocal and interactive, and other lines unique to the second quarto
depict the occasion as an enormous, celebratory, and collaborative community event. As it reports the contributions by those besides Montague,
it continues to represent Elizabeth as especially contented and the entertainment as a joyous one. It identifies that the hunting was "ordered" by
Montague's son Henry and that Elizabeth hunted with the Countess of
Kildare (sig. A4v). Where the first quarto gives the song about the phoenix-
like lover, this version explains that after hunting, "so went all backe to
Cowdrey to supper" (sig. B2v). The word "all" emphasizes the solidifica-
tion of a community, one that includes Elizabeth and her court as well as
local figures. The second quarto also supplies additional narration about
the feasts Elizabeth enjoyed at Cowdray. Her breakfast the first morning
included "three Oxen, and one hundred, and fourtie Geese," and later
she feasted "most sumptuously at a table foure and twentie yards long"
and then one twice that long (sig. A4r, B2v, B4r). These precise details add
something new and specific for Wright's consumers of news, they testify to
the hospitality and therefore status of the host family, and they suggest that

---

[39] Smith, *Vertvovs Lady*. Magadalen came from a family of fervent Catholics, served Mary Tudor as
      a maid of honor, and worked in the Catholic household of Anne Sapcote, Countess of Bedford.
      There is little evidence about her relationship with Elizabeth, but because her Dacre relatives were
      involved in plots against the Queen, it is likely that Elizabeth looked at her with some suspicion.
      After her husband's death, Magdalen's household at Battle Abbey held mass and served as a place
      of refuge for Catholics.
[40] She was quite tall and, in Smith's words, "fat and grosse in body" (*Vertvovs Lady*, sig. F2r).

an enormous number of people dined with the Queen. The book indicates that only those of high status engaged in this part of the entertainment – only "the Lordes and Ladies" feasted at the long tables (sig. B2v) – but it represents the event as a community-wide celebration that demonstrated more unity than division.[41] This perspective is especially clear when the narrator explains that on Thursday evening, "the countrie people presented themselues to hir Maiestie in a pleasant daunce with Taber and Pipe. And the Lord *Montague* and his Lady among them, to the great pleasure of all the beholders, and gentle applause of her Maiestie" (sig. B4r). As with earlier moments in the second quarto, this passage presents a moment of inclusive, festive interaction to argue that the performance succeeded in pleasing Elizabeth and promoting Montague's stature. It insists that Elizabeth is part of the community formed at Cowdray, that the Browne family enjoys her favor, and that Montague is a political insider. Whereas the first quarto represented the performance as a more intimate negotiation between Montague and Elizabeth, this version constructs it as evidence of a larger, idyllic community that glosses over difference.

The final sentence of the second quarto brings our attention back to the royal and local arms hanging on the tree, and it explicitly interprets this display as a symbol of unity rather than resistance. After descriptions of Elizabeth's feasting, the country dance, and the names of the six men she knighted, the book concludes with this line: "The escutchions on the Oke remaine, and there shall hange, till they can hang together one peece by another" (sig. B4v). The arms remain as a memento of the event and suggest continued collaboration in this region. The final phrase implies that more work needs to be done – the book emphasizes the need to maintain and strengthen the collaborative alliance between Elizabeth and local nobility – but it represents the performance as a successful start. Where the first quarto ends with a personal exchange between Montague and Elizabeth, the second leaves us with the hope of regional and national unity. It claims that Elizabeth brings together and controls England – a myth that the first quarto undermines.

The Elvetham Entertainment: Writing England as a World Power

The entertainment at Elvetham was a plea less for equality than for forgiveness, but its objectives and subsequent printed book mostly parallel those

---

[41] The community extended beyond Cowdray as well. This edition of the book situates Elizabeth's visit within her journey across the larger region by saying she dined at Farnham before coming to Cowdray and would travel to Chichester next.

at Cowdray. Like Montague, Hertford identified himself as a marginalized figure who needed to prove his loyalty to Elizabeth and her court and, like the Cowdray book, the Elvetham one both promoted its host's agenda and functioned as political news. It chronicles a recent event in substantial detail and construes its significance as a testament to England's enhanced power on the international stage, and it was popular enough to warrant a revised edition, which amplifies its emphasis on nation-building. Its publisher also imagined a national, diverse readership, but one united in religion as well as language and monarch.

We have already examined the political stakes of the performance from the perspective of Hertford and his wife, and the printed book extends several of their aims. It interprets the entertainment as a successful bid for personal favor and, especially in its first edition, it downplays collaboration to publicize Hertford's prestige. As in the Cowdray book, the first quarto's narrator repeatedly refers to Hertford as "my Lord," which suggests deference and indicates that the narrator may have looked to Hertford as a patron. The narrator even worries at one point about displeasing "the honorable minded Earle," and the book aligns itself with Hertford with an even heavier hand than the Cowdray book praises Montague.[42] Both editions feature Hertford's name and coat of arms on the title page, and both begin with a lengthy "Proeme" that describes his careful preparations for the event (sig. A2r). This preface explains how he hired hundreds of laborers to renovate Elvetham, directed his servants to please Elizabeth, and led the men who greeted her outside Elvetham. It instructs readers to interpret these actions as evidence of Hertford's "vnfained loue, and loyall duetie to her most gratious highnesse" (sig. A2r). In the final paragraph of the first quarto, the narrator once again brings focus to "my Lord of Hertford," refers to the event as "his entertainment," and hopes that "manie, and most happie yeares may her gratious Maiestie continue, to fauor and foster him, and all others which do truly loue and honor her" (sig. E2v). Because this edition identifies no other collaborator except music composer Thomas Morley, it presents the Elvetham entertainment as Hertford's elaborate personal gift to Elizabeth. It excludes even his wife from its descriptions. This especially blatant promotion of Hertford makes it tempting to speculate, as Gabriel Heaton and H. Neville Davies do, that

---

[42] *The Honorable Entertainement Gieuen to the Queenes Maiestie in Progresse, at Eluetham in Hampshire by the Right Honorable the Earle of Hertford. 1591* (London, 1591; *STC* 7583), sig. B4v. This is the first quarto, which I cite hereafter in this chapter unless quotations are explicitly identified as from the second edition.

Hertford subsidized the book to advertise his status and allegiance to the Crown.[43]

Although the first quarto does so more explicitly, both editions claim that the entertainment successfully crafted a reciprocal relationship between Hertford and Elizabeth based on trust and adherence to hierarchy. Hertford is "dutiful," while Elizabeth is "most gratious" and "highly pleased" (sig. A4v, C1r). Just as the performance had Hertford prudently cede authority to Elizabeth, the printed book emphasizes her uncontested power with a string of active verbs: "ruleth," "doth commaund," "gouerns," and "wins" (sig. B3r). It is littered with explanations of her "gratious acceptance" of Hertford's hospitality and delight at the pageantry; twice the narrator claims that the Queen so enjoyed a particular song or performance that she commanded it again (sig. B4r). The book's narration serves Hertford well.

Yet its publisher's interests shaped the book as much as Hertford's did. Both editions were published by printer John Wolfe, whom one book historian calls "the nearest thing to a news-collecting organization" in Elizabethan England, and they continue to reveal how country house pageants served as early sources of printed news.[44] Wolfe called the book *The Honorable Entertainement Gieuen to the Queenes Maiestie in Progresse, at Eluetham in Hampshire, by the Right Honorable the Earle of Hertford. 1591*, a title nearly identical to that of the Cowdray entertainment (see Figure 5.3). Wolfe partnered with both Wright and Scarlet with some regularity, and the nearly matching titles of their entertainment pamphlets suggest that they either consulted or influenced one another. The success of the Cowdray book might have inspired Wolfe to invest in a similar publication, whether or not Hertford solicited him or offered financial support.[45] As the primary agent behind the book's publication, Wolfe shaped its content according to his own interests and sense of its appeal, and his name stamped on the title page would have carried meaning for astute readers. Perhaps best known for his piracy and rebellion against the Stationers' Company early in his career, he consistently endeavored to publish profitable books

---

[43] Gabriel Heaton, *Writing and Reading Royal Entertainments From George Gascoigne to Ben Jonson* (Oxford University Press, 2010), 98; H. Neville Davies, "Looking Again at Elvetham: An Elizabethan Entertainment Revisited" in Margaret Shewring, ed., *Waterborne Pageants and Festivities in the Renaissance: Essays in Honour of J. R. Mulryne* (Farnham and Burlington, VT: Ashgate, 2013), 211–42.

[44] Matthias A. Shaaber, *Some Forerunners of the Newspaper in England: 1476–1622* (Philadelphia: University of Pennsylvania Press, 1929), 288.

[45] There is no definitive evidence that the first edition of Cowdray book was published first, but the importance both publishers placed on timeliness makes it likely that both initial editions were published soon after the performances they describe.

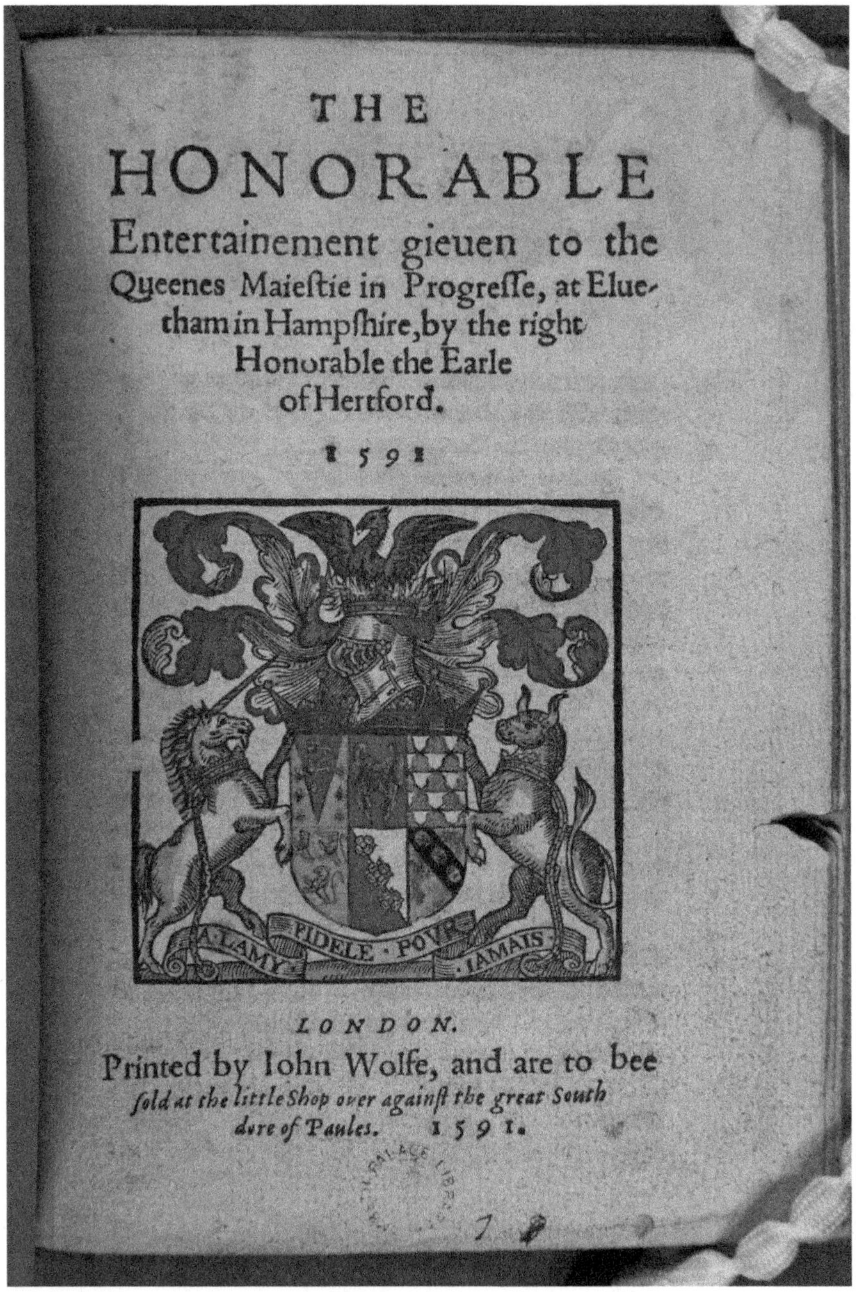

5.3 Title page of the first quarto of the Elvetham entertainment. LPL, shelf mark (zz)
1593.28.07.

that would propagate new and cosmopolitan ideas.[46] His biographers agree that he selected books with care, and, in an extended analysis of his career, Clifford Chalmers Huffman finds that his books tend to confront political problems, offer flexible strategies or adapt old solutions for new purposes, and value new experiences and tolerant attitudes.[47] When we position *The Honorable Entertainement* alongside Wolfe's other books, we might find appeal in its detailed description of a political performance or its renovation of a long-fractured monarch–subject relationship.

Most clearly, a focus on Wolfe's interests highlights the book's function as news. By 1591, he had become one of the most prolific Elizabethan publishers of news, especially foreign political news.[48] He valued these books for their timeliness and therefore published them with great speed. He entered a ballad in the Stationers' Register on November 14, 1588, as *A Joyfull Ballad of the Roiall Entrance of Quene Elizabeth into Her Cyty of London the [ ] Day of November 1588*.[49] He left the date blank because he entered it before the event occurred and before he knew the exact date of Elizabeth's arrival. Wolfe prepared to publish the Elvetham book with almost as much speed. He entered it into the Stationers' Register on October 1, 1591, about a week after its performance, and he likely printed it soon after.[50] Its past-tense descriptions and precise dates corroborate the notion that it was printed after the fact to describe a newsworthy event. The narrator refers to it as a "discourse" (sig. A2r), a term commonly applied to Elizabethan news pamphlets and regularly used in titles of Wolfe's news books.[51] Especially in its first edition, the Elvetham book provides meticulous descriptions of the estate, the host's preparations, the actors' costumes, the fireworks and feasting, and the specific actions and movements during the performance. Its publication shortly after the event

[46] For more on Wolfe's career, see Clifford Chalmers Huffman, *Elizabethan Impressions: John Wolfe and His Press* (New York: AMS Press, 1988), 1–121; Harry R. Hoppe, "John Wolfe, Printer and Publisher, 1579–1601" in *The Library* 4th ser. 14.3 (1933): 241–89; Ian Gadd, "Hunting Down John Wolfe for the New DNB" in Robin Myers, Michael Harris, and Giles Mandelbrote, eds., *Lives in Print: Biography and the Book Trade From the Middle Ages to the 21st Century* (New Castle: Oak Knoll Press, 2002), 193–201; Joseph Loewenstein, "For a History of Literary Property: John Wolfe's Reformation" in *English Literary Renaissance* 18.3 (1988): 389–412; Harry Sellers, "Italian Books Printed in England Before 1640" in *The Library* 4th ser. 5.2 (1924): 108; Shaaber, *Some Forerunners*, 286–8.

[47] Huffman, *Elizabethan Impressions*, esp. 11–19, 83.

[48] Shaaber, *Some Forerunners*, 286–8; Huffman, *Elizabethan Impressions*, 69–98.

[49] Edward Arber, ed., *Stationers' Register: A Transcript of the Registers of the Company of Stationers of London; 1554–1640 A.D.* (1875; reprint, New York: Smith, 1950), 2:506.

[50] Ibid., 2:596.

[51] For lists of Wolfe's publications, see Huffman, *Elizabethan Impressions*, 133–61 and *STC*, 3:186.

was of paramount importance in appealing to readers who desired news of its sights and sounds.

Wolfe's news pamphlets tend to focus on international politics; in 1591 most of his publications offered accounts of the religious wars in France and the Low Countries. Many were newly available in English, several of which were translated by Edward Aggas, and their titles announce the latest happenings, such as *A Most Excellent Exploit Perfourmed by Monsieur de Diguieres, vpon the Popes Armie* and *Nevves Lately Come on the Last Day of Februarie 1591 from Diuers Partes of France, Sauoy, and Tripoli in Soria.*[52] They promise a "Trve Reporte," "Trve Intelligence," "Discourse," "discouery," "Articles," or "Aduertisements" about happenings on the Continent.[53] Wolfe also had a hand in roughly 60 percent of pamphlets about the Spanish Armada published in London in the late 1580s and early 1590s.[54] Although Wolfe's catalog offers a range of political views, his books are mostly anti-Catholic. When he entered *A Joyfull Ballad* about Elizabeth's 1588 civic entry in anticipation of the event, he subtitled the pamphlet "and of the solemnity vsed by her maiestie to the glory of God for the wonderful ouerthrowe of the Spaniardes."[55] Wolfe must have procured a copy of the script before the performance, which he prematurely interpreted as revealing England's increased power following the Armada's failure, and his subtitle anticipates his take on the Elvetham entertainment as well.

This context draws attention to the Elvetham entertainment's celebration of England's successful defense against the Armada – a familiar theme we have seen in most entertainments of the early 1590s.[56] Its water pageant features elements that stage naval prowess: a fort surrounded with armed men and a sailing vessel furnished with masts, cables, and flags. The book

[52] *A Most Excellent Exploit* (London, 1591; *STC* 6878) and *Nevves Lately Come* (London, 1591; *STC* 11283).

[53] *The Trve Reporte of the Seruice in Britanie* (London, 1591; *STC* 18655); *Trve Intelligence Sent from a Gentleman of Account. Concerning the Estate of the English Forces Now in Fraunce* (London, 1591; *STC* 14657.5); *A Discourse vppon a Question of the Estate of This Time* (London, 1591; *STC* 6910); *A Discouery of the Great Svbtiltie and Wonderful Wisedome of the Italians* (London, 1591; *STC* 10638); *Articles Concerning the Yeelding of the Cittie of Grenoble* (London, 1591; *STC* 12359); *Aduertisements from Britany, and from the Lovv Countries, in September and October* (London, 1591; *STC* 3802.5).

[54] Shaaber, *Some Forerunners*, 285.   [55] Arber, ed., *Stationers' Register*, 2:506.

[56] See Harry H. Boyle, "Elizabeth's Entertainment at Elvetham: War Policy in Pageantry" in *Studies in Philology* 68.2 (1971): 146–66. Boyle identifies several allusions to Anglo–Spanish relations and interprets them as a personal tribute to Charles Howard, Hertford's brother-in-law and commander of the English Navy. However, these references make a broader political statement, especially when printed. The entertainment places Elizabeth, not Howard, firmly at the center of England's military success.

attributes England's achievements to Elizabeth's powerful guidance. It figures her not only as a goddess who rules England, but also as an "Empresse" who commands a "hemisphere" and "the wide Oceans" (sig. c3r–c3v). It describes India submitting to England at the mere sight of Elizabeth: "gould-brested *India*, / Who daunted at your sight, leapt to the shoare, / And sprinkling endlesse treasure on this Ile" (sig. c3r). According to the pageant, the sea gods and ocean are Elizabeth's servants, and the waves "haue swallowd vp your foes, / And to your Realme are walles impregnable" (sig. c3r). When it associates Elizabeth with the ocean by calling her a "sea-borne Queene" and imagines her controlling the sea ("More rich then seas, shee doth commaund the seas"), it insinuates that she alone stopped the Armada from reaching England (sig. b3r, d1v). It casts Spain as "Yon vgly monster creeping from the South, / To spoyle these blessed fields of Albion" (sig. c3r), but the sight of Elizabeth's "gracious looks" and virtue have transformed the Spanish monster into a harmless snail, represented by the twenty-foot-tall "Snayl mount" on the side of the pond (sig. a3r, c3r). The book's many references to Elizabeth's wide-reaching power craft England as an emerging empire, and when it vilifies Catholic Spain as a deformed monster, it insinuates that Elizabeth's Protestant rule has made England superior.

The book defines England as centered on Elizabeth and – when read alongside Wolfe's other publications – unlike the Continental nations at war. Elizabeth, it claims, has kept England peaceful and affluent. In the entertainment's first pageant, a Poet greets her with an olive branch to signify peace, and a pageant on the final day praises her for "Inducing peace, subduing warres" (sig. e1v). As we have seen, the book describes a performance filled with "plentifull abundance" (sig. b4v), and through its portrait of a thriving country manor and descriptions of an adored monarch, the Elvetham book indicates that England is more prosperous than ever following the Armada's downfall. It never explicitly argues that Spain's attempt to invade England failed because God has favored the Protestant nation; instead, it gives credit to Elizabeth. Like the Cowdray book, it worships her as a goddess, and all religious language centers on her: she inspires "holy feare" and is "blessed" (sig. b3r, c4v, e1v). It repeatedly insists that England is defined by and organized around its monarch, who has ushered in a peaceful, prosperous age. Although this patriotic rewriting of late Elizabethan England – a place where poverty was fairly widespread and where political power was more dispersed than centralized – may seem unsurprising in an entertainment designed to please the Queen, it

is somewhat unusual for Elizabethan country house entertainment.[57] As
Chapter 3 argued of the performance as well, the generic tendency to
challenge the stability of Elizabeth's control over the provinces is relatively
absent in the Elvetham book, which goes to great lengths to emphasize
her centralized power as it illustrates a harmonious relationship between
Elizabeth and Hertford, as well as between royal governance and local
people.

Besides his specialty in news books, Wolfe's goal of making new perspectives accessible to an English-speaking audience informs an interpretation
of *The Honorable Entertainement*. Although he published several foreign
news books in their original languages, his catalog reveals that he cham-
pioned the vernacular and regularly financed publications translated from
other languages.[58] As many as two-thirds of his publications translated
foreign books of news.[59] Several of his texts were printed in two or more
languages; for example, a 1589 book includes the same material in English
and French in parallel columns.[60] One 1587 title captures Wolfe's approach
to political news especially well:

> *A Briefe Discourse of the Merueylous Victorie Gotten by the King of Nauarre,
> against Those of the Holy League, on the Twentieth of October 1587. Both in
> English, and in French as It Was Printed in Fraunce. Whereunto Is Added
> as Soone as It Came to My Hand since the First Impression, The True Copie
> of a Letter Sent by the King of Nauarre to His Secretary at Rochil, Aswel in
> Confirmation of the Victorie against the Duke Ioyeuse, as Also the Ouerthrow
> That the Switzers Gaue to the Duke of Guise.*[61]

Its language suggests that Wolfe rushed the material to print as soon as
possible; he valued timeliness and expected his readers to do the same.

---

[57] For more on political power and poverty in Elizabethan England, see especially David Loades,
Power in Tudor England (New York: St. Martin's, 1997), 4–16; Jim Sharpe, "Social Strain and
Social Dislocation, 1585–1603" in John Guy, ed., *The Reign of Elizabeth I: Court and Culture in
the Last Decade* (Cambridge University Press, 1995), 192–211. Sarah Crover similarly argues that
Hertford turned Elvetham into a monarch-centered space at the expense of regional specificity,
but while she identifies this approach as typical of country house entertainment, I argue that the
Elvetham pageantry is exceptional and that its printed texts emphasize a nation-building function
that might not have been as apparent in performance. Crover, "A Taste of High Life at Elvetham:
Elizabethan Progresses and the Rural Consumption of Royal Neverwheres" in Susan Bennett and
Mary Polito, eds., *Performing Environments: Site-Specificity in Medieval and Early Modern English
Drama* (Basingstoke: Palgrave, 2014), 180–98.

[58] For more on Wolfe's specialties in Italian books and French news pamphlets, see Huffman, *Elizabethan Impressions*, 1–47 and 69–98.

[59] Shaaber, *Some Forerunners*, 287.

[60] *A Discourse vpon the Declaration, Published by the Lord de la Noue. Discours sur la declaration faicte
parle Sieur de la Noue* (London, 1589; *STC* 15214).

[61] *A Briefe Discourse* (London, 1587; *STC* 13129).

The title also emphasizes accessibility. He extended the book's circulation beyond France and, by printing it in English and French, he could attract cosmopolitan, bilingual readers, as well as those who read only English. Wolfe additionally had an interest in coterie literature and works that enabled popular access to courtly culture, such as the third quarto of Spenser's *Shepheardes Calender* (1586), the 1590 *Faerie Queene*, Thomas Hoby's translation of *The Courtier* (1588), and ballads about Elizabeth's speech at Tilbury (1588).[62] In this group of publications, Wolfe aimed not for a class-based audience of elite or common consumers, but for a broad English readership.

Wolfe's prefatory notes to readers often emphasize national benefit. He procured an English translation of a Dutch text about voyages to the East and West Indies in 1598 because a "learned Gentleman" thought its translation into "our Language" would be "very commodious for our *English Nation*."[63] Wolfe's repeated use of "our" unites his readers around a shared language and nation. He decided to publish this translation "to the ende it might bee made common and knowen to euery body" and "beneficiall to our Countrey and Countrey men."[64] In a 1588 preface, Wolfe writes that the book "will not onely be pleasant, but also verie profitable to our English nation."[65] Another of Wolfe's publications, a Spanish grammar book, includes a note from the translator, who observed that the original book in Spanish and French limited its audience: "none could reape any benefit by reading of it, but such as were acquainted with both the foresayd languages." In response and "mooued with loue and affection toward my country men," he decided to translate it into English so "that any English man may vse it to his profite."[66] One of Wolfe's books begins with a table of authors divided into "Foraine writers" and "Brittaine writers."[67] As these

---

[62] Edmund Spenser, *The Shepheardes Calender* (London, 1586; *STC* 23091); Spenser, *The Faerie Qveene* (London, 1590; *STC* 23080); Baldassare Castiglione, *The Courtier of Count Baldesar Castilio*, trans. Thomas Hoby (London, 1588; *STC* 4781); Thomas Deloney, *The Queenes Visiting of the Campe at Tilsburie with Her Entertainment There, To the Tune of Wilsons Wilde* (London, 1588; *STC* 6565); T.I., *A Ioyful Song of the Royall Receiuing of the Queenes Most Excellent Maiestie into Her Highnesse Campe at Tilsburie in Essex: on Thursday and Fryday the Eight and Ninth of August. 1588. To the Tune of Triumph and Ioy* (London, 1588; *STC* 14067).

[63] Jan Huygen van Linschoten, *Iohn Hvighen van Linschoten. His Discours of Voyages into the Easte and West Indies* (London, 1598; *STC* 15691), sig. A1v.

[64] Ibid., sig. A1v–A2r.

[65] Juan Gonzalez de Mendoza, *The Historie of the Great and Mightie Kingdome of China* (London, 1588; *STC* 12003), sig. ¶4v.

[66] Antonio del Corro, *The Spanish Grammer: VVith Certeine Rules Teaching Both the Spanish and French Tongues*, trans. John Thorius (London, 1590; *STC* 5790), sig. A3r–A3v.

[67] John Leland, *A Learned and True Assertion of the Original, Life, Actes, and Death of the Most Noble, Valiant, and Renoumed Prince Arthure*, trans. Richard Robinson (London, 1582; *STC* 15441), sig. B2v.

examples demonstrate, Wolfe specialized in books that resonated with the interests of a broad English audience. These books do not all advance a kind of Crown-centered patriotism as the Elvetham one does; instead, they together envision a national community of readers united by shared language and history. Wolfe selected books he could market as "profitable" or "commodious" for the creation and advancement of this community.

Wolfe likewise marketed the Elvetham entertainment toward a wide national audience. As *The Honorable Entertainement* depicts England as a flourishing nation with a strong monarch and international reach, it fashions an English readership. The text emphasizes its accessibility to all English readers when it provides a Latin speech from the performance along with an English translation and adds: "Because all our Countrey-men are not Latinists, I thinke it not amisse to set this dovvne in English, that all may bee indifferently partakers of the Poets meaning" (sig. B2v). Like Wolfe's prefatory notes to other books, this aside imagines a unified national community of readers. The book does not translate all Latin – it includes one four-line Latin verse that had been written on a shield during the performance – but the translation of a three-page speech into the vernacular makes it much more accessible to a non-elite literate public. Because this particular speech establishes Hertford's position as a loyal subject and submissive host, Hertford would have favored its reaching a wide audience, but the desire to include "all our Countrey-men" shows Wolfe's influence. Both editions of the book contribute to a central goal of Wolfe's career: making political news accessible to an educated and cosmopolitan English readership.

Like the Cowdray book, the Elvetham pamphlet must have sold well in its first edition because Wolfe published a revised version as soon as he gathered more information, before the year was out.[68] The expanded edition, which announces itself "Newlie corrected and amended" on its title page, continues to function as news and to interpret the event as a personal success for Hertford, but its several revisions alter the book's meaning in

---

[68] *The Honorable Entertainement Geuen to the Queenes Maiestie in Progresse, at Eluetham in Hampshire, by the Right Honorable the Earle of Hertford, 1591. Newlie Corrected and Amended* (London, 1591). A copy of this edition, which has not been assigned an *STC* number, can be found in the Royal Collection at Windsor Castle, shelf mark RCIN 1024755. Wolfe issued at least three versions of the entertainment: a first quarto, a slightly corrected issue of that quarto, and an expanded version. Compared to the first edition, the many spelling and spacing variants of the second quarto reveal that its type was completely reset. To publish this copy, Wolfe probably sold out of the earlier runs and expected enough demand to print it anew. I am indebted to H. Neville Davies, whose recent rediscovery of the second quarto led me there as well. See his detailed introduction to the Elvetham texts in Goldring, et al., *John Nichols's The Progresses*, 3:563–9 and his explanation of the book's history in "Looking Again at Elvetham," 211–42.

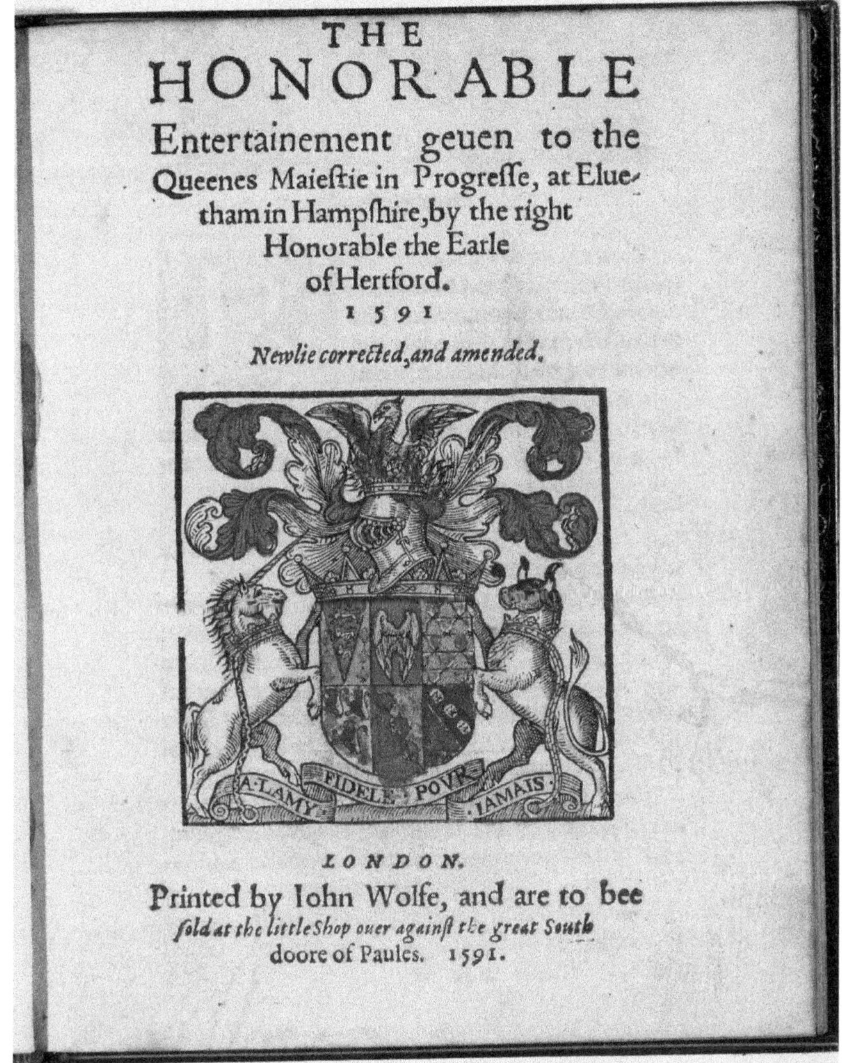

5.4 Title page of the second quarto of the Elvetham entertainment. Royal Collection Trust at Windsor Castle, shelf mark RCIN 1024755.

subtle and crucial ways (see Figure 5.4). Some changes simply clarify or correct errors. Whereas the first quarto claims that Hertford employed three hundred laborers, the corrected version changes the number to "two hundred or therabouts," and offices identified as "new builded" in the earlier quarto are now described as "newlie conuerted" (sig. A2r–A2v). The second edition cuts certain details, such as the distance the Queen traveled, a brief description of the hats worn by Hertford's retinue, and a list of the dishes served at a banquet. Instead, the revised version focuses more intensely on the dramatic shows. It inserts more descriptive song titles that allow a reader to visualize the performance more fully. Instead of "The Sea nymphes Dittie" and "The Plovvmans Song," we get "The song presented by Nereus on the water, sung dialogue wise, euerie fourth verse answered with two Ecchoes" and "The three mens song sung the third morning, vnder hir Maiesties Gallerie window."[69] These expansions enrich the reader's experience of the dramatic part of the entertainment, as the second quarto appears interested in creating a play text that will last beyond the immediate aftermath.

While the first quarto crafts a personal relationship between Elizabeth and a country nobleman, the second quarto describes the occasion more as a communal event centered on a loving and beloved monarch whose presence unifies men and women of all ranks. It places more emphasis on Elizabeth's joyful interactions with performers and spectators as it situates her even more firmly at the center of the entertainment. It adds five song verses that praise "hir sacred name"; reiterate the way her presence "doeth so increase our Climes delight" and benefits "Our happie Soile"; and celebrate her fame beyond compare (sig. C2v–C3r). A spectacle that Elizabeth "desired to see and hear it twise ouer" in the earlier version (sig. EIV) becomes one that "she commanded to heare it sung and to be danced three times ouer, and called for diuers Lords and Ladies to behold it" (sig. D3r). This description makes especially clear Elizabeth's powerful position. She controls the performance and the audience. Nature "yeeldes" to her in the Virgins' song in the second quarto (sig. B3v), whereas it simply "Giues" in the first (sig. B4r). The second quarto's added descriptions of her reactions make her seem even more satisfied with the entertainment. A new marginal note says of the Fairy Queen's song: "It was a most extreame rain and yet it pleased hir Maiestie with great patience to behold and heare the whole action" (sig. D3v). Another marginal note declares of the final song at her departure: "As this song was sung, hir Maiestie nothwithstanding the great raine, staied hir Coach, and pulled off hir mask giuing great thanks" (sig. D4r). Although this obsession with Elizabeth's enjoyment might increase the book's celebration of Hertford's success, it actually moves the focus somewhat away from Hertford as it adopts a more formal tone, changes

---

[69] In the first quarto, see sig. C3v, D3r; in the second quarto, see sig. C2v, DIr.

all insistences of "my Lord" to "the Earl," and describes a wider circle of contributors and spectators.

The second quarto inserts new descriptions of devisers and audience members besides Hertford and the Queen. One of the most striking changes involves Hertford's wife, Frances Howard Seymour. Although the first quarto does not mention her, the second quarto makes apparent her crucial roles as co-host and intermediary when it gives an account of her welcome that, just as the second edition of the Cowdray book does for its household women, represents Frances and Elizabeth as intimate friends.[70] The revised book also adds descriptions of the commoners in attendance, which directs attention slightly away from Hertford and toward Wolfe's emphasis on nation-building. It includes a line about Elizabeth's entrance into the park: "where (to her Maiesties great liking) were by estimat, neer tenne thousand people, from sundrie places" lined up to catch a glimpse of her arrival (sig. A4r). In the narrative about the second day's entertainment, these new lines appear: "And as hir maiestie sate at dinner, there was a dore set wide open for ayer, whereby the people might (to their great comfort) behold hir Maiesties presence in open view" (sig. B4v). Both passages, and especially their parenthetical statements, fashion Elizabeth as affectionate toward and adored by the masses. These added pieces of narration, which represent Elizabeth's common subjects as excited simply to view her, bolster the pageantry's claim that the whole region revels in Elizabeth's arrival and mourns at her departure. William Leahy cautions us not to assume that royal progresses were as successful as some texts claim, and he suggests that the Queen's visits often prompted "mutual suspicion" and fear rather than delight.[71] Yet the Elvetham second quarto insists that all audience members were united in their devotion to Elizabeth and awe at the event. This claim serves the interests of both Hertford and Wolfe.

Some of its additions expose the fiction within its idealism. Its added song lyrics amplify its praise of Elizabeth but undercut its celebration of her unchallenged power over unified subjects in subtle ways. It states that Elizabeth "neuer feares approching night" (sig. C2v), a foreboding line that implies that worst times are ahead. When it wishes that she will never experience "dismall daies or deadly teene" (sig. C3r), it casts her reign as an idyllic "Golden Age," but it again draws attention to the possibility of darker times. Although the second quarto insists that the thousands of spectators worshipped Elizabeth as the center of a unified England, it

---

70 I quote and discuss this passage in Chapter 3.
71 William Leahy, *Elizabethan Triumphal Processions* (Aldershot: Ashgate, 2005), 81–91.

reveals that they were divided by class rank. It includes this description: "*Siluanus*, being so vgly, and running toward the Bower at the ende of the pond, affrighted a number of the countrey people, that they ran from him for feare, and thereby moued great laughter" (sig. c4r). According to the book, country people are simple and easily frightened, and those of higher rank laugh at them. As the second quarto exposes class division, it heightens the representation of Elizabeth as a goddess who sits above and apart from her people. It explains that she heard the final verses from within her coach and reveals that she kept her distance from the performers.

A revised conclusion also reflects slightly altered objectives. At the end of the first edition, the narrator says that the Queen so enjoyed Hertford's entertainment that "hereafter hee should finde the rewarde thereof in her especiall fauour" (sig. E2v), which positions Elizabeth as poised to reciprocate Hertford's hospitality. In the second version, that phrase becomes "shee would not forget the same" (sig. D4v). The revised edition underscores that Elizabeth is in control of their relationship; it promises nothing specific and suggests that she might withhold favor. By this second printing, the possibility that Hertford would enjoy Elizabeth's "especiall fauour" might have already looked doubtful, but it is more likely that Wolfe wanted to make the book about more than Hertford's personal goal. The first quarto fashions an intimate relationship between a generous Elizabeth and a deserving Hertford in a bid for favor. The revised edition, however, moves focus away from Hertford and places even more emphasis on Elizabeth as the powerful leader of an emerging empire.

Both editions of the Elvetham entertainment reveal how printed accounts of pageantry could serve as political news for readers both popular and elite. Although revisions to the second edition help transition it from current news to historical account, later readers may have collected both versions as historical record. All three known copies of the first quarto survive in *Sammelbände*, collections of individually printed pamphlets bound by an owner. Sometime between 1605 and 1610, Richard Bancroft, the Archbishop of Canterbury, bound his copy with nine other pamphlets, including Elizabeth's coronation pageantry, a mayoral speech to Elizabeth, and late Elizabethan foreign political and military news books.[72] A copy at Cambridge University Library is bound with religious, legal, and regional news pamphlets from the mid-1600s.[73] Also in the middle of the seventeenth century, public notary Humphrey Dyson bound his copy with one

---

[72] LPL, (ZZ) 1593.28.07.   [73] Cambridge, Cambridge University Library, bb.11.50.

news pamphlet and twenty-one other Elizabethan and Jacobean pageants and masques.[74] Dyson's library reveals his desire to preserve texts that record important events in English history, and he identified the Elvetham entertainment as one such event.[75] Early modern readers often created *Sammelbände* based on the size or timing of purchases, but these particular collections share similar content and might help us understand how early owners envisioned and used printed country house entertainments.[76] All three collections position the Elvetham entertainment alongside texts that engage with local, national, and international politics and therefore underscore its function as political news. The only known copy of the second quarto is housed in the royal collection at Windsor, and although its provenance is uncertain, all four examples of the Elvetham book probably survived because they were preserved as historical record. They show ownership but do not necessarily prove readership. In fact, none of the known copies of the Elvetham or Cowdray books include marginalia or any other signs of active reading.[77]

My analysis of the Cowdray and Elvetham books extends the claims of Richard Helgerson, Andrew Hadfield, and other literary scholars who have identified multiple "forms" or discourses of emerging nationalism in Elizabethan England.[78] Those searching for "a fully fledged sense of the nation, the feeling shared by rulers and ruled alike of belonging to a common political community" will not find it in Elizabethan country house entertainment.[79] But by envisioning the nation more broadly as Elizabethans did, we can understand the genre as an important space in which elite subjects revealed what England meant to them. In some ways, printed

---

[74] BL, C.33.e.7.   [75] Heaton, *Writing*, 254.

[76] For more on how and why contemporary readers bound books together, see Jeffrey Todd Knight, *Bound to Read: Compilations, Collections, and the Making of Renaissance Literature* (Philadelphia: University of Pennsylvania Press, 2013), esp. 21–53.

[77] The provenance of the two known copies of the Cowdray book can be traced to the nineteenth century. The first quarto (BL, c.33.d.11) was owned by Thomas Jolley in 1810, and the second (BL, c.142.dd.23) was given to John Spencer by his sister Sarah in 1894 as "a relic from our mother's Home." Heaton notes that their mother's home was Cowdray House; it is possible that this book had a connection to the household, although many contents perished in a 1793 fire (*Writing and Reading*, 251–2). It is also possible that later owners or libraries erased marginalia from some of these books in order to preserve them as clean records.

[78] Richard Helgerson, *Forms of Nationhood: The Elizabethan Writing of England* (University of Chicago Press, 1992); Andrew Hadfield, *Literature, Politics and National Identity: Reformation to Renaissance* (Cambridge University Press, 1994). See also Claire McEachern, *The Poetics of English Nationhood, 1590–1612* (Cambridge University Press, 1996); Andrew Escobedo, *Nationalism and Historical Loss in Renaissance England: Foxe, Dee, Spenser, Milton* (Ithaca: Cornell University Press, 2004); Philip Schwyzer, *Literature, Nationalism and Memory in Early Modern England and Wales* (Cambridge University Press, 2004).

[79] Krishan Kumar, *The Making of English National Identity* (Cambridge University Press, 2003), 53–9.

country house entertainments "serve the state by writing the nation," to use Helgerson's phrase, and they sometimes identify England with the person of the sovereign instead of with any larger concept of community.[80] However, their conceptions of Englishness are more nuanced than just the royal patriotism we expect from such texts. Especially in its second edition, the Elvetham entertainment claims that a nation centered on a powerful monarch can also be somewhat populist and inclusive, even though the text exposes a clear division between upper and lower ranks. The Cowdray entertainment, together with Joseph Barnes' *Speeches Delivered* the following year, instead underscores England's heterogeneity and imagines a nation that comprised harmonious but distinct localities. Printed country house entertainments did not imagine a nation fully united around Elizabeth; instead, they explored multiple definitions of nationalism – all of which emphasized diversity, hierarchies, and disagreements in various ways – and demonstrated an active, unresolved debate in the Elizabethan period about what it meant to be English.

[80] Helgerson, *Forms of Nationhood*, 298.

CHAPTER 6

"This paper, which carieth so base names"
The Sidneys, Authorship, and Printed Pageantry as Literature

The previous chapters have emphasized the collaborative devising of country house performances and the printed books that interpret them. This chapter shifts focus from hosts and publishers to two entertainment texts that bolster authorial identity for single authors. We now know the entertainments at Wanstead (1578) and Wilton (1599) by names and authorial attribution given them in print: "The Lady of May" by Philip Sidney and "A Dialogue between Two Shepherds, Thenot and Piers" by Mary Sidney Herbert, Countess of Pembroke.[1] The latter was "performed" only in print because Mary wrote it for a progress visit that never occurred. When she prepared to host the court in the summer of 1599, she planned to entertain Elizabeth with this short pastoral debate and present a copy of the Sidney *Psalms*, including dedications to Philip Sidney and the Queen.[2] But when the final version of the progress route did not include Wilton, there was no reason to perform it. Her brother's literary and political influence is clearly apparent in Mary's plans and printed text; his dialogue between two shepherds, performed at an informal gathering at Wilton, and the country house entertainment he penned probably inspired her entertainment.[3] Although rarely analyzed together, Mary's "Dialogue" and her brother's "Lady of May" share similar critical conversations. Most scholars assume that each presents a debate with a clear winner that we can recover from

---

[1] The editor of Philip Sidney's 1725 *Works* assigned the title "The Lady of May," and the earliest surviving printed text of Mary Sidney's entertainment in *A Poetical Rapsody* (1602) includes its title. The performance (or intended performance) dates of 1578 and 1599 are somewhat speculative but generally accepted as based on compelling archival and thematic evidence. See *The Works of the Honourable Sr. Philip Sidney, Kt.* (London, 1725); W. A. Ringler, ed., *The Poems of Sir Philip Sidney* (Oxford: Clarendon 1962), 362; Mary C. Erler, "Davies's Astraea and Other Contexts of the Countess of Pembroke's 'A Dialogue'" in *SEL: Studies in English Literature, 1500–1900* 30.1 (1990): 41–61.

[2] Margaret P. Hannay, *Philip's Phoenix: Mary Sidney, Countess of Pembroke* (Oxford University Press, 1990), 85.

[3] "A Dialogue between Two Shepherds, Uttered in a Pastoral Show at Wilton" in *Sir Philip Sidney: The Major Works*, ed. Katherine Duncan-Jones (Oxford University Press, 2002), 1–2.

internal evidence, but this approach overlooks each entertainment's development of the pastoral eclogue as a form that presents unresolved tension between opposing views. Both debates highlight the difficulty of pleasing the Queen. In the tone of a pastoral critic, Sidney's entertainment characterizes Elizabethan courtiership as futile. Two decades later, his sister emulates and attempts to surpass his entertainment, according to the Renaissance definition of poetic imitation. Her text exposes the paradoxes inherent in country house performance, especially the courtier's necessary struggle between political ambition and the need to be humble and submissive.

When Mary became agent of their authorial identities in print, she promoted her brother as the father of contemporary English poetry and herself as his literary heir. Both texts promote the country house entertainment not as news, but as politically engaged literature akin to the sonnet or eclogue. When Mary included her brother's country house entertainment in the 1598 folio of *Arcadia* and allowed Francis Davison to print her own in a section of anti-court pastoral poems in the anthology *A Poetical Rapsody* (1602), both entertainments' placement in these collections accentuated their critiques of courtly convention and Elizabeth's hesitancy to offer preferment.

Pastoral Politics in Philip Sidney's "Lady of May"

The initial printing of "The Lady of May" is part of the complicated publication history of Sidney's *Arcadia*. After his death in October 1586, Sidney's works and commemorative volumes celebrating his legacy became highly popular among publishers and readers.[4] Bookseller William Ponsonby found Sidney and his sister especially worth the investment. He published so many of their books that Michael Brennan has called him their authorized publisher, and these books were an instrumental part of Ponsonby's career as a literary publisher.[5] R. B. McKerrow has labeled him "the most important publisher of the Elizabethan period," largely because

---

4 Dominic Baker-Smith, "'Great Expectation': Sidney's Death and the Poets" in Jan van Dorsten, Dominic Baker-Smith, and Arthur F. Kinney, eds., *Sir Philip Sidney: 1586 and the Creation of a Legend* (Leiden: Brill, 1986), 83–103; Gavin Alexander, *Writing After Sidney: The Literary Response to Sir Philip Sidney 1586–1640* (Oxford University Press, 2006), 57–75.
5 Michael Brennan, "William Ponsonby: Elizabethan Stationer" in *Analytical and Enumerative Bibliography* 7.3 (1983): 91–110. Jean R. Brink argues against Brennan's assessment in "William Ponsonby's Rival Publisher" in *Analytical and Enumerative Bibliography* 12.3–4 (2001): 185–205. She emphasizes that Ponsonby was a businessman driven by profit rather than concern with great literature.

of his association with the Sidneys and Spenser.[6] The Sidneys' works also align with Ponsonby's interest in staunchly Protestant politics, as evidenced by his other publications.[7]

There is some evidence that Ponsonby actively sought the opportunity to publish these works. A month after Sidney's death, he approached the late poet's friend Fulke Greville to alert him that another publisher was preparing to issue an unauthorized version of Sidney's prose romance.[8] Although we can interpret this encounter in a variety of ways, it most likely reveals Ponsonby's ulterior motive to secure printing rights himself. Ponsonby entered *Arcadia* in the Stationers' Register on August 23, 1588 and eventually published three editions: the first printed one in 1590, a newly edited version in 1593, and the 1598 folio that included the country house entertainment and other works.[9] The 1590 volume, the unfinished *New Arcadia* edited by Greville, apparently displeased Mary Sidney, but Ponsonby tried to earn her trust and patronage.[10] He dedicated three of his eight books to her in 1590–1, and his publication of her translations of *A Discourse of Life and Death* and *Tragedy of Antony* in 1592 suggests that his attempts were successful.[11] The following year, he published the version of *Arcadia* that Mary sanctioned and probably supervised, and five years later, he issued a folio edition of this version with additional texts appended.[12] Yet once Ponsonby acquired the rights and decided to finance its publication,

[6] R. B. McKerrow, ed., *A Dictionary of Printers and Booksellers in England, Scotland, and Ireland . . . 1557–1640* (London: Bibliographical Society, 1910), 217.

[7] *STC*, 3:136. See also the index in Brennan, "Elizabethan Stationer," 104–6.

[8] Fulke Greville to Francis Walsingham, November 1586, SP Domestic, 12/195; Steven Mentz, "Selling Sidney: William Ponsonby, Thomas Nashe, and the Boundaries of Elizabethan Print and Manuscript Cultures" in *Text* 13 (2000): 151–74.

[9] It was published in all three editions as *The Covntesse of Pembrokes Arcadia*: 1590 (*STC* 22539), 1593 (*STC* 22540), and 1598 (*STC* 22541).

[10] Hugh Sanford wrote in his note to readers in the 1593 *Arcadia*: "The disfigured face, gentle Reader, wherewith this worke not long since appeared to the common view, moued that noble Lady, to whose Honour consecrated, to whose protection it was committed, to take in hand the wiping away those spottes wherewith the beauties thereof were vnworthely blemished" (sig. ¶4r).

[11] *A Discourse of Life and Death. Written in French by Ph. Mornay. Antonius, A Tragoedie written also in French by Ro. Garnier*, trans. Mary Sidney (London, 1592; *STC* 18138). Besides *The Covntess of Pembrokes Arcadia* in 1590, Ponsonby published Abraham Fraunce's *The Countesse of Pembrokes Yuychurch* (London, 1591; *STC* 11340) and *The Countesse of Pembrokes Emanuel* (London, 1591; *STC* 11339).

[12] For fuller discussions of the book history of the *Arcadia*, see Ringler, *Poems*, 337–9; Kenneth Thorpe Rowe, "The Countess of Pembroke's Editorship of the *Arcadia*" in *PMLA* 54 (1939): 122–38; Regina Schneider, *Sidney's (Re)Writing of the Arcadia* (New York: AMS, 2008), 1–36; H. R. Woudhuysen, *Sir Philip Sidney and the Circulation of Manuscripts, 1558–1640* (Oxford: Clarendon, 1996), 224–41; Victor Skretkowicz, "Textual Criticism and the 1593 'Complete' *Arcadia*" in *Sidney Journal* 18.2 (2000): 37–70; Joel B. Davis, *The Countess of Pembrokes Arcadia and the Invention of English Literature* (Basingstoke: Palgrave, 2011).

his agency virtually ended there. He had little (if any) control over the content; instead, members of the Sidney inner circle edited and supervised the three *Arcadias* he published.[13] Ponsonby decided to publish the 1598 folio at a time when he was starting to issue large, expensive volumes with regularity – a venture motivated primarily by profit. Sidney's name was highly marketable, and the volume rested comfortably in Ponsonby's bookshop among other pastoral literature, texts with Protestant politics, and earlier books by Sidney and his sister.

Although the contents of Ponsonby's catalog provide useful context for the publication of this volume, the folio *Arcadia* primarily reflects Mary's vision of her brother's literary career. Its texts probably derived from her own manuscript copies, and she appears to have supervised its editing and publication. The book announces her management of it in several ways. Its title, *The Covntesse of Pembrokes Arcadia*, gives her possession of the book, and it begins with Sidney's note to her, which explains that *Arcadia* was "done onely for you, onely to you" and hopes she will "long liue, to be a principall ornament to the family of the *Sidneis*" (sig. ¶3r–¶3v).[14] Editor Hugh Sanford's note then explains Mary's "protection" and compilation of the book (sig. ¶4r). Sanford praises her "honorable labour" and identifies the book's production as "most by her doing, all by her directing" (sig. ¶4r). He analogizes this supervisory position to that of a housewife or household manager; Mary's correction of the book's faults after its unauthorized publication resembles "repairing a ruinous house" (sig. ¶4r). These notes by Sidney and Sanford together represent Mary as the authoritative protector of her family's literary fame and socio-political reputation. Although Sanford's note claims that Mary was a conservative editor, who aimed to restore her brother's intentions as she understood them, her editorial decisions have shaped the Sidney canon.

In her selection of texts for this volume, Mary identified fictional poetry and prose as the cornerstone of Sidney's legacy. Whereas Greville desired to memorialize Sidney as a serious, moral, Protestant author and hoped to preserve his political and religious writings, Mary did not include Sidney's more explicitly political works (such as his defense of Leicester, discourse on Irish affairs, and letter to the Queen) or his religious translations (*Psalms* and *A Woorke concerning the Trewnesse of the Christian Religion*). This exclusion was not a question of access, but a conscious decision to shape

---

[13] Fulke Greville served as the editor of the 1590 quarto; Hugh Sanford and Mary Sidney edited the 1593 and 1598 versions. See Rowe, "Editorship of the *Arcadia*," 122–38; Skretkowicz, "Textual Criticism," 37–70; Davis, *Invention of English Literature*.

[14] Unless otherwise specified, I quote the 1598 folio of *Arcadia* (*STC* 22541) in this chapter.

his authorial image in a certain way. As the folio downplays Sidney's political and religious messages, it represents him more as an educated courtly poet than as a politician. As the final piece in the collection, "The Lady of May" follows *The Covntesse of Pembrokes Arcadia, Certaine Sonets, The Defence of Poesie,* and *Astrophel and Stella* as the culmination of Sidney's development of English pastoral literature and frustrations about cruel mistresses and courtly life. Together, these texts contemplate the ethics of Elizabethan Petrarchism as they test and rework its conventions.[15] They exemplify the latest literary trends and represent Sidney as a master of those trends. They experiment with and sometimes parody established literary forms and modes, and they expose the tenuous, frustrating position of a courtier poet in Elizabethan England. The collection represents Sidney as an author with a dubious relationship to the court, simultaneously a skilled courtly poet pleading for favor and a marginalized figure defiant in his independence. Although the book serves as a monument to Sidney's literary success, it also points to his political frustrations and missteps. It positions Sidney as an ideal pastoral critic, one who was close enough to the court to conduct an educated assessment but distanced enough to be critical. The inclusion of "The Lady of May" infuses the previous texts with a precise political context and encourages us to locate subtle contemporary allusions in the others. The volume as a whole cements Sidney's reputation as an author of prose, poetry, and pageantry, and, because it is framed as a way to promote Mary, it also advances her reputation.

The text of "The Lady of May" records a single pageant performed in the gardens at Wanstead. When the Queen walks through the gardens, an actor "apparelled like an honest mans wife" emerges "suddenly" in her path (sig. Bbb3v).[16] The wife, labeled in the text as the "woman-suiter," asks the Queen to choose between her daughter's two marriage prospects: the lively forester Therion and the quiet shepherd Espilus (sig. Bbb4r).

---

[15] Several Sidney scholars have identified this anti-Petrarchan thread in certain of these works. Ake Bergvall argues that the *Old Arcadia* and *Astrophel and Stella* provide sustained critique of the Petrarchan system. Jonathan Gibson similarly suggests that both works investigate the ethics of courtier poetry and adds that Sidney's *Defence* develops an alternative poetic theory. Ake Bergvall, "The 'Enabling of Judgement': An Old Reading of the *New Arcadia*" in *Studies in Philology* 85.4 (1988): 472; Jonathan Gibson, "Sidney's Arcadias and Elizabethan Courtiership" in *Essays in Criticism* 52 (2002): 39.

[16] I quote "The Lady of May" from the original printed text, the 1598 folio of *The Covntesse of Pembrokes Arcadia*. The singing match between Therion and Espilus is also printed in the poetic miscellany *Englands Helicon* (London, 1600; *STC* 3191). This excerpt appears among pastoral poems and songs, including the speech by Ceres at Bisham Abbey and the song of Coridon and Phyllida from the Cowdray entertainment, and it is presented as a text written by Philip Sidney for the Queen.

A pompous schoolmaster named Rombus, who parodies elite pretentiousness and Sidney's own learning, delivers exceedingly long-winded speeches filled with Latin that mock academic and courtly rhetoric. The woman-suiter's daughter, the May Lady, interrupts Rombus to introduce her suitors, who engage in a singing match about their love and suitability for her. A group of shepherds and foresters then begin to argue "whether of their fellowes had sung better, and so whether the estate of shepheards or forresters were the more worshipfull," and Dorcas the shepherd and Rixus the forester step forward to debate these questions in prose, while Rombus appoints himself moderator (sig. Bbb5r). Finally, the May Lady steps in again to remind the shepherds and foresters that Queen Elizabeth is the judge, and Elizabeth chooses Espilus.

Twenty years removed from its performance, the printed "Lady of May" no longer serves as news, nor does it record a royal event for posterity. Unlike the entertainment texts discussed in the previous two chapters, this one offers almost no narrative of the progress visit. Its brief header simply explains that the Queen was walking in Wanstead Garden when she encountered the first speaker, and a later passage identifies the Queen's response to the debate without quoting her directly. In performance, the pageant's focus on marriage might have hinted at Leicester's and Sidney's hesitancies about Elizabeth's own marital possibilities and opposition to a French match, but the printed entertainment is distanced from the political context of 1578.[17] It also downplays the contributions of its host, Robert Dudley, the Earl of Leicester. Its two brief references to Leicester are playfully dismissive and emphasize his lack of humility. The text first refers to him as "a certaine Gentleman" who seeks to do the Queen "all the honour he can in his house," but the May Lady quickly decides that Leicester's desire "is not the matter," which pokes fun at his pretensions (sig. Bbb4v). A second self-deprecating allusion, Dorcas' description of courtiers melodramatically complaining "in bushes," playfully mocks the representation at Kenilworth of Leicester trapped in a bush by his cruel mistress Elizabeth (sig. Bbb5v). In performance, this moment must have been funny. In its printed context, Dorcas' emphasis on Elizabeth's "extreame cruelty, some of her too much wit, which made all their loving labours folly" offers a

---

[17] Both Leicester and Sidney opposed a match between Elizabeth and the Duke of Anjou. Although Anjou would not officially revive his suit until the winter of 1578–9, he and Elizabeth started exchanging messages as early as April 1578. Sidney wrote to Elizabeth about the match in 1579: "A Letter Written by Sir Philip Sidney to Queen Elizabeth, Touching her Marriage with Monsieur" in *Miscellaneous Prose of Sir Philip Sidney*, ed. Katherine Duncan-Jones and Jan van Dorsten (Oxford: Clarendon, 1973), 48.

subtle critique of the female patron who denies these courtiers – a critique Sidney's sister will extend in her 1599 entertainment (sig. Bbb6r). Dorcas implicitly advocates a type of male courtier who is independent and needs not rely only on the Queen, and the printed entertainment holds up Sidney as exactly this kind of courtly poet.

Although Leicester seems to have played a less active role in devising this entertainment than he did at Kenilworth, the other extant text of the Wanstead pageantry reveals that the printed version excludes an episode that highlighted Leicester's agency. This manuscript text, known as the Helmingham Hall manuscript, appends a slightly longer version of "The Lady of May" to a copy of the *Old Arcadia*.[18] In an epilogue found only in this manuscript, Rombus presents Elizabeth with a chain of round agates and represents Leicester, whom he praises as "an honeste man," as a beadsman who has dedicated his life to praying for the Queen. Rombus pleads on Leicester's behalf for Elizabeth "to loue me much better then you were wounte."[19] The epilogue explicitly identifies the Wanstead entertainment as a vehicle through which Leicester hoped to win increased favor. It reveals as impossible the earlier image of an independent courtier and represents Leicester as unconditionally loyal to Elizabeth. Through religious imagery, it argues like many other entertainments that its host's true religion was loyalty to Elizabeth. Yet when it analogizes this absolute devotion and Catholic worship, it holds up for critique this kind of worship of the Queen. In their analysis of the epilogue, Robert Kimbrough and Philip Murphy speculate that it may have been dropped in printing because the allusions were dated by 1598 and because the speech offers an anticlimactic ending.[20] I propose instead that the *Arcadia* folio excludes the epilogue to downplay Leicester's role as patron and co-deviser and to showcase Sidney's authorship even more.

---

[18] Of the eleven surviving copies of the *Old Arcadia*, only this manuscript includes "The Lady of May." It belonged to the Tollemache family of Helmingham Hall in Suffolk. Their possession of the manuscript may simply reflect their interest in Sidney or in literature; however, it is possible that Elizabeth visited Helmingham during her 1578 progress, perhaps in August when it was close to her route. If she did or if the Tollemaches attended the nearby progress, the entertainment text may have served as a memento of the occasion, and the attached *Arcadia* would be read in the context of a royal progress. Their presentation together in the same manuscript highlights the structural and thematic similarities between "The Lady of May" and the pastoral singing matches in the *Old Arcadia* eclogues, which may have been court pageants before Sidney incorporated them into the larger project. Woudhuysen, *Circulation of Manuscripts*, 323–4; Schneider, *Sidney's (Re)Writing*, 58–93; Victor Skretkowicz, "'A More Lively Monument': Philisides in *Arcadia*" in M. J. B. Allen, et al., eds., *Sir Philip Sidney's Achievements* (New York: AMS, 1990), 195.

[19] BL, Additional MS 61821, f. 146r.

[20] Robert Kimbrough and Philip Murphy, "The Helmingham Hall Manuscript of Sidney's *The Lady of May*: A Commentary and Transcription" in *Renaissance Drama* n.s. 1 (1968): 103–19.

As part of the folio collection, "The Lady of May" exposes a disgruntled view of the Elizabethan patronage system, and its vexed perspective seems highly personal. Although Steven May argues that Sidney was in Elizabeth's favor when he wrote this piece in the 1570s, most scholars have read their relationship as more trying, and when Sidney's text appears as the culmination of the folio *Arcadia*, it implies a somewhat strained relationship between Sidney and the Queen.[21] It creates an image of a failed courtier thwarted by an unjust monarch, yet the entertainment does not beg to change Sidney's marginal status. Instead, it advertises his wit and independence as a pastoral critic. It presents him not as a deferent courtier who offers only effusive praise, but as a willful advisor unafraid to speak his mind. A parody that exposes frustrated desires in a self-aware manner, the text maintains a witty tone, which helps shape what David Norbrook has called the "detached and critical view of monarchy" that it shares with the *Old Arcadia*.[22] The folio offers as immediate context for "The Lady of May" Sidney's versions of and ruminations on the pastoral and Petrarchan modes of Elizabethan literature. It tempers its praise of the Queen, a crucial component of royal entertainment, with critical reflection on the nature of courtiership and current literary trends. This context highlights how "The Lady of May" represents the country house entertainment as a form that enacts critique and conflict.

Its approach is facilitated by its development of Elizabethan pastoral. As an earlier chapter mentioned, the Wanstead entertainment was composed and performed one year before the publication of Spenser's seminal *Shepheardes Calender* (1579) and may have been the first pastoral singing match in English.[23] As part of a collection including his pastoral romance, *Arcadia*, the printed "Lady of May" marks Sidney as a master of English pastoral. In it, Sidney stages pastoral contradictions, as, within a form designed to celebrate her, his entertainment expresses discontent with the Queen and her system of patronage. As "The Lady of May" offers opposing views and exposes unresolved tensions between ambition and servitude, it helps develop both English pastoral and Elizabethan country house entertainment as ways for devisers to work through frustrations about Elizabeth

---

[21] Steven May, "Sir Philip Sidney and Queen Elizabeth" in *English Manuscript Studies, 1100–1700* 2 (1990): 257–67. For descriptions of Sidney's relationship with the Queen as trying, see especially Katherine Duncan-Jones, *Sir Philip Sidney: Courtier Poet* (New Haven: Yale University Press, 1991), x–xi; Maureen Quilligan, "Sidney and His Queen" in Heather Dubrow and Richard Strier, eds., *The Historical Renaissance* (University of Chicago Press, 1988), 171–96; and Michael Brennan, *Literary Patronage in the English Renaissance: The Pembroke Family* (New York: Routledge, 1988), 47–53.

[22] David Norbrook, *Poetry and Politics in the English Renaissance* (London: Routledge, 1984), 87.

[23] See Chapter 1, pp. 22–3.

and her court. Unlike several other examples of its genre, this entertainment does not try to control the Queen, but emphasizes the impossibility of doing so. It therefore highlights the futility of the male courtier's project, holding up for critique both the courtiers who debase themselves before the Queen and the Queen who expects such flattery.

Most scholarship on "The Lady of May" focuses on the debate between Therion and Espilus and analyzes which suitor Sidney intended to win, and most critics, led by the influential interpretations of Stephen Orgel and David Kalstone, agree that the text favors Therion and the active life he represents.[24] In their view, the entertainment's line about Elizabeth's decision – "it pleased her Maiesty to iudge that *Espilus* did the better deserue her: but what words, what reasons she vsed for it, this paper, which carieth so base names; is not worthy to containe" (sig. bbb6v) – signals the Queen's selection of the wrong suitor. Although it was certainly within Elizabeth's character to interrupt or reject aspects of entertainments that displeased her, the commonplace argument that the debate has a clear winner overlooks internal and intertextual evidence to the contrary. "The Lady of May" does not favor either suitor, but stages a genuinely open-ended debate between two justifiable approaches to life and marriage. Both suitors receive equal promotion from other characters. The six shepherds and six foresters take turns arguing for the superiority of their candidate, and when the Queen first meets them, they are "haling and pulling, to whether side they should draw the Lady of May, who seemed to encline neither to one nor other side" (sig. bbb4r). As the other characters debate the suitors' qualities, the text underscores that neither is an ideal choice: the Queen must choose between a "wild foole" and a "sheepish dolt" (sig. bbb5v). The winning song, presumably written in advance of the Queen's decision, features the forest god Sylvanus and the shepherd god Pan and could be sung by either suitor. Sidney's coy omission of Elizabeth's words probably reveals

---

[24] Stephen Orgel, *The Jonsonian Masque* (Cambridge: Harvard University Press, 1965), 44–54; David Kalstone, *Sidney's Poetry: Contexts and Interpretations* (Cambridge: Harvard University Press, 1965), 42–7. Others who argue that Therion should win include Louis Adrian Montrose, "Celebration and Insinuation: Sir Philip Sidney and the Motives of Elizabethan Courtship" in *Renaissance Drama* n.s. 8 (1977): 3–35; Edward Berry, "Sidney's May Game for the Queen" in *Modern Philology* 86.3 (1989): 252–64; Robert E. Stillman, "Justice and the 'Good Word' in Sidney's *The Lady of May*" in *SEL: Studies in English Literature, 1500–1900* 24.1 (1984): 35–8; Linda Shenk, *Learned Queen: The Image of Elizabeth I in Politics and Poetry* (New York: Palgrave, 2010), 56–88; Kimbrough and Murphy, "Helmingham Hall," 105–6. Notable exceptions to this critical consensus include Derek B. Alwes, *Sons and Authors in Elizabethan England* (Newark: University of Delaware Press, 2004), 65–88; Duncan-Jones, *Courtier Poet*, 149–52; Schneider, *Sidney's (Re)Writing*, 76. Alwes argues that the entertainment inscribes failure and makes the Queen's judgment's irrelevant, Duncan-Jones argues that the text favors Espilus and therefore demonstrates a favorable response from the Queen, and Schneider proposes that the entertainment indeed lets the Queen judge the results.

more about his need for authorial control over the text than about his response to the Queen's selection.[25] Additionally, this rhetorical technique, which allows Sidney to appear both modest and assertive, underscores the entertainment's resistance to "the cult of Elizabeth" and desire for an alternative to the typical Elizabethan courtier–monarch relationship.[26] While other records of royal entertainments fawn over Elizabeth's words, Sidney declares his independence.

An early example of the English pastoral eclogue, "The Lady of May" helps establish that form as one that investigates opposing views about society, politics, leadership, and morality without attempting to resolve them and thus teaches its audience to judge the results independently. In his study of Edmund Spenser, twentieth-century scholar William Nelson writes of *The Shepheardes Calender*, "As Spenser uses it, the dialogue of a pastoral poem is not a Socratic demonstration but a valid disagreement in which the speakers explore what may best be said on either part."[27] When Willye and Perigot ask Cuddie to judge their debate in Spenser's August eclogue, Cuddie decides, "I deeme ech haue gayned," and a gloss by "E.K." adds, "So by enterchaunge of gyfts Cuddie pleaseth both partes."[28] *The Shepheardes Calender* does not initiate this type of dialogue, but builds on Sidney's model. His *Old Arcadia* eclogues, probably written soon after "The Lady of May," explore rival perspectives to raise questions, not to find solutions. In the First Eclogues, Lalus and Dorus debate whose mistress most deserves praise and which singer most deserves compassion. This dialogue between competing views ends not with a resolute winner, but with each shepherd praising the other's argument. Richard McCoy has characterized most of Sidney's works – with the odd exception of "The Lady of May" – as equivocal, ambivalent, and evasive of definite conclusions.[29] "The Lady of May" indeed shares this quality with Sidney's later works and anticipates the open-ended dialogues of the *Old Arcadia* and *The*

---

[25] Wendy Wall similarly posits that the printed entertainment exhibits Sidney's assertion of authorial control; however, she argues that this line reveals his dissatisfaction with the Queen's choice. See *The Imprint of Gender: Authorship and Publication in the English Renaissance* (Ithaca: Cornell University Press, 1993), 144–5.

[26] I take the quoted phrase from Roy Strong, *The Cult of Elizabeth: Elizabethan Portraiture and Pageantry* (London: Thames and Hudson, 1977).

[27] William Nelson, *The Poetry of Edmund Spenser: A Study* (New York: Columbia University Press, 1963), 46.

[28] Edmund Spenser, *The Shepheardes Calender* (London, 1579; *STC* 23089), sig. IIr–I2v.

[29] Richard McCoy, *Sir Philip Sidney: Rebellion in Arcadia* (New Brunswick: Rutgers University Press, 1979). See also Robert E. Stillman, *Sidney's Poetic Justice: The Old Arcadia, Its Eclogues, and Renaissance Pastoral Traditions* (Lewisburg: Bucknell University Press, 1986), 87–97. Stillman argues that few of Sidney's eclogues offer final resolutions; instead, they teach us to judge.

Shepheardes Calender. The performances of Therion and Espilus might have influenced how appealing they appeared to the Queen. In the Italian tradition, the singing quality, not the content of a pastoral debate, often informed the verdict.[30] But because we lack archival evidence of Sidney's intention, the audience's reaction to these performances, or the reasons behind the Queen's selection, we must judge the shepherds on words alone. I would not go so far as to suggest, as do Catherine Bates and Derek Alwes, that Sidney deliberately presents the two suitors as equal in order to make the Queen's choice seem arbitrary and futile.[31] Although the suitors are presented on equal footing, they differ markedly in the values they represent. Instead of asking which suitor should win the debate, we can more productively consider how Elizabeth's choice of Espilus reveals what she valued in suitors and courtiers.

The lively, unpredictable Therion promotes action and individual freedom over monetary riches, while the more passive and wealthier Espilus represents a quieter and milder approach to life. The May Lady introduces Therion as having "many deserts and many faults" (sig. Bbb4v). Although she notes that he "doth me many pleasures, as stealing me venison out of these forrests," he also "growes to such rages, that sometimes he strikes me, sometimes he rails at me" (sig. Bbb4v). Therion might promise excitement and spontaneity, but his tendency toward violence makes him no ideal suitor from a woman's perspective. Espilus, who has "verie small deserts and no faults," is gentler and more predictable (sig. Bbb4v). The May Lady explains that "his fortune hath not bene to do me great seruice, so hath he neuer done me any wrong, but feeding his sheepe, sitting vnder some sweete bush, sometimes they say he recordes my name in dolefull verses" (sig. Bbb4v). As this description reveals, Espilus endorses the conventional pastoral virtues of simplicity, contemplation, and quiet retreat. The foresters criticize him and the other shepherds for idleness as they emphasize their own drive to achieve goals: "wee haue no hopes, but we may quickly go about them, and going about them, we soone obtaine them" (sig. Bbb6r). Espilus and Therion symbolize noticeably different approaches to life and love as they debate the accuracy of the pastoral assumption that the contemplative life carries more virtue than does the active life.[32] Yet both suitors speak of their desired relationship with the

---

[30] Schneider, *Sidney's (Re)Writing*, 74.

[31] Catherine Bates, *The Rhetoric of Courtship in Elizabethan Language and Literature* (Cambridge University Press, 1992), 61–9; Alwes, *Sons and Authors*, 65–74.

[32] The idea that the entertainment debates the merits of the active and contemplative lifestyles has become a truism in contemporary discussions, following Orgel, *Jonsonian Masque*, 44–54 and Kalstone, *Sidney's Poetry*, 42–7.

May Lady, using terms such as "slaue," "possesse," and "Bound," and implicitly represent courtship and marriage as a power struggle between a male wooer and his female beloved (sig. Bbb5r). Rombus later highlights their shared concern with possession and dominance when he explains that either "*Therion* must conquer" or "*Espilus* must ouerthrow" the May Lady (sig. Bbb5v). This language connotes a serious struggle for governing power and represents marriage as an oppressive state for women. If we interpret this competitive wooing as a metaphor for courting the Queen, the dialogue also dramatizes the courtier's conflict between ambition and servitude. In choosing Espilus, Elizabeth not only endorses conventional pastoral ideals, but also selects the suitor without personal ambitions, or at least without the drive to pursue them actively. Dorcas underscores this quality when he draws a parallel between Espilus and his sheep, "among whom there is no enuy, and all obedience" (sig. Bbb5v). Elizabeth's selection of the obedient Espilus suggests her favoring of suitors who are easy to control. Therion, who serves his beloved the best he can but is prone to outbursts, perhaps too closely resembles the male courtiers who fall in and out of her favor.

Although the entertainment is organized around the singing match between Therion and Espilus, that rivalry is not the only one worth considering. The entertainment is filled with explicit debates and implied competition between Rixus the forester and Dorcas the shepherd, Rombus and the May Lady, and the May Lady and Queen Elizabeth. It represents court life as full of debate and conflict, and, through the May Lady and the woman-suiter, it characterizes the Queen's relationships with her female subjects as no easier or less competitive than those with her male courtiers. The woman-suiter, the May Lady's mother, is a rustic figure whose social position and lack of experience make for a bumbling petition to the Queen. As she parodies elite suitors and their deferential relationship to Elizabeth, she alludes specifically to progress hosts who use the Queen's visit to lobby on behalf of their children. She reveals some simple truths: marriage can present an undesirable situation for women, Elizabeth's power is intimidating, and royal favor is difficult to obtain. The woman-suiter opens the entertainment by requesting the Queen's assistance in carrying out the gender-appropriate role of arranging her daughter's marriage. She explains her daughter's situation in these terms: "Other women thinke they may be vnhappily combred with one maister husband, my poore daughter is oppressed with two" (sig. Bbb3v). Underlying this joke about marriage is the more serious assumption, signaled by the phrase "maister husband," that husbands rule their wives and can do so with tyranny.

The woman-suiter keeps her appeal brief, demonstrates appropriate submission by kneeling before Elizabeth, and tries with comic effect to mimic the rhetoric of courtiership. She excuses herself with the line: "I dare stay here no longer, for our men say in the countrey, the sight of you is infectious" (sig. Bbb3v). Several rustic characters in this entertainment playfully and repeatedly differentiate themselves from courtly figures by suggesting that their language might be unique: "which we in countrey call matrimony" and "which we shepheards call a woman" (sig. Bbb3v–Bbb4r). The woman-suiter's line takes this joke further by satirizing the exaggerated language often used by courtiers to declare Elizabeth's power, just as characters in other entertainments claim the inability to survive after the Queen leaves. The word "infectious" carries with it negative connotations (physically and morally damaging, like a disease) along with positive ones (contagious, like laughter or virtue). Her reference to men "in the countrey" suggests on the one hand that poor country folk like the woman-suiter naively use inappropriate language; on the other hand, it references country house owners who flatter the Queen with ridiculous assertions of her power.

The woman-suiter continues her own such assertions in the written supplication she leaves with the Queen. It praises Elizabeth as wiser, more charming, and more powerful than anyone else, but even these positive comparisons employ verbs that can connote danger to others, such as "enchaunt" and "appall" (sig. Bbb3v). The curious phrase, "Your face hurts oft, but still it doth delight," acknowledges Elizabeth's dual role as a feared and beloved leader, but also suggests possible bitterness about her use of power (sig. Bbb3v). Dennis Kay proposes that this line and the earlier reference to "infectious" may refer to Sidney's mother's smallpox, which she contracted from the Queen.[33] According to John Nichols' accounts of Elizabethan progresses, Elizabeth's entourage literally carried contagion and plague into the country.[34] Even if we read these moments less as specific allusions, the humor of these negative phrases thinly veils an expression of resentment toward Elizabeth. The poem figures her as instilling fear and failure when it asks, "How dare I wretch seeke there my woes to rest, / VVhere eares be burnt, eyes dazled, harts opprest?" (sig. Bbb3v). The woman-suiter's fear arises specifically from the vast difference in status

[33] Dennis Kay, "'She Was a Queen, and Therefore Beautiful': Sidney, His Mother, and Queen Elizabeth" in *Review of English Studies* 43.169 (1992): 18–39.

[34] John Nichols, ed., *The Progresses and Public Processions of Queen Elizabeth* (London, 1823), 2:214, n. 1. See also Alan Hager, "Rhomboid Logic: Anti-Idealism and a Cure for Recusancy in Sidney's *Lady of May*" in *ELH* 57.3 (1990): 494.

between herself and the Queen until she decides that the Queen's "gifts enrich euen beggers sight" (sig. ʙʙʙ3v). Still, the supplication's worry about daring to speak to Elizabeth stresses the difficulty of approaching a monarch who might respond cruelly. Later, Rixus mentions they are "in the presence of such a one as euen with her eye only can giue the cruell punishment," and Dorcas responds, "Hold thy peace, I will neither meddle with her nor her eyes, they sayne in our towne they are daungerous both" (sig. ʙʙʙ5v). These hyperbolic statements poke fun at sycophantic courtiers and fearful subjects who grovel before the Queen, but they also release frustrations about Elizabeth's hesitancy to offer the preferment and responsibilities courtiers such as Sidney and Leicester desire. Through the woman-suiter's appeal, the entertainment represents the Queen as difficult to please and a courtier's role as a precarious one.

Where the woman-suiter is bumbling and vulnerable, the May Lady is deliberate and proud. The marriage-ready May Lady presents herself as competition for the unmarried Queen Elizabeth because of the values she represents. The May Lady repeatedly advocates pastoral, local, and country virtues over elite, national, and courtly ones. The entertainment juxtaposes her with the comic figure Rombus, whom the text introduces as "being fully perswaded of his owne learned wisedome" (sig. ʙʙʙ4r). Rombus is characterized by pretentious speech that borders on nonsensical, verbose strings of Latin phrases, and contempt toward the uneducated lower class, whom he calls "the contaminating hands of these plebians" and "these rurall animals" (sig. ʙʙʙ4r). Rombus presents an exaggerated version of a learned scholar and pleading male courtier in love with his own words. The May Lady interrupts Rombus' complaints about the others having not "yeelded" him enough "reuerence" with the simple assertion: "Away away you tedious foole, your eyes are not worthy to looke to yonder Princelie sight, much lesse your foolish tongue to trouble her wise eares" (sig. ʙʙʙ4r). Compared to Rombus' love for garbled Latin and convoluted rhetoric, the May Lady represents vernacular English and directness. She does not endorse national pride or imagine an England unified around this language, but instead promotes local, pastoral virtues over courtly elitism.

This conventional pastoral opposition between the country and the court manifests itself in competition between the May Lady and the Queen. The entertainment's male figures assume that Elizabeth will be offended by a woman whose authority or beauty might upstage her. They assure her that she possesses more beauty and deserves more praise than does the May Lady. One male shepherd begins to praise the May Lady's countenance but then stops and adds for the Queen: "not three quarters so beautious as your selfe" (sig. Bbb4r). Therion gives a similar comparison when he says of the May Lady: "Great sure is she, on whom our hopes do liue, / Greater is she who must the iudgement giue" (sig. Bbb4v). These brief lines do little to counteract the May Lady's competitive attitude toward Elizabeth. Although somewhat deferential and certainly intended to be funny, the May Lady represents herself as the region's democratic ruler and undermines the Queen's centralized power. She kneels before the Queen to show due respect and then discounts possible reasons for her submission:

> Do not thinke (sweete and gallant Lady) that I do abase my selfe thus much vnto you because of your gay apparell, for what is so braue as the naturall beauty of the flowers, nor because a certaine Gentleman hereby seekes to do you all the honour he can in his house; that is not the matter, he is but our neighbour, and these be our owne groues, nor yet because of your great estate, since no estate can be compared to be the Lady of the whole moneth of May as I am. (sig. Bbb4v)

This passage is playful and traditionally pastoral in its language. The May Lady reveals her own limitations as she boasts about ruling only one month, yet the passage challenges Elizabeth's authority through a series of binaries. The May Lady criticizes the extravagance of the Queen's clothing and implicitly the pageantry of progresses, suggesting that her region's natural landscape exceeds the beauty of this showiness. She refers to the surroundings as "our owne groues," a phrase that undermines Elizabeth's control whether it refers to possession by the local community or employs the royal "we" to claim ownership. She compares herself favorably to the sovereign and defies Elizabeth's authority by proposing that her command over this region and claim to the month of May overshadow Elizabeth's rule.

The entertainment continues to expose tensions between local and royal authority and between the fictional maid and the maiden queen when the May Lady says:

> So that since both this place and this time are my seruants, you may be sure I wold looke for reuerence at your hands, if I did not see something in your face which makes me yeeld to you; the troth is, you excell me in that wherein I desire most to excell and that makes me giue this homage vnto you, as to the beautifullest Lady these woods haue euer receiued. (sig. Bbb4v)

This passage suggests that the Queen's beauty is not only her best asset, but also the sole way she might win a competition with the May Lady. However, the May Lady also proudly describes her own situation as follows:

> I am a faire wench or else I am decieued, and therefore by the consent of
> all our neighbours haue bene chosen for the absolute Lady of this mery
> moneth, with me haue bene (alas I am ashamed to tell it) two yong men,
> the one a forrester named *Therion*, the other *Espilus* a shepheard very long
> euen in loue forsooth, I like them both, and loue neither. (sig. вbb4v)

She stresses that she has been chosen by election to serve, and she hesitates
throughout her speech to acknowledge the Queen's authority over the
region she claims as her own. Her authority is, in her own words, "absolute."
As the May Lady explains why she has been elected and why she has
attracted two suitors, she assigns herself the only quality she has admired
in the Queen: beauty. Her concluding speech refers to Elizabeth as "Lady
your selfe, for other titles do rather diminish then adde vnto you" (sig.
вbb6v). She adds, "Therefore I will wish you good night, praying to God
according to the title I possesse, that as hitherto it hath excellently done,
so hence forward the florishing of May, may long remaine in you and
with you" (sig. вbb6v). Although the May Lady dismisses other titles for
the Queen, she claims one for herself. She implies that Elizabeth rules the
court but cannot control the pastoral realm that she symbolically governs.
She may also hint that Elizabeth cannot control the entertainment's author
or the estate's owner. Unlike Elizabeth Brydges at Sudeley and the Russell
women at Bisham, the May Lady does not aspire to serve the Queen, and
unlike the Wild Man and Ceres at Bisham, her subtle threats to Elizabeth's
authority are never explicitly defused. In performance, when it is likely
that a cross-dressed male actor played the May Lady, her pretentions to
beauty and superiority over Elizabeth would have seemed comic. In print,
however, these resonances appear more like serious challenges. Beneath the
humor and parody in "The Lady of May" is the serious insinuation that
Elizabeth's power might not extend to all regions of her kingdom without
struggle.

In his note prefacing the composite *Arcadia*, Sanford accurately predicts
that Mary will persistently promote and develop her brother's works and
agendas in the coming years. His note ends with this prophecy: "Neither
shall these pains be the last (if no vnexpected accident cut off her determination) which the euerlasting loue of her excellent brother, will make her
consecrate to his memory" (sig. ¶4v). Indeed, she foregrounds her identity
as Sidney's sister in her patronage, editing, and writing.[35] She edited and
completed the *Psalms* he began, and the dedicatory poems she wrote to

---

[35] For other illustrations of this point, see especially Hannay, *Philip's Phoenix*, 59–105; Alexander,
Writing After Sidney, 76–127.

preface the *Psalms* urge Elizabeth to adopt a more radical Protestant foreign policy, one of her brother's former goals.[36] In *The Covntesse of Pembrokes Arcadia*, the *Psalms*, and her poem "To the Angel Spirit of Sir Philip Sidney," Mary builds an image of her brother as a passionate, undervalued poet who pioneered English pastoral and who never quite belonged at court. At the same time, she creates her own role as her brother's poetic heir. As her country house entertainment continues and revises aspects of her brother's works, it reformulates the siblings' authorial identities that Mary herself designed.

Mary Sidney's "Dialogue" and the Art of *Imitatio*

When Mary Sidney prepared to host the Queen at Wilton estate in 1599, she wrote "A Dialogue between Two Shepherds, Thenot and Piers," a pastoral debate that, like "The Lady of May," presents unresolved tension in a dialogue between opposing views. Because pastoral literature and eclogues featuring shepherds' praising contests were specialties of Philip Sidney, the very structure and situation of Mary's dialogue alludes to her brother's writing. Mary emulates and "overgoes" the earlier entertainment, according to the Renaissance definition of poetic imitation. *Imitatio*, as defined by such sixteenth-century writers as Roger Asham and Gabriel Harvey, is the art of analyzing and adapting the matter and style of accomplished writers while aspiring to surpass the earlier models.[37] *Imitatio* was a key skill for accomplished scholars and authors to possess. Because Mary attended several earlier progresses and wrote her pageant late in Elizabeth's reign, her text is well poised to reflect upon the country house entertainment's development, functions, and limitations. Although there is no record of her attendance at the Wanstead entertainment, she was probably there, and she accompanied the Queen on visits to Kenilworth, Woodstock,

---

[36] At his death, Philip Sidney left translations of Psalms 1–43; Mary translated the remaining 107 and revised several of her brother's translations. Hannibal Hamlin, Michael G. Brennan, Margaret P. Hannay, and Noel J. Kinnamon, eds., *The Sidney Psalter: The Psalms of Sir Philip and Mary Sidney* (Oxford University Press, 2009), xii–xxxii. For texts and commentary on the dedicatory poems to Elizabeth ("Even now that Care") and Sidney ("To the Angel Spirit of Sir Philip Sidney"), see Margaret P. Hannay, Noel J. Kinnamon, and Michael G. Brennan, eds., *The Collected Works of Mary Sidney Herbert, Countess of Pembroke* (Oxford: Clarendon, 1998), 1:92–115.

[37] Harvey coined the term "overgo" in reference to poetic imitation in a 1580 letter to Spenser, and Asham defines *imitatio* in *The Schoolmaster* (1570) as "similar treatment of dissimilar matter" and "dissimilar treatment of similar matter." Gabriel Harvey, *Three Proper, and Wittie, Familiar Letters: Lately Passed betwene Two Vniuersitie Men* in J. C. Smith and E. de Selincourt, eds., *The Poetical Works of Edmund Spenser* (Oxford University Press, 1912), 628; Roger Asham, *The Schoolmaster*, ed. Lawrence V. Ryan (Ithaca: Cornell University Press, 1967), 117. See also G. W. Pigman III, "Versions of Imitation in the Renaissance" in *Renaissance Quarterly* 33.1 (1980): 1–32.

and several other country estates in 1575.[38] "A Dialogue between Two Shepherds" sympathizes with the male courtiers who have struggled within country house entertainments to please the Queen and promote their own agendas, and it exposes the same generic paradox her brother underscored: the tension between political aspiration and the need to be submissive. But it also uses new strategies appropriate to a different political climate and an exchange between a female courtier and a female monarch. As her brother's posthumous editor and collaborator in *The Covntesse of Pembrokes Arcadia* and the *Psalms*, Mary used his models to showcase her originality as a poet. Her country house entertainment does the same, with added emphasis on her wit. When she demonstrates mastery of two forms – pastoral eclogue and country house entertainment – that attracted her brother, Mary legitimizes her authorial role as her brother's literary heir.

In "A Dialogue between Two Shepherds," Thenot and Piers debate the most effective way to honor their royal mistress, and they employ two competing modes of praise. Thenot speaks first and flatters the Queen in the language of a Petrarchan wooer, while Piers, the pastoral critic, points out the flaws in that language and insists that Elizabeth is above all praise. Piers, whose name recalls *Piers Plowman* and the Protestant shepherd in the May eclogue of *The Shepheardes Calender*, advocates plain speaking and condemns idolatry. While Piers promotes the Puritan ideals of restraint and moderation, Thenot instead represents courtly decadence and advocates the language of the "cult of Elizabeth," including its rhetorical excess and hyperbole. When Thenot asks the muses to "heave my Verses higher," Piers says, "Thou need'st the truth but plainely tell" and suggests that Thenot's inflated rhetoric is disingenuous (sig. B5r).[39] Recalling the praising strategies used in several earlier entertainments, Thenot unwittingly implies that Elizabeth's authority depends upon her physical presence when he celebrates her arrival: "Soone as Astrea shewes her face, / Strait euery ill auoides the place, / And euery good aboundeth" (sig. B5v). Piers counters, "Nay long before her face doth showe, / The last doth come, the first doth goe, / How lowde this lie resoundeth!" (sig. B5v). Just as Piers argues that the Queen's power continues in her absence, he remains skeptical of the ability of any words to capture her magnificence, and he suggests that an accurate tribute is wordless because Elizabeth transcends praise. When an

---

[38] Hannay, *Philip's Phoenix*, 33–5.
[39] I quote "A Dialogue between Two Shepherds" from the first edition of *A Poetical Rapsody Containing, Diuerse Sonnets, Odes, Elegies, Madrigalls, and Other Poesies, Both in Rime, and Measured Verse* (London, 1602; *STC* 6373).

exasperated Thenot finally asks what he can say that will be appropriate, Piers advocates silence. Their final exchange unfolds as follows:

> THENOT. Then *Piers*, of friendship tell me why,
> My meaning true, my words should ly,
> And striue in vaine to raise her.
> PIERS. Words from conceit do only rise,
> Aboue conceit her honour flies,
> But silence, nought can praise her.
>
> (sig. B6r)

Previous scholars have inaccurately interpreted this ending (and the entertainment as a whole) as Mary Sidney's successful repudiation of courtly convention, as represented by Thenot, and promotion of a radical Protestant perspective, as represented by Piers.[40] However, both shepherds employ conventional strategies for tributes to Elizabeth. Piers repeatedly answers Thenot's commonplace panegyric with alternative conventions. For example, when Thenot compares Elizabeth favorably to other figures of power, Piers responds with the popular assertion that Elizabeth is beyond compare: "Compare may thinke where likenesse holds, / Nought like to her the earth enfoldes" (sig. B5r). Furthermore, although Piers has the last word, the entertainment does not necessarily favor his viewpoint. When placed in context with other pastoral eclogues, especially her brother's entertainment, this praising contest offers no clear resolution. It instead presents two equally limiting strategies. It reveals the hypocrisy and contradictory impulses behind Piers' chosen conventions when he advocates silence only after he has spoken at length. His strategy of wordless praise has no practical application within the country house entertainment form. Piers' analysis of Thenot's artificial rhetoric meanwhile underscores its susceptibility to overreading or misreading, especially by Elizabeth. Through Thenot and Piers, the entertainment places in conversation two conventions available to courtiers praising the Queen: excessive praise and humble silence. By cleverly employing and critiquing both strategies, the entertainment is

---

40 Shannon Miller, "Mary Sidney and Gendered Strategies for the Writing of Poetry" in Barbara Smith and Ursula Appelt, eds., *Write or Be Written: Early Modern Women Poets and Cultural Constraints* (Aldershot: Ashgate, 2001), 160–4; G. F. Waller, *Mary Sidney, Countess of Pembroke: A Critical Study of Her Writings and Literary Milieu* (University of Salzburg Press, 1979), 82; Sallye J. Sheppeard, "Mary Herbert's 'A Dialogue between Two Shepherdes': A Study in Renaissance Poetic Method" in *Proceedings of the Conference of College Teachers of English of Texas* 46 (1981): 18–20. Hannay, *Philip's Phoenix*, 165–6 instead suggests that Piers does not necessarily represent the author's perspective because the entertainment explores tensions between the speakers' positions. I extend her argument as I demonstrate how the entertainment exposes the limitations of both sets of conventional rhetoric.

able to praise Elizabeth but also hold up for scrutiny the conventions she expects.

Through this entertainment, Mary does not simply continue her brother's project, but refigures it to fit a different political and personal situation at the end of Elizabeth's reign. Her dialogue unsurprisingly abandons representations of marriage and instead concerns itself with the timely issue of the best way to praise an aging queen. Although its shepherds disagree about the most effective way to do this, they both refer to Elizabeth as Astrea, an especially popular allusion at the end of her reign.[41] Astrea is the virgin goddess of justice whose return to earth is prophesied in Virgil's Fourth Eclogue. Her return will usher in eternal spring and a Golden Age of peace. The allusion to the Astrea myth in "A Dialogue between Two Shepherds" emphasizes Elizabeth's chastity and governing power. It also denies the progression of time and elides the economic and political hardships England faced in the 1590s. According to Thenot and Piers, Elizabeth-as-Astrea radiates beams of light and brings about springtime. Piers' skepticism of Thenot's language of praise is centered on its inability to capture Astrea's transcendence. When Thenot emphasizes Astrea's association with spring and compares her to "heauenly light that guides the day," Piers points out that spring "neuer leaues *Astreas* clime" and "*Astreas* beames no darknes shrowdes" to argue for the stability and permanence of her authority (sig. B5v–B6r). Both shepherds struggle to find a strategy that represents the Queen's control over England as everlasting, even if her control was indeed slipping in the late 1590s amid factionalism at court. This more charged atmosphere, a risky one for courtiers and monarch alike, is reflected in the entertainment's focus on the rhetorical construction of loyalty and especially in Piers' concern about the potential offensiveness of courtly language.

Yet Mary Sidney felt relatively secure in her socio-political power in 1599. Her influence as a literary patron has been well explored, and she held administrative duties for six estates as the wife of Henry Herbert, Earl of Pembroke.[42] Nicholas Breton's *Wits Trenchmour* (1597) describes Wilton

---

[41] Other texts that refer to Elizabeth as Astrea include John Davies' *Hymnes of Astraea* (London, 1599; *STC* 6351), George Peele's *Descensus Astraeae* (n.d. [1591]; *STC* 19532), and the play *Histriomastix* ([London], 1610; *STC* 13529), composed perhaps in 1589 and sometimes attributed to John Marston. See also Erler, "Davies's Astraea," 41–61; Francis Yates, *Astraea: The Imperial Theme in the Sixteenth Century* (London and Boston: Routledge, 1975).

[42] On Mary's literary patronage and circle, see Mary Ellen Lamb, *Gender and Authorship in the Sidney Circle* (Madison: University of Wisconsin Press, 1990), 28–71; Louise Schleiner, *Tudor and Stuart Women Writers* (Bloomington: Indiana University Press, 1994), 52–81; Hannay, *Philip's Phoenix*, 106–42; Hannay, Kinnamon, and Brennan, eds., *Collected Works*, 9–15.

estate as "a kind of little Court" over which Mary ruled.[43] The confident tone of her entertainment indicates that she relied less on the Queen's favor than many previous devisers did. Still, she stood to benefit from Elizabeth's planned visit. She could have used the occasion to encourage Elizabeth to pursue Protestant interests more aggressively or to lobby for a court position for her son William. Her planned gift of the *Psalms* would have highlighted a religious agenda, and her 1601 letter to Elizabeth reveals her desire to secure William a position at court and her relief when Elizabeth welcomed him there. In it, Mary humbly gives "thankfullness unexpresible; not onely for my selfe but for my sonn who of yowr Majestys ever Prinsly Grace yow ar pleased to take into yowr Care."[44] With her husband ill in 1599, she may have been especially eager to establish her son at court.[45] However, her pageant does not explicitly advance this goal or any specific Protestant interests. The text she prepared for this event does not ask for promotion or include a statement of her personal submission to the Queen as many other devisers have done before. We might attribute this exclusion to the text's status as an unperformed and perhaps incomplete country house entertainment. Especially because the dialogue survives in only one early modern source, the printed text might record only an excerpt of the intended event. It might also be edited; compilers of Elizabethan anthologies often revised individual works, or Mary might have edited it herself to recast an intended occasional performance as printed dialogue.[46]

However, the entertainment's simple structure, confident tone, and mastery of the form through *imitatio* highlight the forcefulness of its absences, several of which make space for a new construction of female devising and courtiership. In print this entertainment advances her brother's reputation and advertises her own authorship and wit. Like "The Lady of May," "A Dialogue between Two Shepherds" offers the Queen two different perspectives, but it does not invite her to judge openly and offers her no chance to intervene. Whereas the Bisham and Sudeley entertainments decried the cultural ideal of feminine silence and represented model female courtiers as outspoken, "A Dialogue between Two Shepherds" nearly silences women. It identifies its author and intended auditor in the header, but the pageant dialogue excludes direct references to its female deviser or to the Queen's physical body. In doing so, it may imply that an absent or silent female

---

[43] Nicholas Breton, *Wits Trenchmour* (London, 1597; *STC* 3713), sig. F2v.

[44] Hannay, Kinnamon, and Brennan, eds., *Collected Works*, 291.

[45] Hannay, *Philip's Phoenix*, 163–6; Hannay, Kinnamon, and Brennan, eds., *Collected Works*, 81.

[46] Anne Ferry, *Tradition and the Individual Poem: An Inquiry into Anthologies* (Palo Alto: Stanford University Press, 2001), 77–93.

body is less susceptible to sexual and political control by men. Mary Ellen Lamb has proposed that Mary's three translations exalt feminine silence and obedience as praiseworthy qualities and construct her authorship in terms of female modesty.[47] "A Dialogue between Two Shepherds" represents her similarly. Just as Mary has it both ways when she employs and critiques two praising strategies, she is able to fulfill the ideal of feminine silence while she promotes her authorship.

Because the dialogue maintains a bit of distance from its host, it can adopt a critical stance. As it advocates silence but not necessarily obedience, it fashions Mary Sidney as a different kind of advisor from Leicester, the hosts at Elvetham and Cowdray, or the young women at Bisham and Sudeley. She is poised not simply to boost the Queen's ego or to advertise herself as loyal, but to evaluate the genre and its functions. Her text unapologetically exposes and embraces the genre's inherent paradoxes. It resembles her brother's entertainment as it highlights the difficulty of pleasing the Queen and offers a subtle critique of the Queen's expectations of her courtiers. Yet its lack of a frustrated, desperate tone and its playful emphasis on silence differentiates her approach from that of her brother.

Because the Queen did not visit Wilton in 1599, an early seventeenth-century audience experienced this entertainment only as a text, and although it may have circulated in manuscripts that no longer survive, its only definite public "performance" was its inclusion in the popular printed miscellany *A Poetical Rapsody* (1602).[48] This collection of verse, compiled by Francis Davison, gives voice to its writers' frustrations with the late Elizabethan court, an England in economic crisis, and a stubborn monarch. We have no record of Mary's authorization of this publication, but we also have no evidence to the contrary. The editors of her *Collected Works* assume that she gave Davison permission to print it.[49] Placed in conversation with several anti-court pastoral poems, "A Dialogue between Two Shepherds" holds its own as a critique of Elizabeth's reliance on political Petrarchism, which the collection's other works reveal as destructive

---

[47] Lamb, *Gender and Authorship*, 119.

[48] We might speculate about the reasons for Elizabeth's change in plans – perhaps illness or rumors of a Spanish invasion kept her away from Wilton (see, e.g., Erler, "Davies's Astraea," 42–3) – but her absence in 1599 does not necessarily indicate conflict. A progress gest was always in flux, and the Queen and her advisers often altered it at the last moment. Arthur F. Marotti calls *A Poetical Rapsody* the last great Elizabethan miscellany; for more on this textual form, see *Manuscript, Print, and the English Renaissance Lyric* (Ithaca: Cornell University Press, 1995), 212–35 and Elizabeth Pomeroy, *The Elizabethan Miscellanies: Their Development and Conventions* (Berkeley: University of California Press, 1973).

[49] Hannay, Kinnamon, and Brennan, eds., *Collected Works*, 24.

for her male servants.[50] The entertainment's printed context emphasizes and heightens its subtle dissatisfaction with Elizabeth as the center of a frustrating and sometimes futile courtiership system.

A Poetical Rapsody is framed as a book inspired by and dedicated to the Sidney family. The prefatory matter in all four seventeenth-century editions (1602, 1608, 1611, and 1621) foregrounds an alliance with this family in order to authorize its publication. Francis Davison is particularly anxious to justify his inclusion of verses by unknown poets, including himself, his brother, and several anonymous friends. All editions begin with a dedication to Mary's son William. After praising his "high and noble minde" and "noble high Degree," Davison celebrates him as "Thou Worthy Sonne, vnto a peerlesse MOTHER, / Thou Nephew to great SIDNEY of renowne" and dedicates the anthology to him with this line: "I consecrate these Rimes to thy great NAME" (sig. A2r). Davison emphasizes William's lineage and rank to defend him and his mother during a difficult time; William was imprisoned for adultery in the early part of 1601. The preface insists that William can still lend merit to the printed anthology despite his recent disgrace because of his mother's and uncle's reputations.

Davison's note to the reader, which follows, reveals his anxiety about printing the collection and his desire to legitimize this project. He anticipates readers who will "condemne Poetry in generall, and affirme, that it doth intoxicate the braine, and make men vtterly vnfit, either for more serious studies, or for any actiue course of life," and he defends poetry against such prejudices by explaining that "many excellent spirits with great fame of witt, and no staine of judgement, haue written excellently in this kind, and specially the eucr-praise worthy *Sidney*" (sig. A2v–A3r). *A Poetical Rapsody* is part of a group of lyric anthologies, including Samuel Daniel's *Delia* (1592), Michael Drayton's *Ideas Mirrovr* (1594), and *Englands Helicon* (1600), that invoke Sidney's example in prefatory material to legitimize their printing. By 1602, Davison and many other poets had benefited from what Arthur Marotti identifies as printed lyric poetry's "increased social prestige" following the publication of *Astrophel and Stella*.[51] Although Davison claims to disapprove of the printer's decision to "grace the forefront with Sir *Ph. Sidneys*, and others names," he and the collection's other poets aim

---

50 Richard C. McCoy interprets the book's inclusion of "A Dialogue" similarly. He suggests that several lyrics in the collection "seem designed to undermine rather than support the cult of Elizabeth" and proposes that Mary Sidney's text "strikes a decidedly anti-courtly posture." Richard C. McCoy, "Lord of Liberty: Francis Davison and the Cult of Elizabeth" in John Guy, ed., *The Reign of Elizabeth I: Court and Culture in the Last Decade* (Cambridge University Press, 1995), 216, 225. For more on political Petrarchism, see Chapter 2, pp. 51–61.

51 Marotti, *Manuscript*, 234.

to authorize their writing by exploiting personal, political, and literary connections to the late poet (sig. A3r). The collection begins with two of Sidney's pastoral poems, and his composite *Arcadia* serves as a model for many of the collection's works. Francis and Walter Davison select as their poetry's speakers Strephon and Klaius, the shepherds mentioned in the first sentence of the composite *Arcadia*. Poet A.W.'s dialogue between shepherds Thenot and Perin mourns Sidney's death from the perspective of poets who looked to him for inspiration: "No light we see, / Yet wander wee, / We wander farre and neere without a guide" (sig. C5r). Later in the book, an anonymous poet presents a collection of short poems about Sidney's lasting fame and his own grief at Sidney's death.

As Sidney's own poems illustrate, shared political views and frustrations unite the works in *A Poetical Rapsody*. His first poem, "Vpon his meeting with his two worthy Friends and fellow-Poets," celebrates his friendship with Edward Dyer and Fulke Greville (sig. B1r–B2r). The second poem, "Disprayse of a Courtly life," depicts a male courtier who bemoans his departure from the preferable life of a shepherd (sig. B2r). Condemning "false, fine, Courtly pleasure," he describes courtiers as "pufft in minde" and "birdes of pride" (sig. B3r). The speaker, after listening to these complaints, expresses his gratitude for Dyer and Greville and presents male friend-ship as an appealing alternative to the court, where male courtiers must debase themselves to flatter the female monarch insincerely. This poem conventionally idealizes pastoral life as an escape from court and repre-sents courtiership as disingenuous. Sidney's two lyrics begin the book's first section, "Pastorals and Eclogues," in which most texts employ the pastoral mode to critique Elizabeth and her treatment of male courtiers. In a similar way to how the 1593 miscellany *The Phoenix Nest* invokes praise for Sidney and then presents several anti-courtly poems, Sidney's prece-dent in *A Poetical Rapsody* helps legitimize the printing of anti-courtly verse.[52]

The poems surrounding Mary Sidney's entertainment, which appears as the book's fourth text, represent the pastoral landscape as a male fantasy in which sought-after and resistant women submit to their male suitors. The third poem, by an anonymous poet, tells of a Shepherd who comes across a beautiful sleeping Nymph whose "breast lay bare" (sig. B3v). After the Shepherd "stood and gazde his fill" of the sleeping Nymph, she awakens so distraught that she attacks him with Cupid's arrows (sig. B4r). When the Shepherd only becomes more love-struck, the Nymph remains such an

---

[52] *The Phoenix Nest* (London, 1593; *STC* 21516), sig. B1r–C2r.

unwilling participant in this coupling that she tries to commit suicide by turning Cupid's bow on herself, an action that ends not her life, but her resistance. Once struck by Cupid's arrow, she "seekes for that she shun'd before" (sig. B4v). Although we might assume that both characters are powerless against the god of love, the poem informs us that the Shepherd may have successfully willed this outcome: "Chance *or else perhaps his Will*, / Did guide the God of Loue that way" (sig. B4r; emphasis mine). The poem temporarily invites sympathy for the Nymph by describing her tears and distress, but it ends with Cupid laughing and with the Shepherd victorious. It sends the message that women cannot long deny male desires. Because of its placement in a section filled with anti-courtly verse, this poem's rewriting of the cruel Petrarchan mistress and her love-sick suitor appears as allegorically veiled critique of courtier–monarch relations at the late Elizabethan court. It fantasizes that even the Queen cannot play the cruel mistress forever.

Other poems in the "Pastorals and Eclogues" section judge the Queen more explicitly. Following Mary's text is a series of three poems by Walter and Francis Davison about Strephon and Klaius and their shared mistress, Urania, the love triangle from the Fourth Eclogues of the composite *Arcadia*. These poems offer another fantasy of the Petrarchan lover's triumph over his usually callous mistress. After Strephon angers Urania by making love to another nymph, he begs for forgiveness. Urania, "vnwilling to loose so worthy a seruant," excuses his unfaithfulness immediately and blames her own cruelty for his indiscretion (sig. B8r). She recognizes his value and acknowledges she has been "tormenting" him for too long (sig. B8v). As political allusion, this series of poems represents a courtier–monarch relationship in which the male suitor's pleas are heard and the female monarch apologizes for her cruelty. Francis and Walter Davison had reason to feel resentful toward the Queen because their father had been fined and imprisoned for delivering the warrant for Mary, Queen of Scots' execution, a decision Elizabeth repented too late. The last text in this sequence is Francis Davison's "Eclogue." It expresses sorrow at the Queen's unjust treatment of his father, whom the shepherd Eubulus represents.[53] Eubulus is devastated by "*Astreas* burning-hot Disdaine" and made physically weak by his sadness, while his cruel mistress, Astrea, remains unreasonable and merciless (sig. B11v). Eubulus says, for example, "For all my seruice, faith, and patient minde. . . . A crop of scorne, and of contempt, I finde"

---

53 Hyder Edward Rollins, ed., *A Poetical Rhapsody 1602–1621* (Cambridge: Harvard University Press, 1931), 2:102–3.

(sig. B12r). He emphasizes his loyalty to Astrea, his futile attempts to please her, and his innocence as a victim of undeserved cruelty.

As my discussion of these poems illustrates, *A Poetical Rapsody* is a politically charged book that exposes the emotional dangers of male courtiers using love poetry for political ends. Later sections of the book mirror the pastoral and eclogue section by continuing to demonstrate the interconnectedness of romantic courtship and courtiership: lovesick sonneteers mourn alongside poems from court masques and entertainments.[54] As the book's grouping of these verses exemplifies, wooing the Queen appears no different (and no more successful) than a love-struck Petrarchan poet wooing his desired mistress. When Mary Sidney's entertainment appears alongside these bitter representations of political Petrarchism, its publication emphasizes a similar perspective within her text. The book also frames her entertainment as a continuation of her brother's literary and political work. The book privileges Mary as the author of its fourth text and therefore one of the "others names" that grace its forefront and make it more marketable. The book identifies her dialogue as "made by the excellent Lady, the Lady Mary Countesse of Pembrook, at the Queenes Maiesties being at her house" (sig. B5r). This description highlights Mary's title and proximity to the monarch and fails to mention that this visit never occurred. It gives Mary credit in a volume consisting of many anonymous poems and presumably all male authors, and it situates her in this circle of men by virtue of her family, rank, writing, and politics.[55]

Within the text, Thenot's language resembles that of several other Petrarchan suitors in the collection: earnest and eager yet ineffective and discouraged. Like Strephon, Klaius, and Eubulus, Thenot relies heavily on comparative praise and hyperbole, saying of the Queen, "she is so good, so faire / With all the earth she may compare" and "Astrea is our chiefest joy, / Our chiefest guarde against annoy, / Our chiefest wealth, our treasure" (sig. B5r–B5v). Piers responds by calling Thenot a liar, just as Sidney's speaker in "Disprayse of a Courtly Life" condemns courtiers for lying. Thenot reveals in his final lines that he misunderstands his subservient role when he assumes he has the power to "raise" Queen Elizabeth; however, when read in its printed context, "A Dialogue between Two Shepherds"

---

54 The book includes two poems from the 1594 Gray's Inn masque and "Of Cynthia" performed for the Queen at a May Day show.

55 Several authors are identified as anonymous or only by initials, yet all appear to be male. Besides Philip and Mary Sidney and Francis and Walter Davison, other authors identified by full name include Edmund Spenser and John Davies. Other likely contributors include Henry Constable, Robert Greene, Thomas Watson, and Henry Wotton. See Rollins, ed., *Poetical Rhapsody*, 2:42–51.

encourages sympathy for male courtiers engaged in power struggles with the Queen by representing Thenot as sincere, not manipulative, and without explicit ulterior motives. He asks earnestly why his "words should ly" when they come from good intentions (sig. B6r). When Piers promotes silence, he declares not only that Elizabeth is above all praise, but also that the complications of praising the Queen exceed the rewards. What could have been a dialogue between two equally appropriate praising strategies in performance became in print a debate between two equally limiting approaches and a sly critique of the Queen's endorsement of Petrarchan discourse at court.

Three later editions of the poetry collection (1608, 1611, 1621) reprint "A Dialogue between Two Shepherds" in altered political climates.[56] The 1608 edition includes all the poems from the first edition plus sixty-four new ones, and it rearranges their order. This new arrangement foregrounds courtly entertainment and relies less on the authorizing power of Sidney's lyrics. It begins with excerpts from the Harefield entertainment and the winter pageantry at Hatfield (1602) written by John Davies. These new additions verify the title page's marketing claim that the book includes pieces "neuer yet published," and the increased number of Elizabethan court performances somewhat counteracts the anti-Elizabeth sentiment we saw in the first edition. Furthermore, the pageant texts appear next to two satiric poems that seem to criticize the Stuart court. "Yet Another 12 Wonders of the World," also by Davies, begins with a description of a courtier: "Long haue I liu'd in Court, yet learn'd not all this while" (sig. B1r). This playful humor is juxtaposed with the more derisive line in "The Lie," now attributed to Sir Walter Ralegh, that says the court "glowes / and shines like rotten wood" (sig. B9r). These poems do not refer to a specific court, but their inclusion with pageants that recall positively the late monarch makes them appear critical of the current political atmosphere at the Jacobean court. When Mary's dialogue appears a few poems later, it is no longer listed as royal entertainment or grouped with a collection of similar poems on one subject. The Eubulus eclogue, which appears about fifty pages later, still criticizes Astrea, but without proximity to a dialogue that explicitly codes this figure as Elizabeth, both it and Mary's text lose some of their

---

[56] *A Poetical Rapsodie* (London, 1608; *STC* 6374); *A Poetical Rapsodie* (London, 1611; *STC* 6375); *Dauisons Poems, or, A Poeticall Rapsodie* (London, 1621; *STC* 6376). The miscellany also went through several editions in the nineteenth century: Brydges' edition (1814–17), Nicolas' edition (1826), Collier's reprint (1867), and Bullen's edition (1890–1). Mary Sidney's dialogue was reprinted in *The Monthly Mirror* 11 (1801): 301–3 and Horace Walpole's *A Catalogue of the Royal and Noble Authors of England* 2 (1806): 190–8. For more, see Rollins, ed., *Poetical Rhapsody*, 2:24–35, 100–1.

forceful topicality. Instead of presenting a clear political agenda, the 1608 edition emphasizes variety in perspective, subject, and genre. The collection and Mary's dialogue become more ambivalent about Elizabeth and can be more easily read as a less vexed celebration of her when, after her death, she no longer has power.

The 1611 edition continues to move in a similar direction. It ends with a new collection of epitaphs on monarchs, including a positive one on Elizabeth that celebrates her international Protestant policy and a more subdued one on James that mentions "great Eliza" more than once and includes this passage:

> Our Sun did set with great Elizabeth,
> Before night thou a new day-light didst bring,
> Our sommers peace did close at her cold death,
> Without warres winter thou renewd'st our spring,
> All our liues ioyes with her dead seemd to bee,
> Before intombde they were reuiude by thee.
>
> (sig. K2r)

These lines offer an apt expansion of "The King is dead. Long live the King!" But they also rewrite the collection's attitude toward Elizabeth. Once critical of her cruel treatment of deserving courtiers, this volume now remembers her as a Protestant hero in whose shadow the less impressive James remains. The final early modern edition, published in 1621, foregrounds Davison's authorship after his death with the new title *Davisons Poems, or A Poeticall Rapsodie*. Now divided into six books by genre, it encourages readers to focus on its poems' genres and authors rather than shared political messages. The pastoral section develops from Philip Sidney to Mary Sidney to the Davisons to anonymous poets, which gives the impression of a hierarchy of writers in which the anonymous poets model themselves after the Davisons, who strive to imitate the Sidneys. We have now come full circle: Davison used the Sidneys to legitimize his authorship, and now his authorship is legitimate.

As the three Stuart editions gradually transform the book's arrangement, they alter our interpretations of its content, adding hints of nostalgia for Queen Elizabeth and critique of King James. When they stop labeling Mary's text as performed for the Queen at Wilton, they make it appear more as a commendatory poem than as an interactive entertainment crafted to negotiate multiple agendas and authorities. Together these changes present Mary's text not as a critical reflection on Elizabeth's tactics, but as a clever pastoral eclogue or a posthumous celebration of a renowned monarch. The example of "A Dialogue between Two Shepherds" shows us once again that printed country house entertainments offered more than royal propaganda or even topical news. They also experimented with trends in lyric poetry and entered into conversations with pastoral poems, eclogues, and songs. A single entertainment, although designed for a solitary performance, could produce a range of meanings for diverse audiences depending on the occasion and context.

The Genre's Afterlives in Stuart England

When Elizabeth I died in March 1603 and her successor and his family journeyed from Edinburgh to London, their subjects turned to country house pageantry to negotiate relationships with the new royal family. King James traveled in April for his coronation, and when he stopped at Sir Robert Cecil's Theobalds estate, a young man surprised him with a fourteen-point petition asking for specific policies and for the new ruler to step into the role of loving and beloved monarch vacated by Elizabeth: "Good King, love us and we will love thee."[1] Queen Anna and Prince Henry followed two months later. When they arrived at Althorp, the Northamptonshire estate of Sir Robert Spencer, on June 25, a wild man and fairies jumped out from behind trees to welcome them. The collaborative performance advertised Spencer's prestige, promoted its writer Ben Jonson's skill as a courtly poet, and served as an opportunity for elite women to align themselves with the new English queen. Because Spencer was not present, his wife and three aunts – including Alice Egerton, who hosted Elizabeth less than a year earlier – probably stepped in as hosts.[2] The entertainment fashioned Anna partially after Elizabeth's image by calling her "Oriana" but underscored key differences as well.[3] As queen consort and a powerful patron, Anna could "priuate *Lares* blesse," but she could not transform an estate into a court, as the Harefield entertainment said of Elizabeth.[4] The entertainment proved successful for the absent Spencer, whom James elevated to the peerage a

---

[1] John Nichols, *The Progresses, Processions, and Magnificent Festivities of King James the First, His Royal Consort, Family, and Court* (London, 1828), 1:127.

[2] The other two aunts were Anne (Spencer) Sackville, later Countess of Dorset, and Elizabeth (Spencer) Carey, Baroness Hunsdon. Leeds Barroll proposes their involvement in *Anna of Denmark, Queen of England: A Cultural Biography* (Philadelphia: University of Pennsylvania Press, 2000), 62–5.

[3] Ben Jonson, *A Particvlar Entertainment of the Qveene and Prince Their Highnesse to Althrope*, appended to *B. Ion: His Part of King Iames His Royall and Magnificent Entertainement* (London, 1604; *STC* 14756), sig. A4r.

[4] Ibid., sig. A4r.

month later, but not for the women in his family, none of whom received any specific reward for their contributions.

It also marked the beginning of Jonson's fame as an author of court pageantry. The printed Althorp entertainment claimed him as its primary deviser when it appeared in a 1604 quarto that included Jonson's coronation pageantry and foregrounded his authorship: *B. Ion: His Part of King Iames His Royall and Magnificent Entertainement through His Honorable Cittie of London, Thurseday the 15. of March. 1603.* Its publisher, Edward Blount, specialized in literature, and, like much of his catalog, the Althorp entertainment was presented as a literary work by a prominent male author.[5] It later appeared in the 1616 Folio of Jonson's works, further solidifying the illusion of single-authored entertainment – a movement anticipated by the printed collections of works by Gascoigne and Sidney and fostered by Jonson and the publishers who produced his works.

In many ways, the Theobalds pageant, the Althorp entertainment, and other early Jacobean country house pageantry stressed continuities between the old regime and the new. But they also adapted the genre to a new political atmosphere – one with multiple channels to royal patronage and a patriarch at the helm. As the genre evolved and eventually declined in the next three decades, it reflected and engendered changes in monarch–subject relations, definitions of feminine authority, and representations of devisers in print. This book's methodology and research provide a framework for understanding these shifts and continuities in Stuart country house entertainments, and it opens up new avenues for re-examining two related forms in the seventeenth century: the more canonical Stuart masque and household entertainments performed without a visiting monarch.

In part, the extant records of Jacobean country house entertainments uphold an established narrative about James as withdrawn and awkward. By all accounts, his early progresses drew enormous crowds, which one witness described as so "greedy" to behold the King that "with much vnrulinesse they iniured and hurt one another, some euen hazarded to the daunger of death," and contemporary narratives describe him as overwhelmed or annoyed.[6] Just eleven days into his first progress, he restricted access to "onely those that had affaires" to try to tame the crowds.[7] This approach was

---

[5] Blount published works by Christopher Marlowe, John Lyly, Samuel Daniel, and John Florio and is best known for his involvement in Shakespeare's First Folio. See Sonia Massai, "Edward Blount, the Herberts, and the First Folio" in Marta Straznicky, ed., *Shakespeare's Stationers: Studies in Cultural Bibliography* (Philadelphia: University of Pennsylvania Press, 2012), 132–46.

[6] *The True Narration of the Entertainment of His Royall Maiestie, from the Time of His Departure from Edenbrough; Till His Receiuing at London* (London, 1603; *STC* 17153), sig. F4v.

[7] Ibid., sig. D2r.

not entirely new – as we have seen, Elizabeth ordered that masterless men be banned from her progresses late in her reign – but James gained a reputation of being less patient and more distanced than was his predecessor.[8] The Venetian ambassador would say of James in 1607,

> He does not caress the people nor make them that good cheer that the late Queen did, whereby she won their loves; for the English adore their Sovereigns, and if the King passed through the streets a hundred times a day the people would still run to see him; they like their King to show pleasure at their devotion, as the late Queen knew well how to do; but this King manifests no taste for them but rather contempt and dislike.[9]

James invited less spontaneity than Elizabeth did, as he planned ahead more resolutely and rarely interrupted his pre-determined progress gests, even for emergencies.[10] He approached his visits to country houses more as holidays than as times for political negotiation, and his country house experiences focused more on hunting and field sports than on interactive pageantry. His personality and preferences, along with those of his wife and sons, necessarily altered the genre. For the entertainment at Althorp, Jonson had prepared two farewell speeches that were performed but could not be heard because of "the throng of the Countrey" and "the Multitudinous presse," descriptions that underscore how neither devisers nor honored guests could fully control the genre.[11] This key aspect – the openness that made pageants and persons vulnerable – is exactly why the country house entertainment became less popular under a different kind of monarch.

But the genre was not yet obsolete. James, Charles I, and other members of their family took summer progresses, and their hosts staged country house entertainments when they wanted to negotiate new relationships or return to past traditions. Despite excellent work by James Knowles and Martin Butler, the seventeenth-century country house entertainment has received little critical attention.[12] I noted in the introduction that texts survive from at least twelve Stuart country house performances: Theobalds (1603), Althorp (1603), Highgate (1604), Theobalds (1606), Theobalds

---

[8] As Jonathan Goldberg puts it, "whereas Elizabeth played at being part of the pageants, James played at being apart, separate." See *James I and the Politics of Literature: Jonson, Shakespeare, Donne, and Their Contemporaries* (Baltimore: Johns Hopkins University Press, 1983), 31.

[9] Great Britain Public Record Office, *Calendar of State Papers Relating to English Affairs in the Archives of Venice*, 10:513.

[10] Nichols, *James*, 3:392–3, n. 4.   [11] Jonson, *A Particvlar Entertainment*, sig. B2v, B3v.

[12] See especially Martin Butler, *The Stuart Court Masque and Political Culture* (Cambridge University Press, 2009) and the entertainments edited by James Knowles in David Bevington, Martin Butler, and Ian Donaldson, eds., *The Cambridge Edition of the Works of Ben Jonson* (Cambridge University Press, 2012).

(1607), Caversham (1613), Hoghton (1617), Brougham (1617), Burley-on-the-Hill (1621; known as *Gypsies Metamorphosed* and reprised with new prologues elsewhere), Kenilworth (1624), Welbeck (1633), and Bolsover (1634).[13] These examples, which deserve further study, reveal the continuing influence of their Elizabethan precedents. The entertainment for James and Anna at Highgate in Middlesex used a familiar trope in its invocation when it represented the house and its occupants as yearning for the royal couple to possess them and ceded authority with hospitality encouraging reciprocity. Its host, Sir William Cornwallis, was connected to recusant circles, and it followed the Elizabethan Cowdray pageantry in lobbying for religious tolerance.[14] When James and his brother-in-law, Christian IV of Denmark, visited Theobalds in late July 1606, Latin epigrams delivered outside the house recalled the 1571 Theobalds entertainment by personifying the house as a humble, gracious recipient of royal guests it feared it could not entertain properly.[15] But unlike the earlier Theobalds shows, it made very little mention of host Robert Cecil, his children, or any of Cecil's own agendas. Its lack of direct political pleading demonstrated its host's increased security and responsibility at court, but its exclusion of familial concerns also hinted that country house entertainment might not be the best space for personal lobbying.[16]

In the late Jacobean and Caroline periods, many devisers capitalized on the increased popularity of the indoor court masque by mingling aspects of that form with the already "mixed genre" of country house

[13] Some related Stuart performances also drew influence from the genre. An example is the episodic entertainment at Richmond (1636), which was performed indoors and sponsored by the Prince.

[14] James Knowles also interprets the Highgate entertainment as an argument for religious tolerance. Bevington, Butler, and Donaldson, eds., *Works of Ben Jonson*, 2:485–8.

[15] The 1606 entertainment was popular in print. Published accounts include Ben Jonson, *The Entertainment of the Two Kings of Great Britaine and Denmarke at Theobalds, Iuly 24. 1606* (in *The Workes of Beniamin Ionson* [London, 1616; *STC* 14751], sig. Eeee5r–Eeee6r); *The Most Royall and Honourable Entertainement, of the Famous and Renowmed King, Christiern the Fourth, King of Denmarke* (London, 1606; *STC* 21085); *The King of Denmarkes VVelcome* (London, 1606; *STC* 5194); *Englands Farevvell to Christian the Fourth* (London, 1606; *STC* 21079).

[16] James M. Sutton makes a similar claim in *Materializing Space at an Early Modern Prodigy House: The Cecils at Theobalds, 1564–1607* (Aldershot: Ashgate, 2004), 170–1, but he interprets the entertainment as demonstrating Cecil's slipping hold on Theobalds, a claim that makes sense retrospectively (as James and Anna took ownership of the estate the following year) but that the entertainment text does not support. Instead, like the 1571 Theobalds entertainment, this one indicates a host secure in his position. For more on the 1606 entertainment and the 1607 one, during which Cecil ceded ownership of Theobalds, see Sutton, *Materializing Space*, 144–6; Scott McMillin, "Jonson's Early Entertainments: New Information from Hatfield House" in *Renaissance Drama* n.s. 1 (1968): 153–66; Gabriel Heaton, *Writing and Reading Royal Entertainments From George Gascoigne to Ben Jonson* (Oxford University Press, 2010), 177–8.

entertainment. Some entertainments continued to be staged mostly out-doors, while others added elaborate indoor masques to the genre's trade-mark outdoor episodes. The outdoor, interactive pageants tended to pursue their hosts' agendas most openly, and two entertainments that especially recall Elizabethan models were performed at Hoghton Tower in 1617 and Welbeck Abbey in 1633. The owner of Hoghton Tower in Lancashire, Sir Richard Houghton, needed help following many years of accusations and lawsuits. His family had been affiliated with recusants, he was rumored to have supported Essex's rebellion and exploited his post as sheriff to embez-zle lands, his tenants had accused him of bullying them, and he had many unpaid loans and outstanding lawsuits.[17] His extravagant spending on lav-ish entertainment – providing banquets and other festivities for more than one hundred guests, purportedly carpeting his driveway with red velvet, and sponsoring a folk ceremony that involved morris dancing and strewing rushes – followed tradition in hoping that the gift of an especially elaborate entertainment would encourage the monarch to reciprocate with especially valuable reward.[18] Houghton offered an outdoor welcoming address with familiar rhetoric that tried to balance his and James' dual ownership as it laid open his purpose:

> This House; – this Knight is thyne, he is thy Ward;
> For by thy helping and auspicious hand,
> He and his House shall ever, ever stand
> And flourish.[19]

The tone and circumstance recall the Elizabethan Elvetham entertainment, as each aimed to dismantle its host's old reputation and construct a new one. The next day Houghton took James to his alum works in hopes of selling them to the King, but that attempt failed. James did not purchase the works or relieve Houghton of any debts; Houghton was sent to the Fleet about two years later and continued to struggle financially until his death – an outcome that parallels that of the Earl of Hertford following his entertainment at Elvetham.[20]

When Charles visited Welbeck in Nottinghamshire nearly a decade into his reign, the entertainment devisers called for change by alluding to the past. Sponsored by William Cavendish, Earl of Newcastle and written

---

[17] Rosemary Sgroi, "Houghton, Sir Richard (1569–1630), of Hoghton Tower, Lancs." in Andrew Thrush and John P. Ferris, eds., *The History of Parliament: The House of Commons, 1604–1629* (Cambridge University Press, 2010), 802–3.

[18] George C. Miller, *Hoghton Tower: The History of the Manor, the Hereditary Lords and the Ancient Manor-House of Hoghton in Lancashire* (Preston: Guardian, 1948), 79–85.

[19] Nichols, *James*, 3:399.   [20] Miller, *Hoghton Tower*, 87–90; Sgroi, "Houghton," 802–4.

by Jonson, this entertainment promoted Newcastle's desire to become governor to the future Charles II – a position he eventually obtained – and earned Jonson an opportunity to engage in court politics late in his life.[21] It began not with a seemingly spontaneous welcome when the King arrived, but with a song at the opening banquet. This opening allowed Charles and his entourage to get settled before the entertainment began. It used Elizabethan models to define Welbeck as a great house in the tradition of Kenilworth Castle and to present Newcastle as an advisor to whom Charles should listen.[22] Characters spoke of Newcastle not using his aristocratic titles, but as a military leader in the tradition of Leicester at Kenilworth, Chandos at Sudeley, and Norreys at Rycote to alert Charles to Newcastle's ability to lead this region's military support. Newcastle therefore envisioned a mutually beneficial relationship with Charles. His entertainment urged an environment somewhat like the Elizabethan court and provinces, in which the monarch and his or her elite subjects relied upon one another to govern England – and, in this specific case, to govern a prince.

But its ending reminds us that political circumstances had changed since Elizabeth's reign. After dinner, the King and his lords prepared to take horse when they were stopped by a local antiquarian named Fitz-Ale and a country schoolmaster named Accidence. The two led the crowd to a bride-ale with an "old *May-Lady*" bride and a bridegroom named Stub that alluded to the rustic wedding at Kenilworth in 1575.[23] The entertainment ended with an Officer breaking up the party: "Give end unto your rudenesse. Know at length / Whose time, and patience you have urg'd, the *Kings*."[24] He scolded the actors for interrupting Charles' "serious houres, / With light, impertinent, unworthy objects" and not understanding that "Sports should not be obtruded on great Monarchs, / But wait when they will call for them as servants."[25] These lines were probably playful, as country house pageants often were, but they also questioned whether such

---

[21] James Fitzmaurice, "William Cavendish and Two Entertainments by Ben Jonson," in *Ben Jonson Journal* 5 (1998): 63–80; Anne Barton, "Harking Back to Elizabeth: Ben Jonson and Caroline Nostalgia" in *ELH* 48.4 (1981): 706–31.

[22] For more on the entertainment's Elizabethan nostalgia, see Barton, "Harking Back," 706–31; Lisa Hopkins, "Play Houses: Drama at Bolsover and Welbeck" in *Early Theatre* 2 (1999): 25–44; James Knowles, "'In the purest times of peerless Queen Elizabeth': Nostalgia, Politics, and Jonson's Use of the 1575 Kenilworth Entertainments" in Jayne Elisabeth Archer, Elizabeth Goldring, and Sarah Knight, eds., *The Progresses, Pageants, and Entertainments of Queen Elizabeth I* (Oxford University Press, 2007), 247–67. All three rightly interpret this nostalgia as revealing distrust or critique of Caroline politics.

[23] Jonson, *The Kings Entertainment at Welbeck in Nottingham-shire* in *The VVorkes of Beniamin Ionson* (1641; *STC* 14754a), sig. OO3v.

[24] Ibid., sig. OO4r.   [25] Ibid., sig. OO4r.

a performance could offer both light entertainment and serious advice. Newcastle and Jonson collaborated the following year on an entertainment at Newcastle's nearby estate at Bolsolver Castle, which also exhibited Elizabethan nostalgia to urge the monarch to view the aristocracy and their country estates as powerful, crucial participants in the English system of governing.[26]

Female hosts, performers, and writers are less visible in the records of these Stuart entertainments than they are in their Elizabethan counterparts, yet women still stood behind most progress visits. Robert Cecil was widowed by 1603 and never remarried, but the other Stuart examples I mentioned would have involved female co-hosts. The printed entertainment at Caversham (1613) identifies the performance as hosted by "Lord Knovvles" on its title page but later describes the event as "most nobly performed, by the right honourable the Lord and Ladie of the house."[27] Lucy Neville Cornwallis must have co-hosted at Highgate (1604), as did Catherine Gerard Houghton at Hoghton (1617), Grisold Hughes Clifford at Brougham (1617), and Elizabeth Bassett Cavendish at Welbeck (1633) and Bolsover (1634). These women probably supervised arrangements and sought familiar goals, such as increased royal favor, positions or marriages for their children, and enhanced cachet among their neighbors. Texts routinely mention high-ranking women in the audience because devisers continued to identify them as influential and crucial to please. But because nearly all these entertainments are presented in print as the work of a single male author, there is no evidence of female writers in Stuart country house pageantry. No text indicates female players either.[28]

Perhaps these performance records demonstrate that women were genuinely less involved in Stuart country house pageantry. They might reveal that Elizabeth's queenship indeed positively affected the status of other elite women; after her death, intimate negotiations among women could

---

[26] For more on the Welbeck and Bolsover entertainments and their emphasis on regional location, see Julie Sanders, *The Cultural Geography of Early Modern Drama, 1620–1650* (Cambridge University Press, 2011), 102–21.

[27] Thomas Campion, *A Relation of the Late Royall Entertainment Given by the Right Honorable the Lord Knovvles, at Cawsome-House neere Redding* (London, 1613; STC 4545), sig. B4v.

[28] These entertainments include few female characters. Examples include a Fairy Queen and her fairies at Althorp and several goddesses at Highgate, all of whom were probably played by cross-dressed male actors. Two entertainments feature female parts without dialogue that could have been played by women: the bride and her maids in the bride-ale at Welbeck and "three handsome Countrie Maides" who presented Anna with gifts of rich linen and clothes in the Caversham garden as she departed (Campion, *A Relation*, sig. B3v). These roles recall the kinds of parts played by local and elite women in the Elizabethan period, but we lack internal or contextual evidence that actual women performed them. In fact, no Stuart entertainment I mention appears to have featured performances by members of the household or hopeful courtiers because no performers are identified as such, as they often were in Elizabethan entertainment texts.

no longer include the reigning monarch. The presence of multiple royal guests in Stuart entertainments meant several channels for patronage, but under a king regnant, it might have been more difficult for a female entertainment sponsor to produce an intimate exchange with the head of state. Alternately, we might argue that the gender dynamic within the genre had not changed drastically, but male authors who penned pageantry more routinely erased women's presence to bolster their own authorship. I suspect the answer lies somewhere in the middle: both the reigning monarch's gender and the agendas of those responsible for the textual record produced this result. At the same time, we might discover more evidence of female devising once we know to look for it. This aspect of Stuart country house entertainment especially needs further research so that we can uncover women's specific contributions and understand better what happened to the genre's traditions and practices in this period.

The country house entertainment's trajectory is tied closely to the emerging popularity of the masque, and the two genres together demonstrate how monarchical preference and the increasing professionalization of court pageantry led to the masque surpassing the country house entertainment as the preferred kind of pageantry in Stuart England. When James or Charles presided over a masque as its privileged spectator who received praise and gifts, he did not move with the performers to signify negotiation or shared power, but sat apart as an inaccessible supervisor. While the interactive country house entertainment created the appearance of an accessible monarch, the more rigid structure of the court masque tended to promote an absolutist view of monarchy, a fixed social order, and a powerful, detached king. Many Stuart masques were performed at Whitehall, an indoor space that emphasized the King's authority as England's political center. Although court masques performed several functions beyond royal propaganda and provided devisers opportunities for critique and influence, this more stilted form limited the personalized lobbying we see in Elizabethan country house entertainment. Together the country house entertainment and the court masque reveal that the more outdoor and pastoral an entertainment's structure, the more it introduced possibilities for negotiation with and critique of the monarch.

Many scholars have emphasized the ways in which Stuart masques empowered their female devisers, yet a comparison to Elizabethan country house entertainment encourages us to re-examine the extent to which masques allowed women to intervene in pageantry and policy.[29] An elite

---

[29] Examples of those who highlight the power available to female masquers include Clare McManus, *Women on the Renaissance Stage: Anna of Denmark and Female Masquing in the Stuart Court 1590–1619* (Manchester University Press, 2002); Sophie Tomlinson, *Women on Stage in Stuart Drama*

circle of Jacobean women led by Queen Anna performed silent roles in
The Vision of the Twelve Goddesses (1604), *The Masque of Blackness* (1605),
The Masque of Beauty (1608), *The Masque of Queens* (1609), *Tethys' Festival*
(1610), *Love freed From Ignorance and Folly* (1611), and *Cupid's Banishment*
(1617). Like the high-ranking women who devised Elizabethan entertainments, these female masquers used their contributions to build alliances
or assert oppositional ideologies. But their silent roles and limited interaction with the reigning monarch restricted their possibilities for political
expression. As their masques declared the existence of a female community
at court that held political influence but was separate from the governing
center, they reinforced hierarchies of gender along with rank.[30] Eventually
women took speaking roles again – examples include the late Jacobean
Cupid's Banishment (1617) and the Caroline *Tempe Restored* (1632) – but
these women were professional actors or singers, not female courtiers who
hosted the court for multiple days at their homes. Therefore their opportunities for political intervention differed.

Female devisers played especially central roles in seventeenth-century
household performances that excluded the monarch entirely. John Milton's
Arcades and masque at Ludlow Castle, both performed at country houses
without a visiting monarch, reveal the influence of Elizabethan country
house entertainments particularly well. The three short pastoral songs
and speech delivered by the "Genius of the Wood" in *Arcades* all recall
Elizabethan country house entertainments in their style and language, as
did their performance at Harefield.[31] As Chapter 3 explained, these pageants
celebrate Alice Egerton as a queen and goddess figured in Elizabeth's image:
"A deity so unparalel'd" with a "sudden blaze of majesty" who shines in a
"radiant state" and resides in a "seat of State."[32] The Genius of the Wood
suggested that access to Alice was an exclusive privilege when he advised her
family members to "attend ye toward her glittering state; / Where ye may all
that are of noble stemm / Approach, and kiss her sacred vestures hemm."[33]
This family affair stressed the stability of kinship alliances and the familiar
claim that country estates served as powerful centers of authority. At the

---

(Cambridge University Press, 2005), 18–47; Karen Britland, *Drama at the Courts of Queen Henrietta Maria* (Cambridge University Press, 2006).

[30] Barbara Kiefer Lewalski similarly notes that the separate female community established at Anna's court remained marginalized in *Writing Women in Jacobean England* (Cambridge: Harvard University Press, 1993), 15–44.

[31] I quote *Arcades* from its first printing in *Poems of Mr. John Milton, Both English and Latin* (London, 1645), sig. D3r.

[32] Ibid., sig. D2r–D2v.   [33] Ibid., sig. D4r.

same time, its allusions to the late queen and celebration of domestic power might have indicated subtle resistance to the court or the current regime.

Milton's second aristocratic entertainment, the masque at Ludlow, made such resistance more apparent. Alice's granddaughter and namesake acted the central role in this entertainment, which Milton and musician Henry Lawes devised for John Egerton, Earl of Bridgewater. It was performed at Ludlow Castle in Shropshire on September 29, 1634 to celebrate Bridgewater's installation as Lord President of the Council of Wales and Lord Lieutenant of Wales and the Welsh Marches. Three of his children – his sons aged nine and eleven along with fifteen-year-old Alice – performed speaking parts. The masque began with an "Attendant Spirit" in "a wild wood," who delivered a monologue introducing both the plot and praise of Bridgewater, the guest of honor.[34] Next entered villainous Comus, a god of revelry born of Bacchus and Circe. When the chaste Lady Alice then became separated from her brothers in the woods, Comus tricked her into following him to his palace, where he claimed he would keep her safe. Instead he threatened her chastity and held her hostage until Sabrina, the "Goddess of the River," intervened to rescue Alice from Comus' enchantment.[35] The entertainment ended with a song, dancing, and further praise of Bridgewater's virtuous family. Several scholars have interpreted this performance as a "reformed masque" that responds to the Stuart tradition.[36] Because Egerton's children had danced in masques, Lawes had experience devising them, and an early printed version calls itself a masque, audiences probably connected the Ludlow performance to that tradition.[37] Yet the Egerton family also held close ties to the tradition of country house entertainment, an important precedent that scholars tend to overlook.

If we shift the conversation from its response to the Stuart masque to its adaptation of country house entertainment, a series of related points emerge about the event's political interventions. Its similarities in structure

---

[34] John Milton, "A Masque Presented at Ludlow Castle, 1634" in *Seventeenth-Century Poetry: An Annotated Anthology*, ed. Robert Cummings (Oxford: Blackwell, 2000), 273–302. The quoted phrases come from stage directions preceding the dialogue.

[35] Ibid., line 842.

[36] On Milton's response to the court masque form, see especially John G. Demaray, *Milton and the Masque Tradition: The Early Poems, 'Arcades,' and Comus* (Cambridge: Harvard University Press, 1968); Leah S. Marcus, *The Politics of Mirth: Jonson, Herrick, Milton, Marvell, and the Defense of Old Holiday Pastimes* (University of Chicago Press, 1986), 169–84; Blair Hoxby, "The Wisdom of Their Feet: Meaningful Dance in Milton and the Stuart Masque" in *English Literary Renaissance* 37.1 (2007): 74–99; William Shullenberger, *Lady in the Labyrinth: Milton's Comus as Initiation* (Madison and Teaneck: Fairleigh Dickinson University Press, 2008), 46–81; Ann Baynes Corio, "Anonymous Milton, or *A Maske* Masked" in *ELH* 71.3 (2004): 609–29.

[37] Ian Spink, *Henry Lawes: Cavalier Songwriter* (Oxford University Press, 2000), 51–72.

and style with country house entertainment lend credibility to the theory that it was performed outdoors in full or part – a possibility debated in previous scholarship.[38] The outspoken young virgin at its center did not enact a new role but continued a tradition of female performance from several decades earlier. Like the Bisham and Sudeley entertainments before it, the Ludlow masque featured a male god who tried to intimidate or force a defiant young woman into a sexual relationship. At Bisham, Pan's threats to the shepherdesses were slight, and the women rescued themselves by drawing on the Queen's influence. At Sudeley, Daphne needed Elizabeth to rescue her from the more seriously menacing Apollo. At Ludlow, Alice was saved by a new female protector. Goddess of the nearby Severn River, Sabrina represented the local area rather than royal authority.[39] Sabrina's replacement of Elizabeth's role in this story line signified the region's ability to govern and resolve problems without an intervening monarch. Likewise, the Ludlow masque celebrated Bridgewater as a "noble peer of mickle trust, and power" and Ludlow as the center of local authority, just as a country house entertainment would have done.[40] But it did not praise a monarch or even acknowledge the monarch's authority in absentia. Instead, it implicitly argued for the power of this locality and its aristocracy on their own. Whether or not Milton, Lawes, and Bridgewater looked back consciously, the Ludlow masque evoked Elizabethan nostalgia to imply dissatisfaction with the current, absent monarch and his relations with elite subjects.

Elite women continued to write and stage drama at country houses well into the seventeenth century. Residues of the genre's continuing influence can be seen in the plays of Rachel Fane, Elizabeth Brackley and Jane Cavendish, and Margaret Cavendish. Fane wrote a series of entertainments to be performed at her home at Apthorpe, a country house that James had visited eight times and that had been remodeled at royal command

---

[38] For a compelling argument for hybrid outdoor–indoor performance that would recall country house entertainment and for examination of the "site-specific" nature of the Ludlow masque, see Susan Bennett and Julie Sanders, "Rehearsing Across Space and Place: Rethinking *A Masque Presented at Ludlow Castle*" in Anna Birch and Joanne Tompkins, eds., *Performing Site-Specific Theatre: Politics, Place, Practice* (Basingstoke: Palgrave, 2012), 37–53. For other claims about outdoor or indoor staging, see Demaray, *Milton and the Masque*, 55 and 99; Cedric C. Brown, *John Milton's Aristocratic Entertainments* (Cambridge University Press, 1985), 49–51; William B. Hunter, *Milton's Comus: Family Piece* (Troy, NY: Whitson, 1983), 47–59.

[39] Philip Schwyzer discusses Sabrina, this river, and their meanings at length in "Purity and Danger on the West Bank of the Severn: The Cultural Geography of *A Masque Presented at Ludlow Castle, 1634*" in *Representations* 60 (1997): 22–48. See also John Creaser, "The Original Sabrina?" in *Milton Quarterly* 46.1 (2012): 15–20 about the likelihood that Sabrina was played by a local, non-aristocratic woman.

[40] Milton, "A Maske," line 31.

with a royal subsidy.[41] Her May Day masque, which was probably performed in May 1627 when Fane was fourteen, echoes Elizabethan country house entertainment in several ways. It features a gift-giving episode that recalls the Elizabethan lotteries at Woodstock and Harefield, and it brings familiar pastoral figures and maying festivities indoors. Like *Arcades* and the Ludlow masque, Fane's masque drew on conventions associated with court pageantry but excluded the monarch both physically and rhetorically. Although Elizabethan country house entertainments emphasized women's alliances with the Queen, Fane's masque celebrated women's bonds instead of royal authority and thereby implicitly set those two ideals at odds.[42] Her plays and Milton's entertainments began to gesture toward the ideologies underlying the Civil War by implying that the presence of a monarch was no longer necessary or desirable – a bold extension of the Sidneys' emphasis on the futility of praising a demanding sovereign – and anticipated a time when household drama by the Cavendishes and others would alternately celebrate and lament the monarch's absence. This kind of private household drama existed because the Elizabethan country house entertainment had already located political strength, critique, and power in the country estate.

---

[41] Marion O'Connor, "Rachel Fane's May Masque at Apethorpe, 1627" in *English Literary Renaissance* 36.1 (2006): 90–113. O'Connor includes a transcription of the masque, 105–13.

[42] See Deanne Williams, *Shakespeare and the Performance of Girlhood* (Basingstoke: Palgrave, 2014), 173–83. She argues similarly that the May masque celebrates domestic life, marriage, and women's family ties, although she compares it to the court masque tradition.

Elizabethan Country House Entertainments

Year	Location	Hosts	Contemporary texts
1571	Theobalds, Hertfordshire	William and Mildred Cecil, Lord and Lady Burghley	printed (1571)
1575	Kenilworth Castle, Warwickshire	Robert Dudley, Earl of Leicester	printed in two separate accounts (ca. 1575; 1576), then included in George Gascoigne's authorial collection (1587)
1575	Woodstock, Hertfordshire	Sir Henry Lee	printed in two versions (1579; 1585)
1578	Wanstead, Essex	Robert Dudley, Earl of Leicester	printed in Philip Sidney's authorial collection (1598); manuscript
1591	Theobalds, Hertfordshire	William Cecil, Lord Burghley	manuscript
1591	Cowdray, Sussex	Anthony and Magdalen Browne, Viscount and Lady Montague	printed in two editions (1591)
1591	Elvetham, Hampshire	Edward and Frances Seymour, Earl and Countess of Hertford	printed in two editions (1591); excerpted in poetic miscellany (1600)
1592	Bisham Abbey, Berkshire	Lady Elizabeth Russell	printed with Sudeley and Rycote entertainments (1592); excerpted in poetic miscellany (1600)
1592	Sudeley Castle, Gloucestershire	Giles and Frances Brydges, Lord and Lady Chandos	printed with Bisham and Rycote entertainments (1592); excerpted in poetic miscellany (1600)

Year	Location	Hosts	Contemporary texts
1592	Woodstock and Ditchley, Oxfordshire	Sir Henry Lee	manuscript; excerpted in poetic miscellany (1593)
1592	Rycote Park, Oxfordshire	Henry and Margery, Baron and Lady Norreys	printed with Bisham and Sudeley entertainments (1592)
1594	Theobalds, Hertfordshire	William Cecil, Lord Burghley and Sir Robert Cecil	manuscript
1598	Mitcham, Surrey	Sir Julius and Alice Caesar	manuscript
1599	Wimbledon Manor, Surrey	Thomas and Dorothy Cecil, Lord and Lady Burghley	manuscript
1599	Wilton, Wiltshire (canceled)	Mary Sidney Herbert, Countess of Pembroke	printed in poetic miscellany (1602)
1602	Chiswick, Middlesex	Sir William and Elizabeth Russell	manuscript
1602	Harefield, Middlesex	Thomas Egerton and Alice, Countess of Derby	multiple fragments in print and manuscript

English Translation of Theobalds (1571)
"Congratulatory Poem of the House of Cecil on the Arrival of the Fairest Queen 22 September 1571"

Prosopopoeia of Theobalds

Translated from Latin to English by Jaime Goodrich

We, QUEEN, the rising Roofs of your CECIL
    Stand, not badly built by a private man.
Who, although your Majesty deemed worthy to enter,
    Are indeed worthy of the master, less worthy of a Prince.
Ah, the master laments, because we lie open, not great enough
    Either for you, ELIZABETH, or for your merits.
And we grieve that we do not meet the master's desire,
    Alas, he says, the house is not great enough now.
Granted, it is less than great to you, greatest PRINCE:
    Granted, it is lesser than your splendor, lesser than [your] goodness,
And yet here we have poured forth all [our] might for the time being,
    Roofs, doors, gates, all things revealed lie open.
To meet you, VIRGIN, we run up with peaceful arms,
    The brow is happy, the appearance fair, the face rejoicing.
The master has given these commands. You deserve more,
    But fate, PRINCE, forbids us to convey more.
Majesty, goodness are joined in your heart,
    A strait home for the former, we are great enough for the latter.
And to you we give the master with the house, the children with the dear wife,
    Steadfast bodies, faithful hearts.
Here all things obey your power: to the highest
    Father, leave [their] souls. Take up the rest for yourself.
And lately a famous pillar came to us,
    Here an EARL, here OXFORDIAN Atlas is present:
To whom our ANNA has now been betrothed with matrimonial promise,
    A cherished girl has brought great honor to us.
That young man serves you with youthful strength,
    BURGHLEY serves you with an aged mind.

Neither do you seek more, nor are we able to give more,
    O may Master please, if the roofs [please] you less.
    Happy ELIZABETH, famous Virgin,
    Victorious QUEEN – may she live many blessed ages.

Index

(Bold numbers refer to initial bibliographic references; subsequent references are not indexed unless substantive.)